OVERSEAS AND UNDERGROUND

TRAMOR HAG YN-DANN DHOR

ADVENTURES OF A MODERN CORNISH MINER

ALAN FORRESTER MATTHEWS ACSM

Edited by
JANE HARVEY-BERRICK

HARVEY BERRICK PUBLISHING

CONTENTS

Chronology   ix
About this book   xi

Prologue   1

PART I
THE EARLY DAYS

1. Gold and Tales of Miners   7
2. English China Clays and the Camborne School of Mines   13
3. Summer in Idaho   20
4. Off to the Sun   37
5. Rats   62
6. Abu Dhabi   70
7. The Festival of Santa Barbara   80
8. Leaving the Sunshine   87
9. The Andacaba Lead, Silver-Zinc Mine   95

PART II
FAR FLUNG PLACES

10. Into the Tropics   107
11. The God Miner   131
12. Working for Myself   138
13. Dolly Varden Mine   153
14. The Lion in Sinaloa   167

PART III
USA

15. The Early days of Kernow Resources and Developments Ltd   175
16. The Copper Giant Prospect   186
17. Stanton, Yavapai County, Central Arizona   195
18. Shawnee   202
19. Mina   211

PART IV
PORTUGAL AND THE EAST

20. The Rush for Lithium	219
21. Armenia and the Road to Agarak from Yerevan	228
22. Letter from Portugal	243
23. Jales and Gralheira, Portugal	249
24. Dushanbe to Moscow via Novgorod	269

PART V
RAMBLINGS

25. Don't Get Sick	275
26. Return to Cornwall	289
Glossary	297
A note from the Author	301

Overseas and Underground
Tramor hag yn-dann dhor

Adventures of a Modern Cornish Miner

Copyright © 2022 Alan F Matthews

Editing by Jane Harvey-Berrick

First published in Great Britain, 2022
This book is licensed for your personal enjoyment only. It may not be re-sold or given away to other people.
This work is a memoir, and whilst facts have been checked to the best of ability, it remains dependent on a lifetime of memories.
Alan Forrester Matthews has asserted his right under the Copyright, Designs and Patents Act 1988 to be identified as the author of this work.
All rights reserved; no part of this publication may be reproduced or transmitted by any means, electronic, mechanical, photocopying or otherwise, without the prior permission of the publisher.

Photographs by Alan F Matthews
Front cover: Christian, Adobe Stock
Top to bottom
A mining claim post on the author's Lucky Mica claim, Arizona
The author, his wife, and Minnie
Open pit copper mine, Armenia

Back cover: top to bottom, left to right
The author, Holman's test mine, Troon, Cornwall
Gold field in the snow, Nevada USA
Tunnel entrance, Bradshaw Mountains, Arizona USA
Oil rig, the Arabian Gulf

Cover design by Nicky Stott

ISBN 978-1-912015-15-3

Scan QR code for e-book

DEDICATION

To my amazing wife, Linda, co-pilot on our remarkable journey of fifty years who read and encouraged me to complete this book.
Also to the doctors and nurses at the Oncology department in Treliske Hospital, Cornwall.
In addition, to all the people who have helped make our lives so much fun over the last half-century.

CHRONOLOGY

1969-1971
English Clays Lovering and Pochin: St Austell, Cornwall

1971-1974
Camborne School of Mines, Cornwall
Travelling to Wallace, Idaho, USA

1974-1977
Anglo American: Odendaalsrus, Orange Free State, South Africa

1978-1979
Dowell Schlumberger, Pau, France
Abu Dhabi, United Arab Emirates

1979-1984
Dresser Industries: Mykonos, Greece
Aberfeldy, Scotland
Travelling to Bolivia

1984-1987

Department of Minerals and Energy: Ok Tedi, Western Province, Port Moresby, Papua New Guinea

1987-1989
Melanesian Mining (PNG) Ltd
Travelling to Australia

1989-1991
American Pacific Mining, Vancouver
Dolly Varden, British Columbia
Travelling to Honduras

1991-1996
Arimetco International: Tucson, Arizona, USA
Kernow Resources and Developments Ltd, Scottsdale, Arizona
Travelling to Portugal, Spain, Mexico, Costa Rica, Chile, Brazil

1996-2006
Kernow Mining Portugal: Porto, Portugal
Travelling to Canada, Spain, Armenia, Tajikistan

2006-2017
International Minerals Ltd
Godolphin Mining Services Ltd: Scottsdale, Arizona
Travelling to Ecuador, Peru, New Zealand

2017 forward
Praa Sands and Camborne, Cornwall
Travelling to Ireland, Portugal, Spain, Barriper, Rosudgeon, Plymouth
Capture Results Lda.

ABOUT THIS BOOK

Over the years, on my travels for work and life, I have found myself in mines, restaurants, bars and bizarre accommodations in some very strange places. On my return, people would ask, "What was it like in Tajikistan?" or "Was it difficult to get pasties in Qatar?"

To ensure an accurate recollection of the adventures, I would make notes while sitting in Pablo's Chicken Joint, or after an interesting day in the deserts of central Nevada sitting in the bar of the motel attached to the ubiquitous casino.

These notes and observations have now formed the skeleton of this book on which I have hung the cloak of my memories. It is a memoir, hopefully seasoned with humour, astonishing facts, and with more than a passing nod to my Cornish heritage.

Earth first, we will mine other planets later.

Kernow Bys Vykken!

PROLOGUE

My family had a strong mining background: a great grandfather who mined in Canada, Cornwall and South Africa; a father who worked for Holman Brothers, one of the country's renowned suppliers of mining equipment; a grandfather who was a master mason; as well as uncles who were in the mining business.

My love of mining – minerals, and those subjects that are now known as Geosciences – grew from a desire to find and uncover hidden treasure.

The excitement of discovery first came to the fore when I was eight years old. I unearthed the skull and several bones of a soldier next to the walls of Burgh Castle, a Roman fort just outside of Great Yarmouth.

There was no treasure associated with the skull, but what a find for an eight year old. I took it home, much to the horror of my mum. I've probably horrified a few archaeologists, too, but the skull was given to Norwich Museum.

Later, I would collect unusual looking pebbles from beaches and pull rocks from Cornish hedges that showed signs of mineralisation. Not a pastime appreciated by farmers, but the white quartz rocks would often reveal copper or zinc or occasionally tin ore.

These specimens extracted from the hedges formed the basis of my mineral collection. I am more circumspect now, only searching mining waste dumps.

The desire to travel must have developed during my childhood. My father was an accountant at the forefront of the introduction of business machines, the first of these being those which used punch cards. My parents moved from Camborne to Norfolk and then to Plymouth and Cheltenham and back to Plymouth. Seven locations in fifteen years. There were five moves to different houses in Plymouth alone, one to a different house in the same road. By the time of my parents final return to Plymouth, I had started working for English China Clays in St Austell.

Linda and I have lived in ten different countries over the 48 year span of our travels and moved multiple times in each country; fifteen houses and several apartments. Not forgetting the consulting assignments in Central and South America, as well as traveling to Tajikistan and Armenia.

We have been lucky enough to have canine companions in several countries and have moved them with us: Ransom in South Africa, Misty who moved from Scotland to Papua New Guinea to Canada and on to Arizona, Bear who was rescued in the Arizona desert and came with us to Portugal, and finally Max and Minnie who travelled with us from the US to Cornwall.

Having trained as a miner and graduated as a mining engineer at the Camborne School of Mines, the most exciting part of my career has been in prospecting, the search for and the development of new deposits. There is a huge satisfaction in designing the direction, angle and point of intersection of a diamond drill, and having it intersecting the vein in the right place, even if there is only little mineralisation. There is also a great thrill when the hole intersects a vein with visible gold in the core, a rare event but a great one. However, the thrill of entering an underground tunnel after blasting and to be first to view mineral treasures that may have been exposed can never be surpassed. Never.

As well as the love of travel, I have always craved space. Odd for a career based on going underground into confined spaces. Linda also has a love of open spaces. All of our fifteen houses or apartments, except for our first house in South Africa, have had views either to the sea or to the mountains.

Now back in Cornwall, our house has a fabulous view down to the sea. It is close to several beaches and also close to several mining areas where sometimes valuable mineral specimens can be uncovered in the waste piles. What more could any Cornishman want? Apart from a good pasty.

Join me on my travels around the world, planting the flag of Kernow on four different continents, overseas and underground. My journey is just half a century, but I was following a tradition of Cousin Jacks and Cousin Jennys that goes back many, many hundreds of years.

PART I
THE EARLY DAYS

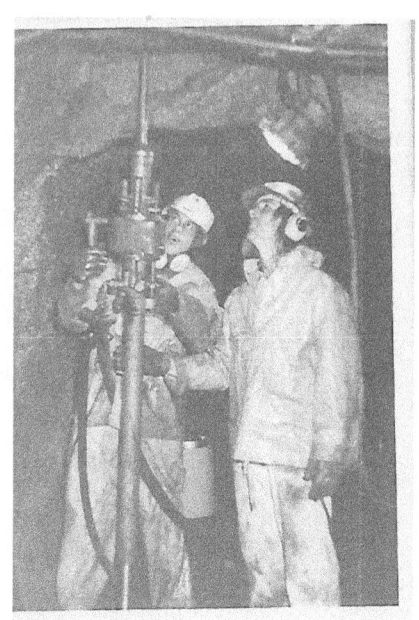

Holman's Test Mine, Troon, Cornwall

1

GOLD AND TALES OF MINERS

In the beginning...

> **Sweat of the Sun, Tears of the Moon**
> *Inca description of gold and silver*

Since the beginning of recorded history and even before that, man has sought the metals and minerals he has needed to make his life better. One of the best examples of early mining is that of Grime's Graves where Neolithic man laboured beneath the Norfolk fields to extract flint using antler horns and fire-hardened pointed wooden sticks as tools, 4,500 years ago.

Next, deposits of copper metal were mined, which, along with gold and silver, is one of the few metals that can be found in its pure form.

Around 3,500BC, the first signs of bronze usage by the ancient Sumerians started to appear in the Tigris–Euphrates valley in western Asia. One theory suggests that bronze may have been discovered when copper and tin-rich rocks were used to build campfire rings. As the stones became heated by the fire, the metals contained in the rocks were melted and mixed.

The Bronze Age finally gave way to the Iron Age around 700BC. This was a much more abundant material and far easier to process into a usable grade of metal.

Often miners and mineral deposits have been the subject of myth and legend. The Golden Fleece that Jason sought was in fact a sheep's fleece which has lanolin in the wool. This, and the woolly fibres, will trap small gold particles which have been separated from the host rock by crushing. The fleece is laid on a gently inclined surface and the crushed rock sluiced over the surface, the gold being trapped in the fleece and the waste washing away. Or the gold may have been from alluvial deposits where the gold has already been separated through natural breakdown of the host rock. The gold would have been winnowed from the rock and redeposited in streams.

In the ninth book of Homer's *Odyssey* (c. 700BC), the hero Odysseus encounters Polyphemus, the son of Poseidon, a one-eyed, man-eating giant who lives with his fellow Cyclopes in a distant land in a cave. Could this have been a miner with a circular lamp strapped to his forehead?

In Homer's story, Polyphemus eats some of Odysseus' men, so Odysseus gives the giant wine and gets him drunk. Polyphemus falls asleep and the remaining men escape from the deep cave where the giant hides his herd of sheep.

Could it be that the cave was a gold mine and Polyphemus was protecting its wealth?

It is not unknown for the location of gold mines to be a closely guarded secret. In Bukarah, Uzbekistan, the fearful and brutal emir Nasrullah (1806-1860) had a secret gold mine, using the proceeds to maintain his awful reign. Its location and existence was the subject of speculation from at least 1840. Before their retirement, miners routinely had their eyes gouged out and their tongues ripped out. Travellers, on the least suspicion that they knew the mine's location, were summarily executed. In the 1960s, the Russians located it and put it back into production.

As evidenced by the above myths and legends, man's fascination with gold dates back to the beginning of time. One or two cultures knew of it but had no use for it because it was too soft to use in the making of tools, and other materials were used as currency. Some saw it as a gift of the gods, and its durability and beauty has given us glimpses of past civilisations from exquisite jewellery recovered from graves of the Etruscans, the Celts of Ireland, the Aztecs and Incas, the Egyptians and very early man in the far reaches of Asia.

The Incas gathered 700 tons of gold (*Sweat of the Sun*) and silver (*Tears of the Moon*) to purchase the freedom of their king, Atahualpa, from Pizarro and his *conquistadors*.

It always astonishes people when I tell them that all the gold ever mined in the whole world since recorded history (going back at least to the time of Egyptian pharaohs) would fit inside a good-sized detached house. It would form a cube with dimensions that are estimated to be 22 meters x 22m x 22m, weighing some 205,238 tonnes. Roughly two-thirds of this has been mined since 1950. Since gold is virtually indestructible, this means that almost all of this metal mined in the past is still around in one form or another.

Other amazing facts about gold are that an ounce of pure gold can be beaten into a sheet with dimensions of 3m x 3m and 0.000018cm thick. That same ounce can be drawn into a wire five microns thick and 80km long. A human hair is 70μm thick. Those fact-checkers can verify this at the World Gold Council website.

Gold does strange things to people, and legends of fabulous deposits have driven prospectors and adventures to unknown faraway lands.

It is understood that King Solomon, in collaboration with the Phoenician King Hiram of Tyre (in present day Lebanon), dispatched expeditions of Phoenician mariners to the lands of Ophir to obtain large tonnages of gold. The location of Ophir mentioned in the Bible has been a subject of speculation for millennia.

The theory that Ophir is located somewhere in the heart of Africa was certainly stimulated in the late nineteenth century by the publication of Rider Haggard's popular adventure novel *King Solomon's Mines* (published 1885). It tells the story of an adventurer by the name of Allan Quartermain and his quest to find his missing brother in an unexplored region of Africa. In this area of Kukuanaland, the group of adventurers unearth the fabled treasure of the biblical king's mines.

The Spaniards in Arizona commanded by Francisco Vásquez de Coronado led an expedition in 1540 in search of the fabled Seven Cities of Gold, also known as the Seven Cities of Cíbola. According to legend, the cities could be found throughout the pueblos of the New Mexico Territory.

Coronado travelled north from the Mexican state of Sonora venturing into what was hostile Native American country. Much of his path was through Apache territory. He eventually came to the Zuni Pueblo in western New Mexico but failed to find the expected riches.

Humphrey Bogart and his crew went on the quest for treasure in *The Treasure of the Sierra Madre*. A classic tale of rookie prospectors not really knowing what they were doing and would have walked over their discovery if the grizzled prospector, played by Walter Brennan, had not noticed a few grains of gold at his feet next to their camp. His 'prospector's dance' makes for memorable viewing, especially to those mining men who are not known for their dancing prowess.

Deserts seem to always attract prospectors, and seemingly disappearing deposits such as the 'Lost Dutchman Mine' in the Superstition Mountains of south central Arizona somewhere close to Thunder Mountain. A familiar story, The Dutchman (who was in fact German), went prospecting in the mountains east of Apache Junction and the tiny community of Tortilla Flats. He discovered an exceedingly rich quartz vein loaded with gold. Myth has it that he came back to Apache Junction from the south, thus throwing would-be claim jumpers off the scent of his discovery.

He brought back specimens, had them assayed, and they were extraordinary in their grade. The mine was never developed and despite numerous low tech and high tech expeditions to find the mine, it remained hidden for 125 years.

Not only have miners sought for legendary deposits of gold but also of silver. In Potosí, Bolivia, miners to this day are extracting silver from the Mountain of Silver or *Cerro Colorado*, named for the colour of the host rock. First noticed and developed by the Spanish *conquistador* Pizarro and his men.

Another legendary mine is known as *Planchas de Plata*, variously translated as 'planks of silver' or 'plates of silver'. Sometimes the ore and product were known as 'balls of silver' (*bolas de plata*). The deposit was alluvial, the silver being washed from a nearby vein and redeposited in an ancient, now dry, riverbed. The rich ore, after extraction, was carried south on the backs of *burros* to a refinery in Mexico or to some shipping place to be sent to Spain.

An old prospector told me that several of the mule trains were hijacked by *desperados*. They took the mules up into the Baboquivari Mountains on an incredibly steep trail and stashed the silver plates and balls in a cave. To this day, no one has ever found the hiding place, although it is generally thought to be on the Papago Reservation in southern Arizona.

Most myths and legends are based around fabulous deposits or vast hoards of gold. Not often does one see a headline about the finding of a legendary mountain of copper or nickel. However, in the 1970s, the nickel miner Poseidon made a huge discovery of nickel in Australia. The shares of Poseidon rose a staggering 125 times in value and crossed the Australian $100 per share mark, even though months before they were trading at a mere Aussie $0.80 per share.

By the time Poseidon actually started producing nickel, the price of nickel had fallen and the mine turned out to be uneconomic; Poseidon went into receivership in 1974.

One of the most spectacular mountains of gold was claimed to have been discovered in Indonesia by a junior mining company called Bre-X. In 1997, its share price rocketed on the announcement that it had discovered possibly the largest gold deposit in the world. There were no qualified reserves yet, but the drilling and assays indicated that it could contain up to 10 million ounces of gold. That's about 312 tonnes which would, if mined, be worth $10,000,000,000 at the time. The share price rose from tens of cents to over $280.00 in the space of a year.

Something was very wrong. Reputable consulting mining engineers went to the site to examine the samples. They were salted – Bre-X was using gold from a totally different source to enhance the value of the samples. Word spread of the fraud and the share price fell to around $100, but still people were buying the shares, not believing the various reports from reputable sources. In a couple of months, the price crashed to $0.10 per share. The geologist who started the whole adventure was reported to have 'fallen' out of a helicopter over the Indonesian jungle and was never heard of again.

Mark Twain was not a great fan of miners and during his time in Virginia City, Nevada, he had occasion to fall foul of a few mining scams.

He is quoted as saying, "A mine is a hole in the ground and the owner is a liar."

The quote has been adapted by various parties and used in the *Detroit Free Press* in 1881 as, "A mine is a hole in the ground. The discoverer of it is a natural liar. The hole in the ground and the liar combine and issue shares and trap fools."

Perhaps not the most ringing of endorsements for the profession.

But when I started at the Camborne School of Mines in 1971, I was told, "Mining is an ancient and honourable profession."

Over the years, I have found most miners to be honest, hardworking people who care about the society around them and take great respect in managing the environment.

Society needs metals and miners to extract them. Mining will be around as long as civilisation is in place.

Remember, "If it can't be grown it has to be mined."

2

ENGLISH CHINA CLAYS AND THE CAMBORNE SCHOOL OF MINES

1969-1974: St Austell and Camborne, Cornwall

In the early summer of 1969, my father and I left our house in Paddocks Lane, Cheltenham in the family Wolsey Hornet with my 49cc Puch Maxi Moped strapped to the roof and set off for the deep southwest of England, St Austell, Cornwall, via Plymouth. The Puch had been bought by my parents to enable me to take up a position as a Trainee Mine Captain with English China Clays Lovering and Pochin or ECLP for short. We left early in the morning and set off along the A38 arriving in Plymouth at 4.00pm.

Dad and I knew the route well as he'd commuted from Plymouth to Cheltenham for a couple of years prior. It was a difficult road then, passing beneath the bridge that spans the Avonmouth gorge and winding its way over the Mendip Hills, past what is now the road skirting Bristol airport. We passed Bridgwater, having survived the three-lane stretch of the A38 known as 'suicide alley' and always recognisable by the reek of the nearby cellophane works.

In Plymouth, we unloaded the Puch and stayed the night with a family friend. Next morning, we set off to St Austell. This convoy consisted of me on my Puch Maxi Moped (registration TDD 1H) with Dad following on behind in the Wolsley Hornet.

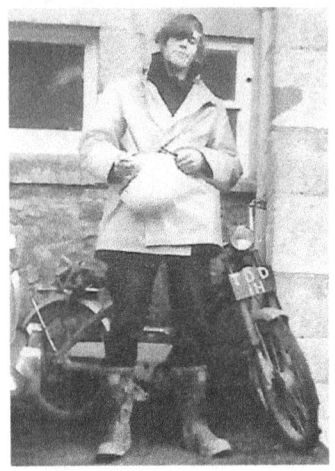
Outside ECLP

The Maxi's top speed was 40mph downhill with a following wind, and it took over an hour to reach St Austell and Cusgarne Hall of Residence. A beautiful granite built gentleman's house from the late 1800s, it was where ECLP housed their apprentices, trainee mine captains, and those undertaking HNC and ONC courses in engineering, a mix of all the trades that would lead along the pathways to a successful career with ECLP. The charge to stay at this august establishment was £5.00 per week, full board – my pay was £7.00 per week.

Dad saw me checked in and went back to Cheltenham.

Next morning, I reported in at John Keay House, the dreadful 1960s architecture having produced the flat pancake headquarters of ECLP.

I was introduced to my training officer, and the course I'd be following was outlined. I was told to report to the Goonbarrow mine offices at 7.00am the next day. The Mine Captain would be expecting me.

The first couple of months were to be spent at Goonbarrow, a china clay pit close to the village of Bugle – mildly famous as the location of a mass meeting of striking miners in the summer of 1913. The strike was led by a Joseph Matthews – not a relation, as far as I know. Initially, over 200 police were drafted in from Plymouth to control the miners but they proved too unruly for them, and a special force of police trained in strike-breaking was brought in from Glamorgan. The strikers eventually went back to work in October.

So as not be late for my first day after leaving John Keay House, I decided to locate the mine offices at Goonbarrow. I jumped on TDD 1H and drove to Bugle. The offices were up a small lane and housed in an Edwardian family house which had been overtaken by the expansion of the pit, and was now perched on the very edge of it. The family were long since gone.

The reason for joining ECLP was that I hoped that the Mine Captain training course would help gain me entry to the world famous Camborne School of Mines (CSM) to qualify as a mining engineer. This consisted of a day release course: four days at work, and one day in technical college at Pool near Camborne, studying for the Ordinary National Certificate in Engineering (ONC).

Most recently, I'd been at Cheltenham Grammar School, and in the past I'd been the recipient of elocution lessons to smooth out my Cornish accent, so when one of the first tasks I was assigned at Goonbarrow was to man the crib hut, it was eye-opening.

The crib hut was a sort of dining room rest area at the bottom of the pit, where the workers, hose men, front-end loader operators, lorry drivers, and fitters would have their lunch. My job was to keep the coke-fired Rayburn range hot enough so the water in the half-dozen kettles would boil at crib time. Also, there was the huge responsibility of ensuring that the pasties handed to me at the beginning of the shift were warmed up and ready at lunchtime. If the water was not hot enough, the tea in the miners' tin mugs would not steep properly and there would be 'hell up'. I guess I managed okay because I became friendly with the men and would join in the games of euchre at crib time. I was fortunate to remember my Cornish roots, and my Cheltenham accent dropped away quickly.

During my three months in the pit, I experienced various jobs. This included using the giant hoses known as 'monitors', where a stream of high pressure water was directed at the blasted faces of pure white china clay. The resultant milk-white liquid flowed to the bottom of the pit where the quartz and mica waste was separated from the mixture. From here, the liquid known as 'slurry' was pumped up to the treatment works a mile or so away in Bugle. The mica was separated from the slurry in large settling tanks; the clay was dried and then sacked or put in railway wagons, and shipped all over the UK. The quartz sand was hoisted to the top of the pyramid shaped hills which for years formed an iconic emblem of central Cornwall: the Tip and Pit.

Passing on down the job line, as it were, I was assigned to assist Tom Hancock in his duties as fitter, blacksmith and pump specialist.

Tom was a man of three sections: a round bald head, a rotund torso which may have been the result of over indulging in many pints of St Austell ales, and a lower section of stocky legs ending in leather boots of great age. Tom smoked Woodbine cigarettes, untipped, and there was always a fag hanging from his lower lip. The fag generally lasted until saliva dribbled down the cigarette and put it out. It stayed there until the next was lit.

Tom had great experience with fixing pumps – the heart of the clay business. He was able to fix the big slurry pumps that pumped the fluids out of the pit, or the smaller centrifugal pumps that moved the clay mixture through the various parts of the operation. Tom worked closely with Jimmy Christmas, a man of small stature, and possibly the first 'entrepreneur' I had ever met. He had bought a tractor and fitted it out with welding gear and oxy acetylene cutting gear which he contracted out to ECLP, and he also had a smallholding where he raised calves and sheep. There was nowhere that Jimmy would not go to weld a broken pump case or cut out a section of pipe that was blocked.

So my experience went on – some of the tasks were onerous and some a lot of fun. Through it all, I relied on TDD 1H as my main mode of transport, using it on many occasions to travel along the A389 from St Austell to Liskeard, and then the A38 onward to Plymouth to spend a weekend at home with my parents. There are hills on that route where I had to pedal hard to get the moped up and over, and times when about to run out of petrol, I would tip the machine on its side to get that last drop from the tank into the carburettor to prevent being stranded halfway up the hill to Dobwalls where I could get some 2 stroke petrol.

Then in the summer of 1971, I had my interview with the Principal of the Camborne School of Mines, Dr Peter Hackett, to see if I was a suitable candidate. Although from Nottingham, Doc Hackett knew the value of having a rugby playing local fellow at the school. So on the proviso that I obtained the correct results for my ONC, I would be granted admittance.

Fortunately (or not), in the late spring of 1971, I broke my knee playing soccer and had to stay at home in Plymouth where I studied and revised like crazy for the finals of the ONC. I passed with the required grades and won the ECLP Apprentice of the Year award.

In October 1971, I joined thirty other first year students at the CSM, many of whom are friends to this day. Others, sadly, have died, although none from industrial accidents.

ECLP did not follow through on their promise to sponsor me through CSM, and at a rather late stage I was left to apply for a grant from Cornwall County Council, which did come through with a reduced allowance but paid all tuition. ECLP did provide a grant of £100 per year. That represented quite a few pints of beer in 1971.

A lot of people look forward to leaving their home town to go to college, and while I looked forward to the chance and opportunity, I was a bit wary. I had so many relations in Camborne, it would be difficult to stay under the radar when carousing or getting up to student hijinks without reports getting back to the parents. But it did have the great advantage of being able to have tea most Sundays with my Granny Matthews. She would bake scones and provide lovely ham sandwiches.

"Come on eat up," she would say. "I made those special for you."

She also gave me a 10 shilling note or 50p every visit in order to, "Buy something sweet."

The three years at Camborne were a lot of fun, mixed with anxiety related to my hopeless ability to conquer the riddles of Strength of Materials, and calculus. I enjoyed learning about the geology of Cornwall; the intricacies of surveying, taught by a superb Cornishman Ron Hooper; the basics of mining, and tips on how to use a gold pan and vanning shovel. Often on Saturdays and during the vacations, I would work underground at Pendarves tin mine. This helped pay the expenses of being at CSM.

Rugby, surfing and dating took up far too much time. The dating proved fruitful as I met my wonderful wife Linda outside Camborne church where she and my one time girlfriend, Lindsey, were selling buttonholes for Alexandra Rose Day. Linda was from Camborne and knew about the School of Mines and the students who frequented the bars. I am not so sure her mum was initially keen but she baked me a pasty most Saturdays after I'd played rugby. Sitting in front of the fire after the pasty watching the television, I usually fell asleep. Perhaps a taste of things to come! The pasty was always excellent, no mean feat for an Austrian lady who married a Cornish soldier and moved with him to Cornwall after the war.

There was a wonderful cast of characters during my time at CSM. There were men from Ghana, Sierra Leone, Southern Rhodesia (now Zimbabwe), Zambia and South Africa. At any one time in the common room you could hear South Africans talking with their – to me, at the time – exotic accents, Africans with their sometimes pedantic slow way of talking, dialect from deepest Cornwall, and the occasional educated speech patterns associated with an English public school. There were men from the Caribbean, Guyana, Malay, Iran and Ireland. All countries with an established mining industry, and all were sending their brightest men to Cornwall to the best School of Mines in the world.

A few of them had been at CSM on and off for five years, repeating a year after failing the final exams. Often they were sponsored by the companies they worked for and would return to the mine for a year and come back. Several of these men were mature students and seemed quite sophisticated to most of the people in my year. The international nature of the mature student body helped those of us who had yet to travel abroad get an inkling of what life was like in mining camps and towns throughout the world. The older South African fellows also tended to be excellent rugby players.

So in July of 1974, after sitting my finals, Linda and I set the date for our wedding – hoping I would pass and not have to re-sit any of the dreaded engineering subjects. I did pass with the standard 2:2, and I was offered several jobs in South Africa, Sierra Leone and Zambia.

We took the offer in South Africa and left Camborne in November of 1974.

3

SUMMER IN IDAHO

1973: USA

The houses of ill repute, The Morning Star Mine, 72 hours on a Greyhound Bus, Posnick's Bar, the Wallace Hotel and Shorty

In the summer of 1973 while at the Camborne School of Mines, I was lucky enough to work in the Star Morning mine located in the panhandle region of northern Idaho in the United States. The mine produced silver, lead and zinc and was one of several mines in the area known as the 'Silver Valley'. It was a requirement of our degree course to gain practical mining experience in a foreign country and then to write a comprehensive report on the mine. To enable us to work in the US, we were sponsored on J2 visas by BUNAC (the British University North America Club).

1973 was the summer of the televised testimony of the trials and impeachment hearings of the Watergate scandal, of Reggie Jackson hitting home runs for the Oakland A's, Tying a Yellow Ribbon Around the Old Oak Tree, Crocodile Rock and blistering August heat in the panhandle of northern Idaho.

Leaving the UK for the first time by plane, I flew from Gatwick into La Guardia with Northwest Airlines on a 707. The flight seemed to be full of students, including my friend Dingo Edwards who originated from Guyana. Dingo was off to work in the New Jersey zinc mines and was met at the airport by his relatives from New York who had emigrated from Guyana. They bundled Dingo up in a huge family hug and spirited him away to New Jersey.

Left by myself, I ventured into Manhattan on the airport bus to my hotel which was located close to the Port Terminal Authority of New York. The University Hotel, recommended by BUNAC, turned out to be a multi-storeyed modern budget residence. I checked in and went to my room. To my surprise, BUNAC had booked another student into the room as well. Not to worry – we had separate beds.

Next morning, I ventured out to find the Port Terminal Authority which housed the Greyhound Bus Station. Having a little difficulty finding the place, I approached a policeman and asked if he could direct me to it.

He looked over my shoulder and said, "Sonny, go buy a streetmap."

I found the place and located the window to purchase a one-way ticket to Wallace, Idaho, which was the nearest town of any size to the mine and where the headquarters of the Hecla Mining Company were located. The guy behind the window had never heard of Wallace and wanted to send to me Walla Walla as that was the nearest town that started with a W in that region in his fare book. Eventually, we located Wallace and he sold me the ticket for about $20, less than I had budgeted.

Flushed with commercial success, I then decided to purchase a packet of cigarettes. Following the advice given at the BUNAC induction course, I was to avoid using 'please' and 'thank you'. So I said in my best American accent, "Gimmie a pack of Marlboro."

The lady replied, "Soft or hard, filter or no?"

I had no idea what she meant so asked her, "Would you please explain what that is?"

She was very nice and gave me a soft pack of Marlboro and, as a bonus, a book of matches.

I said, "Thank you very much!"

The bus was to pass through Cleveland, Chicago, Minneapolis, Fargo, Sioux Falls, Billings and Butte. In Butte, there was a huge open pit copper mine right beside the highway, and the restaurant where we stopped to pick up and drop off passengers sold Cornish pasties!

The series of buses I took travelled through the night. I would doze and occasionally drop into a deeper sleep waking up to find myself seated next to a cowboy or a fellow student who had got on while I slept.

There were many interesting experiences on that 72 hour journey. Leaving New York on the New Jersey turnpike, the two girls seated behind me started singing the Simon and Garfunkel song *America* just as we set out.

> *Counting the cars on the New Jersey Turnpike*
>   *They've all come to look for America.*

Later, they tried to get me in trouble, saying I was smoking a cigar which was a no-no on the bus. The bus driver admonished me, but nothing really came of it.

Changing buses in Chicago, I had time for a burger with the works, and coffee. The sign said: 'Coffee – bottomless cup $0.50'.

I had never heard of this and asked the man who looked like a manager what this meant.

"Do I, for my fifty cents, get to drink coffee all through my meal and after, if I wish?"

He was effusive in his response: "Yes!" he said and took me over to the counter and said to the waitress, "Fill this young man's cup and keep it coming."

Crossing the Great Plains from Minneapolis toward the Rockies, passing through Fargo and many of the smaller towns, it seemed as though I was travelling on a sailing ship that was making stops at small islands, dropping off and picking up packages and passengers from the depots and cafés that served as Greyhound bus stops.

Eventually after 72 hours or so riding the bus, we arrived in Wallace. A small mining community, its buildings and streets were clustered in the bottom of a narrow valley between two steep sided pine tree clad mountains. For years, Interstate 90, one of the main cross-country highways of the United States, passed through the small town. Amazingly, a single set of traffic lights controlled the east–west traffic across the continent. This was where, on 6th July 1973 the Greyhound bus, one of many I had travelled on from New York, made a stop at the Sweet's Motel and Restaurant.

It was a typical diner with booths for four people lining one side and on the other a long counter with chrome stools, the seats of red plastic. The tables had small replicas of a juke box on the wall which accepted 25¢ for three selections and was somehow connected to a large Wurlitzer. I liked to play a song by the Eagles, *Take it Easy*. For some reason, I also liked Charlie Pride's *Goodtime Charlie's got the Blues* which was playing the morning of my arrival. My first experience of Country & Western music.

It was all so strange, most unlike the Wimpy Bar back in Camborne. Even though the menu was in English, there were items I did not want to try: mac and cheese, being as my father was known as Mac and I really did not like macaroni. I stuck mostly to burgers of various types. I had never had a pickled gherkin before nor Cowboy Beans and was initially confused by getting crisps when I wanted chips/fries. In addition, there was a bewildering choice of eggs, never heard of by me in Cornwall, but familiar to Americans: scrambled, over-easy, over-medium, over-hard, sunny-side up, as an omelette; and, "What sort of bread would you like? White, brown, wholemeal, rye," and so on. Other items such as chilli and chowder were tasted but forsaken in favour of the humble burger. Best of all were the hash browns, and I would see if I could get them with everything. I guess they were touted as being of superior quality because Idaho is known as the Potato State, growing the best in America.

I often wondered how this was possible, only ever having seen this part of Idaho which was in the Rockies and there did not seem to be anywhere to grow the prodigious amounts of spuds. Later, I found out that to the south and west of the Rockies down toward Nevada, there are rolling plains and hills that are perfect for growing potatoes.

The Silver Dollar Diner also served pancakes of varying sizes. There was a sign in the window that said if you could eat the supersized huge 12 inch pancake in one sitting you could have it for free. I never attempted it. In fact, I didn't eat pancakes as they came with maple syrup or fruit. Neither of which I liked at breakfast.

Silver was in demand, the economy was booming, and miners were earning good money. It was still okay to cut down trees, and lumberjacks worked in the woods in the summer, returning to the mines in the winter as carpenters and drillers.

After arriving at Sweet's Motel, I reported to the mining company's offices at 7.30am. I think they were rather surprised to see a 21 year old mining student from England turn up on their doorstep armed with a letter they had written in January saying report for work in early July. Nevertheless, I was hired on and told to come back to the offices next morning for transport to the Morning Star Mine, some eight miles up the valley in the village of Burke. In the interim, I was to find somewhere to stay in Wallace.

The personnel man at the offices told me that accommodations in Wallace were limited. I wondered about this as there were a number of redbrick buildings with such names as Oasis Rooms, the Sahara, the U&I Rooms, and the Lux Rooms.

Prior to leaving the UK, I had been on an induction course with several other students on American culture, organised and run by BUNAC. They sponsored students on temporary visas to work in the US, aimed mainly at camp counsellors and waitresses. Their advice, whilst not sage, proved useful in some instances. For example, they recommended always asking for weekly or monthly rates when taking a room in a hotel.

So, after checking in with the personnel man at Hecla at 8.30am and armed with the BUNAC advice, I walked to the building with a flashing neon sign that proclaimed Oasis Rooms. I boldly knocked on the front door and waited. After a while a blonde woman of what then seemed to be middle age, opened the door dressed in a pink, flowing, see-through peignoir.

"What d'ya want?" she asked.

"I'd like a room," I said, "but I want weekly rates..." (using the abrupt manner we had been told to use by BUNAC).

She looked me up and down and then said in quite a disdainful tone, "Sonny, I don't think you could stand the pace," and closed the door.

Thinking how rude she was and wondering why she, as the proprietress of a boarding house was dressed so at that time in the morning, I proceeded fifty yards down the road to the Wallace Hotel where I found a room for $12 per week. I subsequently discovered that the Wallace Hotel was indeed the only hotel in Wallace. At the time, I didn't actually know that a motel was also considered a hotel. All of the other establishments that offered accommodations or rooms were, in fact, whorehouses, including the Oasis Rooms. Over the years, I have met several Americans and Canadians who were introduced to the charms of ladies of the night in Wallace.

The Wallace Hotel was owned by Keith Murray and his wife. They had an owners' suite at the top of the stairs. Every Saturday, I would hand over my weekly rent of $12 and sit and chat with Keith. He was a retired serviceman and had fought in the Second World War in France. He told me that while in the UK waiting for the invasion of Normandy, he became fond of Guinness, not a drink that I particularly liked. However, for some strange reason, Keith had bottles of the evil-tasting brew in a large wooden crate, and every Saturday morning when I went to pay the rent for my room he would open two bottles, one for me, one for him, and we would drink while Keith told tales of his time in the UK and France. It tasted horrible, I had no idea where it came from and it was possibly at best 27 years old, if brought from Europe. Or maybe he bought it in the US for sentimental reasons and only drank it on special occasions. But it was worthwhile to hear stories of the dames in Devon, and the Frenchies and their wine.

Posnick's Bar occupied the whole of the ground floor of the Wallace Hotel but was in no way associated with the hotel. It was a soda joint that served milkshakes, ice cream and icy cold beer, and if it was late at night, you could maybe squeeze a Jack Daniels out of Posnick Junior. It also sold newspapers, magazines, postcards and strange fishing lures, bait and hunting accessories.

The zinc-topped bar was some 30ft long and fronted by several fixed pedestal chrome-plated swivel stools whose seats were covered with pink plastic. The patrons ranged in age from five to fifty, and everyone was served in a rapid and efficient manner by either Posnick senior or his son. At times, there was the hum of a homogeniser whipping up ice cream sodas with some amazing flavours. There was also a pool table, which to me was a joke, as it was so small compared to the full size billiard tables we had back at college in the UK. It took me a few games to learn the rules of 8 Ball, but after a while I became proficient enough to occasionally earn a few beers from the locals.

Another feature of the bar, which was new to me, was the presence of a television. I imagine there were not too many channels available in that neck of the woods, but it was always tuned to whatever baseball game was showing, or the Watergate investigation. John Erlichman, one of the participants in the whole deal, was from Idaho, so there was quite an interest in the proceedings.

Posnick senior was a rotund man of late middle age who wore thick black rimmed spectacles, had slick-backed thinning black hair, a large hook nose and knew everything about American sports. To look at him you would have sworn he was from the Lebanon or Greece. I guess he was a second-generation Polish immigrant but his physical features were more middle European than anything else.

This was my first experience of the American fascination with sports statistics and facts. He always wanted to know how fast I could run a hundred yards. I had no idea and said in 11 seconds. He then wanted me to race against the local high school quarterback. I declined saying I could not run in all that gear they wore.

Senior also ran a pretty serious poker school at nights. Coming back to the hotel at around 11pm after an afternoon shift at the mine, it was not uncommon to find several local notables of the town in the backroom wreathed in a haze of cigarette and cigar smoke, dealing up a storm.

Posnick Junior and I got pretty friendly and we played a lot of cribbage that summer. He beat me most of the time but I always beat him on the pool table. His dad bought him a Corvette and he showed me how to leave rubber on the street running the engine up to high, high revs and letting the clutch out quickly resulting in the squealing of tyres and leaving black rubber marks on the road. This resulted in the car fishtailing down the street at high speed and, so we thought impressing the girls who stood on the corner. Junior had a first name but I never heard him called anything but Junior. He wasn't big enough to be a football player and was waiting to go back to college in Moscow, a city in northern Idaho, where he played basketball.

Whilst everyone in Wallace was a character, Shorty stands out in my memory. He was a dwarf or midget standing 4'6" or so and was quite heavy. I know that because sometimes coming back to the hotel from night shift, I would find him passed out at the bottom of the stairs which led from just outside Posnick's Bar to the first floor, and I would carry him up to his room and drop him on his bed.

He lived across the hall from me and lent me a radio so that at night I could listen to the AM stations from California, and sometimes the signals bounced up all the way from Mexico. His room also looked out over the flat roof of the Lux Rooms where the girls (ladies of the night) would sunbathe. Oddly, they were quite modestly dressed, and Shorty didn't pay much attention to them.

Shorty lived on welfare and seemed to spend all his money on white bread, baloney and beer that he kept in a small fridge in his room. He used to let me keep my sandwich fixings in the fridge, and on some nights I would drink a few beers and watch baseball with him on the tiny black and white television he had in his room.

Shopping was also a unique experience. Being a frugal student, I would check the prices of the items I needed to buy, totalling the cost as I went. For ages, I was always surprised when the cashier said that will be $5 and $5.50 with tax, and I would then fumble for the change. All the purchases were put in a brown paper bag. The real miners used to call us summer hires 'paper bag miners' as we always carried our lunches in paper bags. Before too long, I got fed up with that and splashed out on an aluminium lunch pail which also held a thermos flask in the lid. I was very proud of this and when I thought about it, I would get coffee from the diner 'to go' and fill the thermos.

It was, to me, extraordinarily hot that year, and the smell of hot pine, and later in the summer, the smell of smoke from the forest fires pervaded the atmosphere. The temperature was always known from the revolving neon sign on the corner of the hotel, on one side with WALLACE CORNER in bold letters and showing the current temperature on the other. Temperatures reached the high 90s in early August but by the end of my stay in late September, night time temperatures dropped down to the 30s, only a few degrees above freezing.

Several of the bars in town boasted cold, really cold air conditioned premises where you could buy a gin and tonic without having to knock it back in one gulp as you had to with Posnick's illicit whiskey. Shorty always seemed to be in one or other of these bars and usually drunk, which resulted in falling off his barstool. Folks were kind and helped him back on the stool.

Posnick's Bar was probably no different from any other small town bar in the western United States at that time, but it was an eye-opener for a young man from the UK who had to produce his passport as a form of photo ID to show he was over 21. One bar in Washington refused to accept the blue UK passport as valid ID. The draft beer served was Olympia or Rainier, named after two mountains in Washington State. You could also get Schlitz, and several other beers like Blue Ribbon and Budweiser in cans. None of them tasted anything like beer back home, and I suppose they were basically lagers. A couple of places served the beer in jugs, the first time I had seen that.

The Star Morning Mine was located up Burke Canyon Road, at the community of Burke where there was a Post Office. Oddly, there was a small community a couple of miles downstream from Burke called Cornwall.

If you carried on up FR50 (FR=Fire Route) past the mine buildings, you came across a timber log cabin structure that hosted a restaurant which sold bear steaks.

From the mine, the road ran along the valley bottom and next to the river. At Wallace, the river joined the South Fork of the Coeur d'Alene River which ultimately flowed into the Columbia River and the Pacific.

The mine was, at the time, very profitable and hosted a large milling operation, sending its concentrate by specially built rail line to the smelter in Kellogg, 12 miles west of Wallace. Emissions from the smelter were for years unregulated, and the hills above Kellogg were covered with stumps of dead pine trees: some dying as the result of waste gases from the smelter, and some as the result of fires over the years. The mine buildings seemed very permanent and the mine offices were extensive, as was the 'dry' or changing rooms for the miners. The mine where I had worked in Cornwall was a series of portacabins, with limited showering facilities. Here, miners had lockers in which to keep their overalls, towels and personal gear. There were also communal showers, and probably the weirdest thing I had seen in the US was a line of 20 or so toilets with only a low dividing wall separating each throne. So, in the mornings and after day shift, one would see a line of twenty men ensconced on the thrones doing their business and chatting to each other.

The mine employed some 227 underground miners and about 100 people in the mill and engineering offices. Many of the men wore what we would call boiler suits or overalls. The clothing was straight out of an American television show such as *Casey Jones*: button-up bibs made of white calico and printed with thin blue stripes. Others, like me, wore Levis and woollen lumberjack shirts. The mine issued us with slickers (oilskins to us in the UK), steel toe capped boots and a wide webbing waist belt with a large aluminium ring at the back with which to attach yourself to something when working in high places. It also had an attachment for a lamp battery and, importantly, the Self-Rescuer which was about the size of a six-ounce coffee jar. When opened, the miner could take out the small device which provided sufficient clean air through a filter and mouthpiece to enable him to reach fresh air.

After undertaking a mandatory course in the use of a Self-Rescuer, I had a tour of the mine facilities and the mill, then had a lesson in basic first aid. To go underground the next day, I was paired with an old timer who repaired track and did some carpentry work. I don't think they believed me when I told them I knew how to drive the small battery run locomotive used to haul the ore cars, or that I could use an Eimco overshot shovel used to load blasted rock in tunnels, a pneumatic drill, and knew the rudiments of railway track laying. All skills learnt last summer in the local Pendarves tin mine in Camborne. By the end of the summer, I was accepted as a legitimate partner for the miners.

The Self-Rescuer course and the carrying of the equipment was implemented as a result of a dreadful disaster that took place at the Sunshine Mine in Kellogg the previous year. On the morning of 2nd May 1972 at around 11.40am, smoke was noted on the 3700 level (3,700 ft below ground) indicating fire was burning somewhere in the mine. Underground fires are deadly as they produce large amounts of carbon monoxide from the incomplete combustion of wooden timbers that support the tunnels and the shafts. Of the 173 men in the mine at the time of the fire, 80 were able to evacuate, with the last one reaching the surface by 1.30pm. Two men, able to find a safe zone on the 4800 level near the number 12 borehole, were rescued a staggering 175 hours later. The remaining 91 men died of carbon monoxide poisoning.

Many lives would have been saved had the miners had access to Self-Rescuers. Knowing of the time taken to rescue the two men at the number 12 borehole, I always carried an 'emergency' sandwich and beef jerky, as did many of the miners.

The engineers, geologists and mine officials helped me a lot, from ensuring I had a ride to work, to providing me with engineering data and a tour of the mill so that I could compile my report for CSM. The training officer put me in touch with a guy who gave me a lift to and from work. I never knew his name and he was always referred to as 'the Polack'. He was a man of few emotions, and I could never figure out if he was pleased to have company back and forth to the mine or if he was naturally taciturn. He spoke very little English. Conversations were limited.

Me: *Have a good day?*
Polack: *One hundred dollar day.*
Me: *That's pretty good money.*
Polack: *[Grunt]*
Me: *Well, my partner and I put up three timber sets today and that will be $60 bonus between us.*
Polack: *[Grunt] Good.*
Me: *[Generally babbling until we got to the Wallace Corner]*
Me: *See you tomorrow.*
Polack: *Okay.*

A one hundred dollar bonus shift was pretty extraordinary as he and his partner must have drilled and blasted their development tunnel at least twice during their shift.

Occasionally Polack would say, "Tomorrow, night shift," and I would have to get a ride with someone else. Or he would say, "Bad day, no bonus," and not elaborate.

The work was fairly standard with the mining method being cut and fill, which was relatively safe. I was mostly paid at the day rate which was between $3.00 and $5.00 per hour.

On occasion, if one of the miners didn't turn up for work, I was paired with one of the stope miners or one of the development miners who drilled, blasted and mucked out the tunnels. The stopes were where the action of extracting the silver ore was undertaken. When working with these skilled miners, I would earn a production bonus and extra pay. I remember at the end of the trip I had saved up $800 and had enough to pay off the loans provided to me by relations to undertake the trip, *and* to buy a second hand car.

In the stopes, which are like short tunnels some 15ft wide, 90ft long and 8ft high, the mining method required the roof to be secured by putting timber posts and horizontal timber beams between the posts in place and then drilling and blasting the 15 x 8ft face. Blasting would advance the face of the stope by 6ft or so until it reached the end of the stope at the 90ft mark. When completed, the space from where the ore was extracted was filled with fine sand and cement pumped from surface through boreholes. The sand was a portion of the finely ground ore from which the mineral value had been extracted. This then formed the floor of the next stope. Access to the stopes was gained by ladder-ways boxed in with timber. These were divided in two, one half holding ladders for men to ascend into the stope, also to carry the compressed air and water pipes required for mining; the other half was used as a chute to drop the blasted ore down to the tunnel level so that it could be collected by small rail cars and transported along the small narrow gauge rail track back to the main shaft and then hoisted up to surface for milling.

To complete all these tasks required a team of several people including two miners who stayed at the working face, and a 'nipper' who stayed in the access tunnels below and delivered the explosives, timber and all the other material the miners required. There were also timber men who built the chutes and the 'Cousin Jack' boxes that controlled the flow of the broken ore to the railcars. A tramming crew collected the ore from the chutes and drove back to the shaft in the three-ton railcars.

At the end of the summer, I became familiar with all of these operations and even had a few shifts as a development miner. This involved drilling and blasting a tunnel to allow access to new areas of the mine, and in one case, creating a tunnel to connect the Star

Morning to the Lucky Friday mine on the other side of the mountain. Development miners were the top of the pile and earned more money than anyone else. Being a nipper was a pretty specialised task, so I never got to do that. The nipper on the level where I did most of my work was a Native American named Randy who used to chant songs while driving his three-ton rail-bound supply locomotive up and down the tunnels.

I was somewhat fortunate that a fellow second year student on the same course as me at the CSM had landed a job in the Sunshine Mine in Kellogg some 10 miles up the road from Wallace. Mike was a mature student and an experienced miner having worked in Cornish mines before entering the School of Mines. In addition, there was Julian, a CSM graduate who was the Contract Engineer at the same mine, and on occasion he took myself and Mike out on excursions at weekends.

These included a visit to Ellensburg in Washington State where Julian's brother was completing a graduate course in Undersea Surveying (or something to do with the sea, which was a little weird as Ellensburg is some distance from the coast). There was a river that ran through the city, and on the weekends students would float down the river on large inner tubes and drink beer. Of course, Mike and I tried this. It was fun, except at the end where you had to get to the right side of the river to disembark or be swept over a weir and end up in the Pacific Ocean.

Julian also took us to a bar in a log cabin on Rose Lake, 15 miles west of Kellogg, where he kept his Bottle Match mug. This was a pint mug made of Cornish tin and awarded to members of the winning team of the annual rugby match between the Royal School of Mines in London and the Camborne School of Mines. He preferred not to go out for drinks in Kellogg as the miners did not like him, not because of his personality, but because his position as contract engineer gave him the power to award or cut bonus payments at the mine. Most of the miners worked on a bonus system as the base rate was pretty low, so cuts in their bonus were not appreciated for what they may have considered spurious reasons.

Then, toward the end of the summer, disaster struck. A forest fire swept through the Rose Lake area, burnt the bar to the ground and melted the prized Bottle Match mug.

Julian once took me to a Toast Masters meeting at a bar in Murray, a little town between Kellogg and Wallace. I had never heard of the organisation but understood it was formed to help people of all walks of life become proficient at public speaking. There I met a DJ from the local radio station KWAL. It broadcast to the Silver Valley on a low power AM transmitter. KWAL provided coverage on football and basketball for the three local high schools in the Silver Valley, Wallace, Kellogg and Mullan High School, with live play-by-play action on all away and home games.

The DJ also did an early form of a talk show with phone-ins. He interviewed me one morning while I was on afternoon shift and apparently he had a lot of calls from local girls wanting to meet me. I didn't take up any of the offers, but in Wallace most people knew me anyway and would call out, "Hey Limey, heard you on the Radio."

Fame at last.

Mining wasn't the only industry in the region. There was a tremendous amount of logging taking place. There were a couple of timber mills in the valley and on the road up to the mine, as well as on the road between Wallace and Kellogg where conical structures with domed perforated tops spewed red sparks out into the night. They looked like something from *War of the Worlds*. Or maybe Daleks who had lost their shooting sticks from an episode of *Doctor Who*. In fact, they were built to dispose of sawdust from the mills by burning it in these domed structures.

August passed into September and the two American students who were working in the mine, Chuck and Jimmy Junior, left a week before Labor Day to return to college in California.

In mid-September, the Safety Department held a raffle. Your name was entered into the draw if you had worked three months without a loss-time accident. Astonishingly, my name was drawn out of the hard hat. The prize I had won was a top-of-the-line Winchester hunting rifle. I was thrilled but knew there was no way I could ship a rifle back to the UK. Fortunately, I was allowed to choose goods to the value of the rifle from the Outdoor Sportsman shop in town. The rifle was valued at $120, and so, armed with my voucher, I went to the shop and proceeded to buy clothes and ski gear that I kept for years. My favourites were a duck down ski jacket and a knitted woollen crew-neck ski sweater with a flag of the USA on the front. I had the jacket until 1985.

In preparation for my return to the UK, I went into the JCPenney department store and bought a couple of fleecy brushed cotton, check-patterned lumberjack shirts. These I also kept for years. In addition, I bought a small brown canvas bag that would be suitable as carry-on luggage for the trip home. Into this I packed a few clothes and most importantly several what I thought to be spectacular mineral specimens gathered at the working face in the mine: mostly composed of silver, lead and zinc. These were very heavy and would have put me way over the hold luggage allowance. In fact, the small bag weighed around 40 pounds. It, too, survived for years.

My return flight was scheduled for two weeks before our term started at Camborne. It was probably a good thing that I was pre-booked to fly home as I was having a great time in Wallace. I was earning good money, I had a couple of girlfriends (before meeting Linda, by the way), and the living was easy. I could have quite happily stayed there for another year. However, my visa was due to expire in a couple of months and Cornwall was calling me back home. So in late September with my pockets full of 'dough' – and to avoid taking another 72 hour bus ride back to New York – I bought a first class ticket on Northwest Orient from Spokane to JFK airport, to arrive in time for my flight back to the UK.

I was quite sad to leave the area, and the owners of the diner where I ate most of my meals bought me a present of a bottle of aftershave. Posnick Junior and I went out for a night on the town, and one of the girls gave me a bandana which I kept for years. The engineers and guys at the mine also bade me farewell and I was given a great reference by the mine manager. In fact, after completing my degree I wrote to Hecla to see if I could get a job with them. They offered me a position at their mine in Casa Grande, Arizona. However, after leaving the US, I met the love my life, married her, and after careful consideration (and as well as the US embassy refusing to issue us a visa), we decided to take a job with Anglo American and took off for South Africa for a three-year stint on the gold mines. Many years later, Linda and I spent a good portion of our working career in the US in both Tucson and Phoenix. Casa Grande is located midway between the two cities and we would often drive through Casa Grande and wonder how life would have been if we had taken up the offer.

I took Linda to Wallace some twenty-four years later to find that traffic on I-10 had finally made it through the town without having to stop on a red light. I-10 had now been raised on stilts, leaving the town in peace below. The Wallace Hotel is closed and Posnick Junior now owns a bar across the street. Wallace has become a Historic Mining District and the silver mines are closed.

I can't help but wonder what happened to Shorty.

4

OFF TO THE SUN

1974-1977: South Africa

The truly 'Orange' Free State, deep gold mines, rescue training, underground schools, black miners, friends from CSM, horses and rugby

"Off to the sun!" read the banner above the photo of Linda and myself in the wedding report page of the *West Briton*, August 1974.

Having graduated from the Camborne School of Mines, I accepted a job as a graduate mining engineer with Anglo American Mining Corporation of 44 Main Street, Johannesburg, South Africa; a company closely associated with the Oppenheimer family and Barney Barnato, the famous mining entrepreneur. This was one of several jobs that were on offer to us as mining was in a boom time and graduates were in high demand. We later found out that jobs at Anglo were so plentiful because 75% of the graduates who went out to SA returned to the UK or left for other jobs after the first three-year contract. Not that work was hard or the living conditions poor, but those that left were either homesick or looking for something more than advancing up the Anglo corporate ladder. Nevertheless, those that remained had a pretty good time of it.

It was the ideal life for a mining engineer just out of university. So, in early November 1974, we boarded flight SA237 on a South African Airways 747 that left from Heathrow, stopping to refuel in Cape Verde islands, where we all had to disembark and cross the tarmac to the transit lounge. The stop was our first experience of tropical humidity and heat, as well as our first sight of armed soldiers who were guarding the plane and ensuring we went to and stayed in the transit lounge before re-boarding. We were not the only celebrities on board as behind us in economy was a very young Jimmy Connors the tennis player with what must have been his entire family.

On arrival at Jan Smuts airport in Johannesburg, we were met by Mr Lehman from the company. He took us to the New Library Hotel in Jo'burg where all incoming graduates were put up before travelling down to the mines in the Orange Free State or were shipped off to the far west Rand. Safely ensconced and having eaten, we were surprised when one of the fellows from Camborne came and had a drink with us. Apparently the Camborne School of Mines mafia who worked in head office knew of our arrival and sent Ally to meet us. He briefed us on some of the do's-and-don'ts of working for Anglo. He, nor it seemed anyone else, had heard of the mine we were to be stationed at nor knew the name of the town in which it was located, Odendaalsrus.

In any event, next morning Mr Lehmann picked us up, took us to 44 Main Street, and after a brief welcome cup of tea and biscuits, we had a meeting with the head of personnel, Mr Penny, who outlined the Anglo Graduate Training scheme which provided the pathway to riches and the fabled company car. We were then driven back to Jan Smuts airport and took the afternoon flight to Welkom which lies in the centre of the mining district in the middle of the Orange Free State.

Never having been in a prop-driven, unpressurised plane before, it was quite an adventure boarding the DC3. That morning, it had flown up from Welkom loaded with the gold that was produced from several of the mines in the area. In the afternoon, the plane returned with passengers bound for the Free State, home of the Afrikaner Boer farmer and gold miner.

Looking out of the window at an altitude of what the pilot said was 10,000ft, the ground seemed very close, which was in fact true, as the average height of the countryside or *veldt* is around 5,000ft above sea level, which brought the plane 5,000ft closer to the ground.

No jungle to be seen, and not a lot of geographical relief apart from the occasional *kopje* and small lakes that were likely cattle watering holes. As we flew south, the fields became greener with a crop which we guessed was maize. On arrival in Welkom, we were met by Mr Van der Merwe a young Afrikaner who barely spoke any English. Linda asked him a couple of questions about the agriculture and forestry on the way to the mine site to which he didn't respond, either not knowing the answer or not knowing the answer in English.

He checked us in to the Oranje Hotel in Odendaalsrus (or OD) which was 11 miles from the main mining centre of Welkom where all the Camborne and Royal School of Mines graduates were based. OD, at that time, still had several unpaved streets of compacted dirt the same orange colour as the rest of the State. The hotel was dark, clean but somehow seemed dingy, with bare floors and furnished almost entirely with furniture upholstered in different shades of orange and green vinyl.

We were the only ones in the large echoing dining room, so for our first meal in the Free State we ate some kind of meat not really knowing what it was as we had to order from the menu which was in Afrikaans and the word *fleiss* seemed to fit the description of meat. Somewhat easier to understand, we ordered *aartappel*, which were what we thought to be potatoes.

Aartappels were indeed potatoes boiled to destruction, and the meal also arrived with an orange vegetable on the side which turned out to be carrots boiled to a mush and heavily dosed with sugar. We were starting to despair of the situation as the dessert of canned pears in syrup and ice cream was delivered to the table, when at that moment another Camborne School of Mines man blew into the dining room: Sluggo, a rugby player and generally good fellow. He couldn't have been a more welcome sight. He had been in country a couple of years and knew the ropes.

During the next few weeks, he directed us along the path of getting a small furnished flat in Nyala House in Welkom, and a few other invaluable tips, while I completed the Miners Certification. This entailed getting my blasting licence in the Learner Officials Training Centre, the classroom of which was 3,500ft below surface at the Welkom mine in a room blasted out of the living rock.

Back to school and new accommodations

A part of the certification was to pass the blasting course which I had done both in the US and Cornwall. One had to learn the rules that applied in South Africa, which were all common sense apart from those concerning the handling of explosives by the black workers. White miners were supposed to closely supervise the handling and storage of explosives. This was often not the case as a miner in charge of two working places could not be expected to oversee all of the steps related to charging the holes drilled for blasting. Much of the supervision was delegated to Bantu known as 'Boss Boys' who acted as a foreman for each of the miner's working crew. Also, some miners were so lazy that they delegated all of the work of charging the faces to the Boss Boys. In fact many of the Boss Boys had more experience than the miners themselves.

The course also focused on personal safety and those around you. One thing which I will always remember was the Quebec Safety System. This consisted of five rules that were to be applied on a daily and continuous basis:

1. Check the entrance to the place of work
2. Are workplace and equipment in good working order?

3. Are men working properly?
4. Do an act of safety.
5. Can and will men continue to work properly?

It was a requirement to write in your Shift Boss daily log book that you had completed one of the actions in each working place visited.

The most important part of the course was to recognise deadly explosive methane gas in a miners' lamp (good old Sir Humphry Davy). After passing the methane recognition test examination conducted by one of the many Inspectors of Mines and passing the blasting test, one went to the mine to which you were allocated. This allocation was determined in London before leaving the UK, so we knew we were going to a mine called 'Freddie's Consolidated Lease Area', a mine of three shafts recently having been brought into the Anglo group. Being the new boy to the group, the mine had only one other graduate, a Civil Engineering type and a Scot.

As graduates, our accommodations were reasonable and generally 'miners cottages': two bedroomed bungalows with a small garden. Here, one could happily live until rising to the position of shift boss when a new, more palatial house, would be allocated. Single men were housed in Protea House, a building with small self-contained rooms or mini flats where meals were served and all laundry was done. We stayed for six weeks in the furnished flat in Nyala House in Welkom until housing became available in Odendaalsrus.

After completing the certification, we were assigned a modest bungalow close to the mine. As in most mining camps, there was a strict hierarchy associated with the allocation of the accommodations. As one climbed the Anglo ladder, the houses had an increasing number of toilets and bathrooms. In addition, the size and quality of the detached servants' quarters increased. It appeared that when one rose to the dizzy heights of Section Manager (third from the top in the chain of command at a mine), there would be a minimum of three toilets, two bathrooms and palatial servants' quarters (two rooms instead of one), plus a company car.

On arrival, Anglo very kindly gave us a settling-in allowance of a massive (to us) 500 Rand. This was a full month's salary and we could spend it on what we wanted. Generally, people put a deposit down on a car and then bought some furniture from the OK Bazaars. As the Bazaars were owned by Anglo, we were able to get the goods on hire purchase if we wanted. The graduates pretty much all bought the same stuff: a sofa and two or three armchairs made of dark *imbuia* wood, a dining room set of bleached pine, and a bed. Oh yes, and then a horse.

The colour of the sofa and soft furnishings were of a very hip orange. Our wedding presents, carefully packed in a tea chest along with two zinc trunks contained much of our crockery, also in seventies orange. For a while, the shipment travelling by boat to Cape Town from the UK went missing but eventually was located at the docks and placed on a train to Ventersdorp, twenty miles from OD. We went to retrieve them in our Volkswagen Beetle and found them sitting unattended on the platform. The zinc trunks survive to this day.

After completing the Miners Training Course and obtaining my blasting certificate, we moved to OD to our house, 13 Taljaard Street, where we lived for three years. It was in sight of the mine headgear and with an excellent view of the drive-in cinema screen.

As 90% of the miners and tradesmen that did the hard and dangerous work were black, or as they were known *Bantu*, one was required to learn the lingua franca of the mines, *Fanakalo*, so as to give instructions and orders to the Bantu. At Freddie's, all of the white miners were Afrikaners, and very few of them spoke English. A couple of them still held grudges against the English dating back to the Boer Wars. I found it very difficult to manage the Fanakalo but at least grasped the basics of Afrikaans. A couple of phrases in Fanakalo stick in the mind: *Sindile* meaning 'work safely', which also acted as a greeting. The other was the first one I learnt, *Nika mina lo manzi,* 'give me the water'. Very important, as it was hot underground.

The next step in the Anglo training course was to be placed with a miner as an assistant to learn the ropes, and learn the tricks that were played on the other miners and shift bosses. It also helped to understand the mentality of the miners: childishly competitive and seldom professional, although those that knew what they were doing produced excellent results and earned good money.

Following that stint, I was placed in charge of a team of black miners on night shift whose job it was to clean the rock and ore that was blasted in the stopes by the day shift. The working areas known as stopes were mostly slightly inclined, at an angle of 25 degrees, and only 1-1.5m in height. The rock from the blasted faces was cleaned using scrapers or scoops attached by wires to a system of pulleys to a winch. The scraper pulled the broken ore to a vertical tunnel or box hole that connected to a tunnel beneath the stope. The tunnel acted as a storage area, and at the bottom of the box hole, a chute stopped the ore from falling on to the rail track. From here, the broken ore was taken back to the shaft and dumped into a holding pocket before being hoisted back to surface.

As well as ensuring the stopes were cleaned, other crews moved the broken rock from horizontal tunnels which radiated out from the shaft to access the areas where the gold lay in the veins known as the 'reef'. The tunnels were of standard dimensions, some 12 x 16ft. These tunnels were equipped with the rails on which the ore cars travelled from the stopes to the shaft. As well as ore from the stopes, waste rock was hauled to surface. The waste rock was from the access tunnels and had to be taken up for disposal on the huge waste tips, a feature of the city scape in Jo'bug.

The rock sides of these tunnels when penetrating areas away from the main shafts got hotter and hotter as the mine went deeper. The temperature of the quartzite rock in the sides and roofs of the tunnels when first blasted was hot to the touch. In deeper mines, it could reach 120°F. This was known as the 'virgin rock temperature'.

To keep the workings cool, air from surface was funnelled down the shafts and sucked out of the mine by giant fans. On frosty mornings in winter, you could spot the location of the fans by the plumes of dense, white condensation rising up into the cool, high, *veldt* air.

As these tunnels were reaching out into virgin ground, the rock they were going through became stressed, and on occasion the tunnel walls would burst as if they had been shattered by an explosive force. Thankfully, these seemed to occur after blasting when the mine and tunnels affected were empty of personnel.

Challenges at work for both of us

Everything was new to us. Linda took a job as a Steel Estimator working for OD Engineering, a private company based in Welkom that fabricated steel structures for the mines, and in particular, several of the new processing components at my mine, Freddie's.

Surface at Freddie's was 5,700ft above the last working level. Workings known as levels started at 3,000ft below the surface; an ever present thought when working in a narrow 3ft (90cm) high stope, knowing that there was an awful lot of rock above you. The roof of the narrow stopes were supported by timber logs known as 'packs', stacked on top of each other, three foot long and some eight inches square, which were reinforced with interconnected concrete blocks. They were secured by hammering wooden wedges into them between the roof and the pack. Sounds secure, but one could see stopes in old working areas where the roof had collapsed and crushed the timber to a height of 12 inches or so. Not enough room to survive if trapped in there. And while supporting the roof, the packs were liable to catch fire through poor blasting procedures. Occasionally, a disgruntled miner who had lost his bonus or wanted to go on leave, or a black activist striking a blow for emancipation would ensure an outbreak of fire by setting flammable material in a place where it would otherwise be unlikely catch light from the blasting.

The fires mainly started in the stopes using the wooden packs that supported the roofs. I also saw fires start in heavily timbered tunnels where the timber caps and uprights supported the roof. These were always away from an area where spontaneous combustion or blasting may have started the fire, and were obviously started on purpose. Very scary, because as the fire burned, the caps and timbers would fail, causing the roof to fall.

Each mine had its own Proto team, and all the personal rescue equipment was stored at the mine. If there was a fire on one of the other mines, we would be called out to help fight their fires as well as looking after our own mine. There was also an aviary that held several canaries. As the newest member in the team at Freddie's, I was placed in charge of the canaries, and had to ensure one was with us every time we went to a fire. Being the graduate and, latterly, as the only one in the team with the Mine Manager's Certificate, I also took care of the gas testing equipment.

The incomplete combustion of the timber and the burning of plastic pipes that carried water to the working areas produced a suite of noxious gases. The worst was carbon monoxide. On occasion, when underground fighting a fire, the atmosphere while being visually clear contained fatal amounts of CO (carbon monoxide). Using the Drager gas detector, we could tell how much gas was present, not just CO but CO_2 (carbon dioxide) as well. It's a really scary feeling being in an area where the air looks clear as a bell but one small breath would kill almost instantly.

The earthquake in Welkom

In the second year we were there, one of our fellow graduates from Strathclyde was caught in a roof fall in his mine and was killed, crushed. It was dangerous work.

So it was no surprise that people were very worried about their husbands and other members of their families when the earthquake struck on 8th December 1976. The quake measured 5.2 on the Richter scale. At the time, there were an estimated 4,000 men underground in various mines in the Welkom area, including me.

Initially, we knew nothing of the quake as the shock waves passed above us in my section. Friends and miners on the upper levels told of the roof opening and closing in the stopes. Our first indication that something was wrong was when another shift boss and I went back to the shaft to take the cage to surface. Instead of the usual well behaved group of Bantu, the men were grumbling, complaining and generally causing a ruckus.

After an event of such magnitude, it was required to inspect every foot of the shaft, checking the guides, rails and supports that kept the cage carrying up to fifty miners at a time on track. This was done by the Shaft Mine Captain and the Mine Manager standing on top of the cage and being slowly lowered.

If all was clear, they were hoisted back to surface, inside the cage this time. After this, the hoist driver would run the cage up and down the shaft at high speed. This was essential as the cage would be travelling at 36mph to reach the bottom of our 5,700ft shaft.

Pushing our way through the crowd of black miners, we reached the shaft station and called back to surface on the cable wire phone. We were informed of the earthquake and given an estimate of when we could all expect to be hoisted back to surface. It was now about 1.30pm, and some of the miners had been underground since 4.00am with little food. They were justifiably upset and even more so when one of the first cages to come down was loaded with Black Mine Police and a couple of Alsatian dogs to maintain order. By now, there were about ten white miners and two shift bosses gathered on the back side of the shaft away from the side where the workers were gathered. Eventually, after a four hour wait, we were hoisted back to surface where each of us were trying to get to a phone so we could let our wives and families know we were okay.

Linda was working in her office in Welkom when the quake occurred and saw the floor move and the ceiling ripple as the shock waves passed through. Phineas, the teaboy, was entering the offices with a tray, and the sensible lad dropped it and ran outside. The only major damage was done to a six-storey block of flats which collapsed 75 minutes after the event. I still find it amazing that there were no fatalities related to the quake.

It made the BBC news in the UK, "not yet known how many killed and injured."

We had no idea that this had been reported at home. Linda's Mum tried to call us and eventually got through after a couple of days. The delay was probably because the telephone exchange was relocated away from where it was housed in case its building collapsed. This made communications with the outside world difficult.

Progressing along the Anglo career path

Most of the cleaning operation from the blasting of the stopes and development tunnels was done on the night shift from 8pm to 4am. Night shift cleaning was about the bottom of the white miners' job ladder. As graduates, we passed quickly from that onerous duty to managing a track laying team of 12 or so black workers laying the rails for transporting the ore on mini railways and delivering the supplies to the working areas.

Next, one progressed to filling in for miners who were sick or on holiday. After this, you would be allocated your own stope, managing a team of thirty black miners. If you were unpopular with the management or had a mine captain or shaft manager who didn't like graduates or Englishmen (or Cornishmen), you could get stuck for months on night shift or would end up being placed in the most difficult of working areas.

So, this was the path to be followed to reach the exalted status of Mine Manager: from miner to Shift Boss, to Mine Captain, to Section Manager and finally General Manager. The only way to rise above shift boss was to obtain the Mine Captain's Certificate of Competency and then on to the Mine Manager's Certificate of Competency. By passing the Mine Captain's certificate I obtained the Mine Manager's Certificate, but I never made it beyond shift boss. Partly because I was assigned to the planning office after snapping the tendons in my foot playing rugby and could not go underground, and partly as I liked working in the planning office. However, the pay was good and the income was supplemented by my joining the Proto Underground Fire Fighting team (named after the antiquated rebreathing apparatus we wore), plus we had Linda's salary, as possibly the only female Steel Estimator in the country. This meant we could save a little while enjoying life. It was quite difficult to send money out of South Africa but we managed it, in one instance paying a courier who had a tin false leg to smuggle small gold bars out of the country.

It wasn't all work; after all, it was Africa and we had come to see lions, zebras and to feel the sun on our faces. However, it was a six-day work week and there were only four public holidays a year. Freddie's had its own nine-hole golf course, and on a certain portion a few animals were allowed to roam at will. There was a camel, a couple of zebra, wildebeest and an enormous tortoise. Oddly, the animals stayed away from the greens where they would have been safe from errant golf balls sliced off the tee or from the fairway.

It was important to be seen playing golf and we used to call it 'promotion sticks'. Most of the mines had a nine-hole course, but Freddie's was the best as it had nine holes but played twice from different tees. Usually on Sunday mornings, a few graduates or friends would play either at Freddie's or one of the other courses in Welkom and then have a *braai* after the game.

These Sunday barbeques were a lot of fun. There would be new and old friends, a lot of meat: steak, lamb chops, occasionally chicken, and of course, *boerewors* – a spicy game sausage. The Afrikaners liked to marinade their steak and *boerewors* in coke. Not so for us.

Life in a small mining town in the Orange Free State

Living in OD had its advantages, well at least two: the drive-in cinema and the stables.

The mine had its own riding stables where Linda kept her horse Espanje. It was a toss-up as to which was purchased first, the horse or the car. The car won by a nose.

The horse was bought from a stable in Welkom, 14 miles away. Not having a horse trailer Linda had to ride Espanje from Welkom to OD on the main road. So having just bought the VW Beetle I was able to ride shotgun for her along the side of the road.

Our home was about a five minute drive from the stables where Espanje was kept. We also had the advantage of being able to see the drive-in movie screen from our front window. Not such a great thing, as we couldn't hear the sound. But as there was no TV, it would sometimes provide two or three minutes of fun trying to guess what was being said. Another advantage of being close to the drive-in was that an ancillary takeaway shack was 300 yards from the house. They served the most amazing sandwich known as a Dagwood which contained sliced tomatoes, cheese, bacon, ham, and a fried egg, all captured between two pieces of toasted white bread and optional mayo or tomato ketchup.

It was a strange country and a strange time: *apartheid* was in full swing, petrol rationing was introduced during the oil crisis in 1975 with petrol stations closing at 6pm on a Friday and not opening again until 8am on Monday. If you were caught carrying petrol in cans, there were huge fines.

If we wanted to go to Jo'burg, I would have to pull an early shift at the mine on Friday going underground at 4am coming back to surface at 12 noon, getting back to the house at 1pm, and ready to drive to Jo'burg. The early shift combined with taking a holiday on Saturday meant we could drive toward Jo'burg and then fill up at the last moment at a few minutes before 6 o'clock on Friday night. This, and a litre of petrol in a lemonade bottle, would just about see us and the VW around Jo'burg and back to OD.

Initially, there were no TV broadcasts in the country and we listened to the BBC World Service on a very small shortwave radio, stringing bits of wire around the room to try and improve reception. Alternatively, Radio Springbok was very good. I still remember some of the jingles: "Black Cat Peanut Butter, Take a new look at Blue." (Not sure what Blue was.)

The programmes were quite good and had quizzes such as, 'Test the team' or 'Does the team think?' People would send in questions to be answered by 'three wise men' to ponder and answer, one in Jo'burg, one in Cape Town and one in Pretoria. If you beat the team, you won a small prize. They had no wise man in the Free State.

Another radio series that we listened to on Friday nights was *Squad Car: Tales of John Vorster Square*, the main police station in Jo'burg. (This is where the black activist Steve Biko 'fell' out of his cell located on the fifth floor of the building.) The programme started with dramatic music and the sound of police sirens, then a deep voice would say, "They roam the empty streets at night." Very entertaining! There were characters such as Shady Lanes and Fingers Lockpick the burglar. On Sundays, we listened to, "The story of the conversion of Saul of Tharsis."

Occasionally, we hired 16mm projectors and rented a film ('fil-lum' as the Afrikaners say), and showed movies on a white bed sheet pinned to the wall of the lounge. We took it in turns visiting each other's houses for the showings. We usually finished by 9pm as most of us had to be underground by 7am the next morning.

Ah, happy days, with no decision on which TV channel to choose. We also listened to music on Radio LM, broadcast, oddly, from Lourenco Marques in Mozambique. It was a time when colonial powers were letting go of their African possessions. Angola and Mozambique were the closest to us, and there were Portuguese refugees crossing the borders leaving behind an uncertain future in a post-colonial communist regime

Even in the Free State, which was somewhat removed from the coast and the borders, there was a strong Portuguese presence, and they seemed to have a monopoly on fresh fruit and vegetable shops. These were invariably known as 'Alonso' or 'Paulo's Portuguese Market Garden'. They were the Afrikaner version of the corner shop, and would open all hours.

Although it was a six-day week at the mine, the Saturday shift was two hours shorter than the normal eight hours. Not a lot of free time to explore and check out your surroundings, not much got done underground on a Saturday. At Freddie's, because it was not a fiery mine where deadly methane was present, the miners would congregate around their work stations, make a small fire and grill lamb chops or the steak marinated in Coca Cola, plus *boerewors*. The fire was strictly illegal but tolerated. When reaching a more senior position, one did not go underground on a Saturday.

The work station would be close to designated stopes and development tunnels, at the junction of two tunnels or an area where there was a little space to congregate. It held a wooden 3 x 4ft box which stored tools, spray paint and often blasting fuse. Next to the box miners would build a chair and spend most of the working day there. Some of the white miners would only go into the working areas to mark the working faces with red spray paint, showing the black miners where to drill, and go back to their work station.

Most of the white miners would oversee the process where the holes were then filled with explosives. In the stopes, they would ensure that the roof supports were properly installed and that the blasted rock was removed. Some miners left all of the supervision to the Boss Boys, only visiting the working areas once a day.

Time off and trips away

The four designated public holidays in South Africa were Christmas Day, New Year's Day, Easter Friday and *Dingaans Day*, also known as Day of the Covenant, celebrating the Battle of Blood River.

Even with the limited holiday structure, we managed to see some of the Free State which was basically a large field of maize. However, exciting trips were made to Allemanskraal Dam on the appropriately named Sand River, about a two-hour drive to the southeast. And in the Willem Pretorius Game Preserve, a few wildebeest, giraffe, Eland antelope, meerkats, and a lone cheetah were enclosed in a large safari park. There were convenient picnic areas where baboons stole fruit and cakes. Photos were taken of distant animals with Kodak cameras that provided coloured memories of our fun. See that dot there? That's an antelope, and that one is a wildebeest. The photos were carefully placed in albums and although now faded, the memories are vivid.

A short ninety minute drive from OD through an even bigger field of maize brought us to the Bloemhof Dam situated on the Vaal River. To get there you passed through several small *dorps* or one-horse towns that consisted of a main street with a general store, a feed merchant, a grain silo, and hotel. I played rugby at a couple of these places: Wesselsbron and Hoopstad. The pitches consisted of *kikuyu* grass, dried and burnt by the winter sun. Being tackled and skidding along that was like falling onto a very hard coconut mat. Much skin was lost from elbows and knees.

Playing rugby for the mine and OD helped me integrate and get on with the miners. It was very hard rugby and I was known as, '*Saute the hartlooper*,' roughly translated as 'the Englishman who could run fast'. The speed was in direct proportion to the need to escape from enormous, tough Afrikaners, whose greatest desire was to have the opportunity to squash an Englishman. However, I enjoyed it immensely.

At the dam, there were a few places for a picnic and some open space where we could look at the river that formed the boundary between the Cape Province and the OFS. The Vaal eventually became the Orange River after passing the famous diamond mining town of Kimberley.

Optimistically, I thought I might be able to pan up some diamonds in the river which, at one time, led prospectors to the famous Kimberley Mine. No such luck. Ransom, our rescue cross-breed Alsatian, did however plunge into the river chasing a meerkat. Not to worry, until we realised there were crocodiles in the river.

"Here, boy! Ransom, come! Good boy."

Fortunately, the slow current had pushed him only a little way downstream and he emerged without a croc on his tail.

On a couple of occasions, we made the four-hour journey to the Golden Gate national park lodge to roam the valleys and sandstone cliffs, viewing the spectacular scenery. Once, we hired ponies for a two-hour slow-paced walk out to a view point ... and a thirty minute gallop back to the lodge. At no time were any of us in control of the speed of the horse. And probably not in charge of the direction they were taking.

The route from OD took us through Bethlehem to the small town of Clarens, along some of the most boring scenery we had ever experienced. However, the park is close to the border of Northern Lesotho situated in the Maluti Mountains with wonderful topography. The scenery changed dramatically as we neared the park. The 'Golden Gate' refers to the sandstone cliffs on either side of the valley at the Golden Gate dam. In 1875, a farmer called JNR Van Reenen and his wife stopped here as they travelled to their new farm in Vuurland. He named the location Golden Gate when he saw the last rays of the setting sun falling on the cliffs.

As with most of the place names in the Free State and Northern Cape, the villages and towns were named by the *voortrekkers* – the Dutch immigrants who populated the country from the 1830s to the 1890s at the start of the Boer War.

They trekked seeking to live beyond the Cape's British colonial administration. The Great Trek was the culmination of tensions between rural descendants of the Cape's original European settlers, known collectively as Boers, and the British. Eventually, this led to the Boer War and the founding of several autonomous Boer Republics, namely the South African Republic known simply as the *Transvaal*, the Orange Free State, and Natal. It was one of several decisive factors influencing the decline and collapse of the Zulu Kingdom.

Our little bungalow had a small garden at the front and back. The front had two large palm trees in the middle of the lawn; a narrow paved drive led to the back garden that held a couple of apricot trees and a mulberry tree. We planted maize, but were surprised when its ripened colour was white and not the familiar golden yellow. It turned out to be mealie pap, a corn fed to cattle and enjoyed by the Afrikaners.

The garden also housed the maid's quarters, a single-roomed, brick built structure with an *en suite* toilet. Our maid, named Florence, only came three days a week and travelled back to the township every night where all the black people lived, and didn't use the not so salubrious accommodation in the back garden.

Again, a new experience for us was having a 'garden boy'. Ours was named Journal 17 and came from Mozambique. As well as being our gardener, he worked at the mine as an assistant mechanic. For some reason, all the workers from Mozambique were employed as mechanics and riggers.

It did appear that Journal and Florence would occasionally have a liaison in the maid's quarters, so at least it had some use. This was evidenced by the huge grin on Journal's face one day as he watered the lawn.

I asked him, "*Kungani?*" (*How are you?* in Fanakalo.)

Normally he would have said, "Okay, but I miss home," or "it was hard at the mine today," but on this day, as Florence progressed back home across the small park in front of us, she swung her hips in a way that only joyful African ladies can, and Journal gazed appreciatively at the movement and grinned, "Today I am happy man, boss..."

Journal cut the grass every couple of weeks with a long bladed knife known as a *panga* instead of a lawn mower. He was paid very little but enjoyed coming to the house to get away from the compound where the black workers were housed. Occasionally, I gave him a bottle of Lion beer and practised my Fanakalo with him.

We never experienced any trouble with the local population apart from having the tarpaulin covering the bed of our pickup truck known as a *bakkie* stolen by a couple of Bantu just before our big holiday to Durban.

An incident that was uncomfortable at the time, occurred one morning after I left for work for a 5am early shift. After leaving, I didn't lock the door to the house, and a young Bantu came in and then into the bedroom where Linda was asleep. Linda woke as he was reaching for the bedside cabinet where she kept her jewellery. As she looked up, the thief said, "Good morning, missus," pocketed her necklace and left the house.

Almost all of our communication with home was by letter. Every Sunday, we used the wafer-thin airmail envelopes to write our news, and posted them on the Monday. The post was amazingly efficient, airmail envelopes reaching the UK in three or four days. Any packages that weren't sent by airmail would have to go by ship on the Union Castle line.

We did have a phone on a party line and very occasionally would call back to the UK, and on one occasion to the US to speak to my cousin. As a member of the Mine Rescue Team, it was important for me to have a phone in order to respond to the call for team members to gather at the shaft to deploy to where we were needed.

Proto and the fires

The Proto equipment was very old, most of it bought from the Royal Navy submarine service where it was used for submariners trapped beneath the waves so they had at least a few hours' breathing time in which to escape before running out of air. These were known as re-breathers. They were airtight self-contained units mounted on a harness around the waist and over the chest. Reinforced rubber tubes fed air from a large rubber bag strapped to your chest, containing chemicals that absorbed the carbon monoxide and CO^2 exhaled from the lungs. In addition, there was a top-up cylinder of oxygen positioned on your back which, correctly administered, allowed you to work in the kit for about two hours. The rubber hoses led to a mouthpiece that was securely fastened in place with head straps. In many areas of the fires, if you took out the mouthpiece you were likely to die very quickly from CO_2, CO or some other poisonous gas.

All very scary, and as a team we relied on each other to stay safe. There was an intensive training course that needed to be completed to qualify as a member. It dealt with the equipment and its maintenance, and the rules of staying alive. Every three months, we underwent a physical examination which involved 'steppies'. To pass the physical, you were required to step up onto and down from a one-foot high step for a period of fifteen minutes. Your heart was monitored and checked, and you couldn't go above a certain heart rate and, more importantly, your recovery rate was measured to gauge your fitness level.

Most of us in the team who worked underground would, once or twice a week, take the inclined ladder-way from one level to next two levels to keep fit – a vertical distance of 600ft.

The Proto team were a good bunch of guys and it didn't matter if you couldn't speak Afrikaans as all the communication when kitted up was by plunging a klaxon horn: one honk, *all okay*; two honks, *stop*; five honks, *Danger! Retreat!* Our captain was Hennie De Witt, a bear of a man, an Afrikaner who, whilst he seemed to like me, would always take the opportunity to pinch me or pull out one of the few hairs I had on my chest when in the cage on the two-minute plunge into the mine shaft. As the cage barely had room for twenty-five men, conditions were cramped and there was no escape from the horseplay, which was strictly forbidden. In any event, I suspect it was his way of saying, "you are now one of the gang."

Other memorable members were Villem Smit, a very swarthy Afrikaner who was teased endlessly about his dark complexion; and Harry Prinsloo, who played scrum half with me in the mine and town rugby teams, as did Hennie de Witt.

Harry was short, well-muscled and very agile. Once, when we were underground at a fire, he fell 15ft down a box hole, a small vertical shaft down which the broken ore was passed to the transport levels. His fall was cushioned by four feet of water which had collected in the tunnel below where we had gathered after using the rope to descend the box hole. Harry had reached for the rope hanging down at the top of the box hole, missed, and instead clamped on to his breathing tubes. Harry hit the water and sank. We rushed to help him, but he would not let go of those tubes. It was as if he had hold of a snake which was attacking him. Quickly, we flashed our lights into his eyes to tell him it was okay. Finally, he let go, we propped him up, and order was restored.

Nick Van de Merve, the electrician, made up the team – again, an Afrikaner and a rugby player. As I was the operator and guardian of the Drager gas detector, it was me who gave the all clear to remove the mouthpieces and turn off the oxygen when we reached our already established fresh air base. It was the one instance when they really listened to me.

Managing the miners

After a couple of years, graduates were sent on a management training course in a town just south of Jo'burg called Maccauvlei, which the graduates called the 'the duck pond'.

Managing the white miners could be a challenge as most of my team were Afrikaners who spoke very little English. One was Bill Hearn, who spoke some English and was rather shunned by the other miners. Apparently, he had been charged with murdering his wife but the case was not proven so he returned to work. Another, Piet Van Rensburg, asked for a day off to have all of his teeth extracted. Not wishing to seem unsympathetic, I told him to take a couple of days. He refused, and the day after the extraction he appeared with no teeth, but at work. Unsurprisingly, I could not understand a word he was saying.

Another memorable miner was Farnie Voogt who could be described as mentally unstable, and had a reputation for treating the black workers badly. For some reason, he was allocated one of the most difficult areas of the mine to work in. It was at the end of a long tunnel a mile or so from the main shaft, and getting the timber and other supplies to him was a challenge. Nevertheless, he always made the production targets set by management.

One day, during my rounds as shift boss, I could see Farnie hauling an unfortunate black worker along by the scruff of the neck, and occasionally taking a swing at him with a clenched fist. Having just completed the management course at Maccauvlei, I felt that I could handle the situation. According to the lessons learned in the psychology class, the first step was to get between the aggressor and the victim. I bravely stepped forward, getting between Farnie and the poor black worker. Farnie was swearing in English, Fanakalo and Afrikaans, and lunging for the man. One of the haymakers swung toward the black missed him and caught me square on the point of jaw.

I went down in a heap, and my hard hat flew off along with my cap lamp. Farnie was now distraught because striking a mine official was a serious offence. If charges were brought, he would be dismissed and probably not be able to get a job in any other mine. I didn't report him.

Despite his predilection for thumping people, he was not a bad fellow. He was also a devout Christian and would preach the Bible on a street corner in Welkom's Horseshoe shopping plaza. A couple of times he saw me and directed his preaching at me switching from Afrikaans to English, and I was caught in the flow of the strange logic of the Dutch Reform Church.

Occasionally, on Saturdays after the early shift, we would drive into Welkom and gather at Schoernicks Café to drink iced coffees and cappuccinos, believing we were quite sophisticated. Next to Schoernicks was the Red Ox restaurant run by a fierce German. It served excellent steaks and not much else. It had booths that seated six, which was an unfamiliar arrangement to us. There were a couple of pizza joints, and the hotels in Welkom had restaurants. No one ventured out to OD to eat at the Oranje.

Holidays and travelling around

If not playing golf or rugby or having a barbeque on Sundays, we would occasionally go the mine compound where the black workers were housed. They had purpose-built sports arenas where at least once a month there would be exhibitions of tribal dancing. Each of the tribes that worked on the mines had different dances which they would perform, sometimes competing against other mines. Some of the more memorable were the Zulu stamping and leaping dance, and the gumboot dance performed by the Baca Gumboot boys. The dance originated in Durban where the Bantu were issued with wellingtons to work on the docks. The dancers would perform a series of steps and in unison slap their hands against the sides of their wellies in an African syncopated rhythm. The Pondo tribe also did a stamping dance, and the Mandaus tribe performed an acrobatic tumbling dance and were always in fine tribal dress. One tribe performed in their white underground overalls, the Xhosa Amakwenkwe performed a rippling snake type dance, all the movements controlled by football whistles.

After 18 months, it was required by law for us to take at least a two-week continuous break from the mine. So, using time accrued from the four weeks a year holiday allowance, most of us saved up for a full three week break mid-contract. We used a fair number of days spending time in Southern Rhodesia at Kariba and Victoria Falls, and the Wankie Game Reserve (now Hwange National Park). At last, real lions and elephants, warthogs, and the full range of African wildlife, a spectacular country. We also went camping south of Durban, where Linda was attacked by a horde of jellyfish whilst swimming in the Indian Ocean. The tentacles of the jellyfish left nasty looking wheals around her calf and thigh. As Linda was writhing in agony on the beach, several people came to help. We were told to rub the juice from the fleshy triangular stems of the Hottentot Fig onto the area where the tentacles had left marks. Massaging would also help, as the poison from these jellies apparently attacks the lymph system. So Linda lay back and I massaged the nearest point of the accessible lymph node being at the junction of her leg and torso. This looked quite weird...

For our long vacation, we went west, travelling to Kimberley, on past the singing sands of the Kalahari into Upington. Passing through towns with such exotic names such as Olifantshoek, Vroeggedeel, and off to the side, a dirt road striking north to Wincanton. We stopped in Upington as it had one of the few petrol stations along the way, of which there were not too many in the Northern Cape. There was a hotel with a spectacular mineral collection where we were viewed with suspicion, perhaps for being English. After leaving Upington and its secret airbase, which then was not marked on the map, we went onto Ai-Ais in the Fish River Canyon in South West Africa (Namibia). It's the largest gorge in Africa, and it also has hot springs in the Ai-Ais camping facility.

On the way into the gorge, we saw a large pink quartz vein in a scar on a cliff. Not wanting to miss the opportunity to collect some of the famous rose quartz, we parked and I climbed the cliff. When I was halfway up another vehicle came down the road and as it passed a man leaned out of the passenger widow and shouted out, "*Vrei State!*" ('Free State'), because our car's number plate had an Orange Free State designation.

Then we headed south to Cape Town across Namaqualand, wondering at the spectacular display of wild flowers that sprang from the dry desert every spring. The most prolific was the Namaqualand daisy which can be yellow to deep orange and everything in between. There were carpets of them stretching to the horizon. We could not reach Cape Town in one day, so stopped in Clanwilliam, a quaint town on the Olifants River and known as the Rooibos capital of the world. In Afrikaans it means 'red bush' which makes delicious caffeine-free tea brewed from its fine needle-like flowers. The town was established in 1806 but was populated by Irish and English settlers in the 1820s.

From Cape Town, we went to Oudtshoorn to ride on tame ostriches farmed for their meat now rather than their tail feathers, then along the Garden Route, travelling through the tropical jungles of the coast to Plettenburg Bay, and finally north again toward OD.

On the way, I wanted to pass through Ladysmith, scene of a famous siege during the Boer War that the Brits lost. During the battle, the Boers fired a blank artillery shell into Ladysmith, which contained a Christmas pudding, two Union Flags and the message, 'compliments of the season'. This was well before Paul Simon hooked up with the Ladysmith Black Mambazo Band.

It was quite an adventure, well planned, clocking up 3,000km.

After three years, we decided that while the living was easy, we wanted to leave for more adventures. We were the first of the graduates who started on the mines in the same year as we did to pack up our tents and return to the UK. We left many good friends behind, all of whom eventually left South Africa. It was a tough decision, and although I wouldn't say we were homesick, we needed to at least see family and friends in Cornwall and expand our horizons a little.

The timing was also dictated by the fact that if you left before a 36-month period from being employed, you were required to repay your shipping costs, airfares and settling-in allowance. We flew back a few days before Christmas, 36 months and two weeks from the start of the contract. We flew with our good friends Liz and Phil, who were from Cornwall. They were returning home for their mid-contract leave. As they had a rented car, they kindly agreed to pick up our unaccompanied baggage, in the form of a large zinc trunk, and take us down to Camborne.

It was good to be home for Christmas, to see family and friends, and have a proper-job pasty made by Linda's Mum.

5
RATS

1977: South Africa: a little fiction along the way

"So put your faith in the Lord above as you go underground"
(Cornish saying)

Most people hate rats, some more than others.
Some people apparently actually like them.
Scientists use them in experiments because of their supposed intelligence and their ability to survive when being used in horrible ways to test new cosmetics or inhale noxious fumes and other cancer-causing chemicals. These experiments, mostly of a gruesome nature, could well mean that as a species they may have some bones to pick with the human race. That's about it, I think, for the likes.
There are many, many dislikes ... as we will see.
Personally, I hate them intensely, having been bitten by one as a young boy while playing in a derelict 18th century barn close to my home. Of course, I couldn't tell mother that I'd been bitten as we weren't supposed to play in the barn and, of course, the bite got

infected. The infection was so bad, they had to take the finger off, so I was never able to play the violin. However, I did gain the nickname 'stumpy'.

Later in life and as a college student, I had a dread of the little bastards. Coming home from a late night session to my shared accommodations, a rat and I had a standoff in the front porch. I threw a rock at it, and I swear it stood on its hind legs and hissed at me. It was quite large, so I backed off and allowed it free passage to the garden.

There were three of us living in the flat and we decided to get a cat. One of chaps had a cat at home that his sister no longer liked and so Tiddles became our guardian. However, after two weeks, Tiddles disappeared and we later found his body lifeless and partially consumed in the garden. The rodent in the garden was not quite a King Rat, but a big one nevertheless. Tiddles must have cornered him and then been set upon by *Rattus Maximus* and his followers.

As a mining engineering student, during the summer vacations we would work underground to gain experience whilst earning good money at the same time. In the local mine, the miners were quite superstitious and would leave a small piece of their pasty or a corner of their sandwich for the 'Knockers'. Also known as 'Buccas', some believed they were the souls of departed restless spirits who had died underground throughout the ages. Of course, the offerings disappeared over night and some of the miners believed the Knockers had taken them. Hmm, either that or rodents.

Being in Cornwall, some of the smaller mines came to the surface, so it was conceivable that rats had come down the tunnels to live in the stygian darkness, feeding off the miners' offerings, small insects, and probably wood taken underground for use as props and supports for weak places in the tunnels.

Working in a mine in the US, one of the shift bosses had a pet rat that would come to the underground meal room which was hewn out of solid rock. Not sure where the rat came from, probably hitched a ride in one of the timber cars. The shift boss, 'Slim', an enormously fat man, would feed the damn rat from his hand. Even this relationship soured, and one day the rat bit Slim and ran off with a choice piece of salami. Subsequently, Slim sought out and destroyed the rat.

When I was working in a South African mine, there was no exit to surface other than a vertical shaft that reached some 5,000ft below. I suppose a rat could have climbed down the shaft timbers or compressed air pipes if it really wanted to get underground, and believe me, there were a lot of rats underground.

Otherwise, the method of entry could have also been in the honey wagon, a delightful name for a toilet mounted on a small railcar where desperate miners could relieve themselves without going back to surface. You had to be desperate, as the smell from the 'honey' could knock you over. One sat on a tank like structure that had a circular opening which served as a seat. A lot of business was conducted here. The car was taken back to surface once a week and emptied, then taken back underground. Possibly a route for the rats.

Despite the regulations and efforts of all to keep rats out of the mine, there was plenty of evidence they were with us underground. In addition to riding in the honey wagon, they were known to get into the mine by hiding in the rail cars that were taken down into the mine every day, wagons which held the pit props and timber used for roof support. Snakes also got into the mine the same way causing great consternation amongst the Bantu miners. The snakes were tolerated as they pursued the rats.

In some of the mines, the rat problem was so bad that you had to make absolutely sure your lunch was kept in a canvas duffle bag with a rope drawstring securely fastened and hung up on a nail where the rats could not get to it.

Nothing worse than coming back to the miners' box where we congregated for lunch break, taking down your bag and have three or four rats spring out of it. I was unable to bring myself to eat my rat-nibbled peanut butter and jam sandwiches, or my meat pie, or the apple now scored with grooves of rat incisors.

So I hear some saying, "No problem, they're just rats."

Perhaps those people were not plagued by bad rat memories, or brought up on tales of rat catchers abducting children, or not having the knowledge of rats carrying fleas that spread the plague in medieval times, or of rats leaving sinking ships, of rats on tropical islands eating local potentates out of house and home, and nasty tales of seagulls swallowing a rat and the rat eating its way out of the seagull's belly to tumble into the harbour.

However, generally speaking, the buggers would have eaten through anything other than a hard plastic container to get to the food. So not usually having had any breakfast, and another three hours before you could get back to surface, the rats figured high on the hate list.

The only thing that helped to reduce the population was fire. Often, the timbers that supported the roof of the working areas and sometimes in the tunnels would catch fire.

The fires had to be extinguished by the Proto teams of volunteers. The teams would go underground to attempt to stop the fire from spreading by trying to starve it of oxygen. In some cases, water sprays would be installed to wet the wooden packs and timbers that held up the roof to isolate the fire. Sometimes, fireproof brattices and walls were built across the tunnels leading to the stopes and working places where most fires started.

The atmosphere in the vicinity of the fire was deadly, the air being contaminated with the products of incomplete combustion of the timber such as carbon monoxide and carbon dioxide. In addition, there were other deadly gases such as hydrogen cyanide released from burning plastic-wrapped electrical cables and rubber hoses.

The Proto equipment, while very old, did a good job. It relied on the principle of rebreathing a fixed amount of air. This meant the equipment recycled the air one was breathing by filtering it through a chemical that absorbed the exhaled carbon dioxide and other gases. This air was mixed with and supplemented by oxygen from a small cylinder strapped to your back. Air was supplied to a mouthpiece by a rubber canvas-covered hose, and expelled air was carried away by another hose. The mouthpiece was securely strapped to your head. If it slipped or dislodged, it was highly likely one would die in a couple of breaths from carbon monoxide poisoning. Concentrations of the deadly gas in the atmosphere often exceeded 5,000 parts per million. A level of 50 parts per million was lethal.

Somehow, many of the rats survived the fires and noxious gases.

On my mine, there was a Proto team with nine members, but only five at a time were required to go underground, the others being held in reserve. I went most of the time as I had a qualification to operate the equipment that measured noxious gas levels, a mine manager's certificate, and oh yes, I was in charge of the canary.

On one of the fires I attended with the team, there was so much smoke it was hard to see beyond a metre or so, and I became separated from my team. Crawling along almost blind, suddenly, I fell into a vertical shaft, a box hole, 25ft deep. This was where broken ore was loaded into rail cars. It was a rail spur from the main tunnels, an area seldom visited and only when miners were removing the broken rock.

I survived the fall, but my cap lamp did not seem to be working properly and was flickering. While trying to get back to my team, I became disorientated and entered a very old part of the mine. In the dim light, I failed to notice the poorly constructed barricade supposed to keep miners out of the area. It looked like no one had been in there for many years, judging by the amount of dust on the footwall and the way the timbers were crushed by the enormous weight of the rock above.

I realised I was in a bad place and should have turned around immediately, but with the weakening cap lamp and being disorientated from the fall, I moved further into the stope. Suddenly, there was an ominous cracking and a large piece of rock fell from the roof and pinned my legs to the floor. The pain was intense, and I must have passed out for a while. I tried to move the rock but it was too heavy. I still had my Proto gear on and the mouthpiece was still in place. My cap lamp was working, but the light was feeble.

Frighteningly, I had no idea if the atmosphere here was breathable. I knew that by keeping still and breathing slowly the rebreather and oxygen mixture would last for about an hour. After that, the air would become unbearably hot to the extent that it would melt the rubber in the rebreathing sack.

Pain dulled my senses, but I could just feel my feet and wiggle my toes on my right leg, my left leg felt slightly damp, and I realised that I was bleeding. I had no way of knowing how serious the injury was. I was alone, and there was no way I could call for help or contact anyone. Communication between team members was by means of a klaxon, operated by manually pushing a plunger. The signal for help was five short blasts.

I tried this every ten minutes but realised the effort was consuming oxygen, so I stopped. I was either going to die of asphyxiation or die of gas inhalation.

At least I had a choice.

Looking back to where I came from, I saw several pin pricks of light coming toward me. Could this be the team coming to rescue me?

It was odd, the lights moved jerkily and didn't seem to get any bigger. Then, to my horror, I realised it was a pack of rats coming toward me. I could do nothing. I pushed the plunger on the klaxon. The rats stopped for a moment and then came on. I pushed the plunger again and the noise halted their progress, but for not as long as the first time. They were now within a metre of me; I could see their little sharp teeth, the twitching whiskers. Then they all rushed behind the rock pinning my legs. I thought for a moment they had moved on. A sharp pain seared through my left leg, then another, and again and again. I let out a muffled howl. The bastard rats were nibbling on my leg, attracted by the blood which must be seeping from whatever wound I had.

Rather than be eaten alive, and in a panic, I threw caution to the wind and loosened the straps securing my mouthpiece and took a short tentative breath. Nothing happened, I was alive. There wasn't even the unmistakable stench of burning timber, so the ventilation must have been blowing fresh air into the stope from above.

I was at least safe from death from poisonous gases. Safe, but which was worse, a quick death from the inhalation of CO or being eaten by rodents? Safe, but possibly dying alone from dehydration or from further rock falls. A desperate situation.

I could do very little. At least now I could make noise with the klaxon which would hopefully keep the rats at bay for a few moments.

Then I felt an excruciating sharp pain in my left leg. With the mouthpiece gone, I let out a scream, and as the rats kept gnawing, I screamed louder and louder. Then I passed out.

The next thing I remember was a lady dressed in white looking at me, asking my name, telling me I was in the hospital in Odendaalsrus, and saying that I was lucky to be alive. However, she said the surgeon would see me later and explain all.

Apparently, several Proto teams had been searching for me since my disappearance, and it was only when they heard my screams of agony that they found me. They had to call in a specialist team to shore up the area where I was trapped and to get the slab of rock off my legs. The medic had given me a shot of morphine, so I don't really remember anything at all.

The surgeon arrived at my bedside and again told me I was doing well and my vitals were perfect considering the trauma I had experienced. He went on to say that due to the extreme damage caused by the rock fall to my left leg, and given that the rodents had eaten a few of my toes and infected the wound where my fibia and tibula had been crushed, he was sorry to tell me that he had to amputate my left leg below the knee.

When I played rugby for the mine, I was known as *Saute the hartlooper*. Now, I am sometimes known by the Afrikaners as, *Saute Two Stumps*.

I just need one more to make up a set of wickets for cricket.

Well, that's a bit of a tall story since I still have all of my digits, if somewhat bent in places, as well as both legs.

But I really do hate rats, and have seen packs of them underground, along with them jumping from my lunch sack.

Damn those rodents.

6

ABU DHABI

1978-79 June to September: United Arab Emirates

Oil rigs, more schooling, new skills, new friends, new horses, more adventures in the desert

On leaving South Africa in December 1977, I was looking for a new job. The mining industry was in a deep recession and I was directed to look at the oil industry by the Principal at Camborne School of Mines. After sending out a few letters of enquiry, I was called up to London for an interview with Dowell Schlumberger, an oilfield service company. I fitted their bill and was hired immediately to gain some practical experience in the natural gas fields of Northern Germany. Not a pretty place, and incredibly cold in winter. The salary was good and the benefits excellent.

After six bitterly cold weeks, I was sent to Pau in the southwest of France. It was much warmer, and I was to spend three months on a training course to become an oil well service engineer. The training centre was on the edge of the city and had its own drilling rig, workshops and lecture rooms. The job would mainly involve the cementing of steel liners into oil wells so that the oil and gas intersected by the drilling would not escape from the well. The steel pipes would prevent blowouts. We were also taught to use Drill Stem Testing Equipment, tools that measured the pressure and temperature of the oil at the bottom of the well. They were used in conjunction with equipment known as 'packers' that were lowered into the oil well on the drill pipe. These devices were then manipulated from surface by lifting, lowering and turning the drill pipe in a specific sequence. All very complicated, especially when giving instructions in French. The tools were very heavy, needing two people to carry them. We were also taught the basics of fracking which relied on some of the downhole equipment. There were fifteen people on the course, their nationalities representing all the major oil- and gas-producing countries of the world, some of which I never knew had production, including Iran, Argentina, France, Nigeria, Holland, USA, the UK and Italy.

We all got on very well, and of course, in any group of young men there were one or two who came in for ribbing.

Paul from Nigeria suffered; when Paul asked Kurt, an ex-soldier from the USA, what his first name was, Kurt replied, "You can call me Mr Bishop – that's what people call me."

Raul, from Mozambique, after repeatedly being told of the dangers of working on the demonstration oil well rig, lost most of his right index finger within a couple of hours of being on the rig floor.

Every morning on the way to the training school, Alexandro Smilovitch from Argentina would exclaim, "Look at Moun-tains, how wonderful is the moun-tains".

One of the guys from the US fell desperately in love with a girl who worked on the cafeteria food line in the Carrefour Café, but not knowing a word of French, asked me to help him get acquainted with Mimi. He thought his first attempt at communicating would be by saying, "Nothing, thank you," when she offered him a helping of *petit pois* from her vegetable selection.

"Chuck," I said, "just say, *'Rien, merci'*."

Chuck tried this. Unfortunately, Chuck was from Texas, and *rien, merci* came out as 'rain mercy'. Nevertheless, he did end up with a girlfriend who had a small chateau, and his French improved a lot over the time of the course.

On completing the course, I was initially told we were being posted to Saudi Arabia, which we were not thrilled about. However, during a stopover in Tehran *en-route* to Saudi, I was told we would be posted to Abu Dhabi instead. This was better as the restrictions on foreigners in Abu Dhabi were far less stringent than those in Saudi. You could even get a drink without having twenty lashes if discovered, or getting sick from drinking homemade 'flash' that expats made in Saudi.

I was directed to the regional office in Tehran, a much hotter place than Pau. It was fascinating, and my first experience of the chaos that whirls around the traffic in most large cities in the Middle East. On the main boulevard leading into town from the airport, the driver of the company car negotiated his way through four lanes of traffic that were subsequently squashed into three marked lanes then funnelled into two. Indicators were ignored, even if they existed; signalling was replaced by constant honking. Aggressive pushing with one's bumper to change lanes seemed to be normal practise. The atmosphere was thick with dust and diesel fumes, filtering the sunlight in the late afternoon, a shimmering golden haze over the Shahyad Tower (now known as the Azadi Tower). The side streets were jammed with vehicles parked haphazardly almost blocking the road, but not quite, leaving room for street vendors. The Dowell offices were in a modern high-rise. Now knowing we were to go to Abu Dhabi where friends from the training course were based, I called Linda and gave her the good news.

Abu Dhabi was a very different place in 1978 than now; there were only five or six high-rise buildings, a few three- and four-storey buildings, and a couple of Western-style hotels –plus plenty of places to park your camel. The Corniche was not yet fully developed, and if one ventured onto the beach for a swim in the bath-warm sea, one might occasionally find on exiting from the water a group of Arab ladies in traditional clothing appear, settling uncomfortably close to one's towel and staring.

So instead, for a cooling dip, the pool at the Khalidiya Palace Hotel or the club where one could swim in isolation and sip on a cool beer was the place to go.

Our apartment was on Electra Road, close to what was then the Grand Mosque and was within hearing distance of the muezzin. He called the faithful to *adhān,* daily prayer five times a day: at dawn, noon, mid-afternoon, sunset, and nightfall. The middle three were fine but the dawn call amplified by huge speakers on the towers got to be a pain. It seemed to be especially loud on Fridays.

From seeing photos of the city or TV programmes today, Abu Dhabi is so very different from how it was in 1978. Now, there are a multitude of high-rise buildings, our apartment block is dwarfed by what is reputed to be the largest and probably the most costly mosque in the world. It can hold 41,000 faithful and cost two billion *dirhams* (US $545 million) to build.

The locals and immigrants were devout Muslims, to the point that often taxi drivers would pull over to the side of the road, pull out a prayer mat, turn toward Mecca and pray. Not a problem, unless one was on the way to the airport to catch a flight, or a chopper out to the rig.

I spent a lot of time offshore supplying two French rigs with engineering services, the *Île de Amsterdam* and the *Île de France*. As the Gulf is quite shallow, both were jack-up rigs which were owned by the French drilling company Foramer. They were drilling on contract for the Abu Dhabi Oil Company (ADNOC). I was appointed to service these two rigs because the staff in Pau had told the Dowell management here that I spoke French. That was true to a certain extent, but the French of grammar school and the Jockey Bar in our hotel in Pau was a lot different to the French spoken on board the rigs, which was somewhat rougher and more colloquial than that I was used to.

I was to operate the pumping and cement mixing machinery

which was located in the bowels of the rig where the temperature was often more than 40°C with 100% humidity. I had a helper, Yousef, and after about five minutes preparing the equipment for the job, we were both drenched in sweat. Initially, it seemed that previous engineers from Dowell had not been very popular due to a couple of costly mistakes that caused a great deal of lost rig time. After a couple of months, I was accepted by the crew, the chief driller and the company man who supposedly ran the whole operation. All the staff rotated in and out every two weeks, most going back to south western France.

The company man spent thirty days on the rig before returning home and coming back after another thirty days. One was an American from Louisiana who spoke appalling French with a strong Bayou accent which was impossible to understand. In addition, he liked more than drop to drink and spent most of the time in the radio room/control centre, never going out to the drill platform. I was often called in to translate his instructions. My acceptance was aided somewhat by the fact that my boss in town told me to buy a bottle of Pernod and a bottle of gin, and place them on the bar in the canteen every time I went on board. These were the only two French rigs operating in the Gulf at that time, and the only two that allowed alcohol on board. One can imagine the consternation in a French crew if no wine was served with the daily meal.

The rigs were well run, and the meals served at dinner were very good. I know the food contained large amounts of garlic and were – in the way of all French meals – accompanied by fairly decent red wine. I would come back from the rig exuding garlic and be cloaked in the odour of diesel for a couple of days.

The work was interesting and hard, but there were moments of levity.

The communication system for the crew was through ship to shore radio telephone system and it was an open mic so you could hear everything being said by everyone. This included marital disputes, good and bad news. On one occasion, I was talking to

Linda who was in our apartment in Abu Dhabi when there was a tremendous crash accompanied by the sound of breaking glass.

"What's wrong?" I asked. "Are you okay?"

"I've just fallen through the top of the glass coffee table and I'm sitting in a small pile of broken glass," Linda replied. "And I'm also stuck! My legs and arms are hooked over the rim of the table."

Not a lot I could do, so she hung up and managed to extricate herself.

The radio was positioned in the ops room and there was a dedicated telephone link back to ADNOC headquarters in Abu Dhabi. It was here that I saw my first fax machine. Written communications were sent by telex, but on the rig, sometimes we needed instructions and technical drawings from ADNOC. They would normally have been in the mail pouch in the chopper that flew out from Abu Dhabi every morning and afternoon.

However, one day the rig received a fax machine which consisted of a metal cylinder about four inches in diameter that rotated and was attached to an integral handset. Over the cylinder was a bar along which a stylus was attached in the manner of a recording device on a seismometer. To receive a fax, you fastened a single sheet of heat sensitive paper onto the metal cylinder, dialled the sender, and placed the receiver in its cradle. When the connection was established, the cylinder rotated, and as it did so, the stylus moved across the paper and started to make dots on the heat-proof paper. When all the dots were connected, a diagram of the well completion pipework was shown. Quite ingenious. The first time the machine was put in to operation, there were ten people crowded into the control room being amazed by the new technology.

Back onshore, there was not much time for recreation or exploring. Just out of the city was an area known as Umm Al Nar, which was the site of an archaeological dig with remains of buildings and walls from 4,000BC. It was deserted, and you could swim in the nearby creek.

After an interview with the *Chef d' Equipe* of the Zayeed stable,

Linda was selected to exercise the Sheik's horses, engendering a lifelong love of Arabian horses. If the Sheik's family came to ride, the western ladies who exercised the horses had to leave the grounds so as not to be seen in their jodhpurs.

As we hadn't seen any of the surrounding countryside, one day we decided to visit the oasis at Al Buraimi. It was once the site of a contentious border dispute between Saudi, Oman and the Trucial States (until 1971, the name for UAE).

The oasis dominated Anglo-Saudi relations for more than thirty years, and the dispute was only really settled in 1974. Apparently, it was also an important centre for the slave trade until just after World War Two, and the setting for Hammond Innes's novel *The Doomed Oasis*. In 1978, it was unclear as to whether the oasis was in Oman or not.

The oasis was close to the city of Al Ain in the UAE which had a very old covered *souk*. The road leading to it from Abu Dhabi was a single-lane highway. It looked like a long strip of liquorice laid out on the desert threading between the dunes. It had been laid mostly straight onto the desert floor with a very thin sub-base and a thicker layer of tarmac right on top. As there were no kerbs, and because of the intense desert heat, the tarmac spread over the edges of the roadway and heavy traffic created parallel channels. Fine if your vehicle was the same axle width as the heavy trucks that had created the ruts, but it was a bit of a struggle for our Honda Civic. I had to drive with the left-hand wheels in the rut and the right-hand pair on the ridge between the ruts.

The journey gave a glimpse of the raw desert, and we saw Bedouin on the horizon with camels heading to town, which gave a sense of the past.

The drive didn't take very long as it was only just over 100 miles from Abu Dhabi to Al Ain.

The oasis was fascinating. It had all of the characteristics one would expect of an oasis in the desert: date palms, ladies in traditional costume, a small lake fringed with greenery. There were raised pathways defined by whitewashed, waist-high walls leading through the date palms and cisterns. People were living in and around the lake in small white buildings. The water in the oasis was fed by the Jabal Hafeet Al Hajar Mountains twenty miles to the east, and it arrived by tunnels in underground canals built around 1,000BC.

As we drove toward the oasis, we noticed a fort off to the left which looked like something from the silent movie era, a place where Beau Geste and his cohorts would be stationed. It was the Al Jahili Fort, one of the largest forts in the UAE. It was built on the orders of Sheikh Zayed bin Khalifa Al Nahyan, also known as Zayed the First (1835-1909), as the home to members of the ruling Al Nahyan family. The fort was established in 1891 close to the Buraimi oasis for the protection of the date palm farmers. At one stage, it was seized by the former Omani coastal scouts for their operation to protect the mountain lanes and to preserve the inter-tribal peace.

We parked about 100 yards from the arched gateway, and the fort gates were flanked by several tribesmen who had Martini-Henry rifles cradled in the crooks of their arms with bandoliers over their shoulders. Thinking I would like a photo, I got out of the car and approached the men with caution, knowing that the border here was undefined and we could be in Oman and the guards may be hostile.

I gestured to the guards pointing to my camera and trying to indicate that I would like to take a picture of them and the fort. They seemed to agree, nodding and smiling, and lined up in the arched gateway shouldering their arms and posing. I had what I thought was a pretty sophisticated camera with a telephoto lens, adjustable F-Stops and other such items which could have produced a great picture. So I snapped away, probably taking a dozen or so pictures. Finishing, I put the lens cap back on the camera, made a *salaam* and turned back to the Honda Civic. There were a few shouts, and I saw the tribesmen shouting and gesticulating toward me and the camera. I was at a loss to understand what they wanted and walked backward to the Honda Civic calling out to Linda, "Start the engine and get ready to drive fast."

I turned and ran the last few yards to the car and we sped away, well, went quickly, in the Honda Civic. Trying to analyse the situation later on, we decided that the guards were used to tourists with Polaroid cameras and they wanted a picture of themselves. Foregoing the delights of the Al Ain Hilton, we headed back home.

During the time we spent in Abu Dhabi, I was asked to relieve a guy who single-handedly ran the company's Doha outpost in Qatar. He had not had leave for six months and needed to get home for Christmas.

In early December, I flew the short distance to Doha on a Qatar Airways flight. You were allowed to take your falcon on board. On my flight, there were a couple of sheiks who had bought new falcons in Abu Dhabi and were bringing them back to Doha.

The airport in Doha was quite small with one arrival gate. As I walked out, I spied a westerner who smiled at me and greeted me with the words, "Wass she like, boy?" a typical Cornish greeting.

The man I was to relieve came from Camborne; he even knew a couple of my uncles and had worked with them for Holmans, a world renowned manufacturer of air compressors and rock drills. He, like many before him, had worked for Holmans in the Middle East and Iran, and learned of the high wages paid by the oilfield service companies to practical engineering types, and joined Dowell a few years before me. We got on together very well, sharing many mutual acquaintances, but after a few short days he flew back to Camborne. Via Heathrow.

Christmas in a Muslim country wasn't such a big deal, but the company flew Linda over to Doha just before Christmas, and we were able to buy each other excellent presents in Fortnum & Mason who had a shop in the foyer of the Hilton Hotel in Doha.

In Abu Dhabi, we could get most food items except for pork products. However, our neighbours at our apartment worked for the British Embassy, and occasionally we would be supplied with a few rashers of bacon and a couple of pork sausages courtesy of the Diplomatic Bag.

During the 18 months we were in the Gulf, I spent a lot of time offshore on the rigs, and Linda was working, so we saved a fair bit of money. It was a very different life from a mining assignment, and so after a year, we headed back to the UK.

The day we left Abu Dhabi it was 113°F and 98% humidity. It was a little cooler in Camborne.

7

THE FESTIVAL OF SANTA BARBARA

4th December 1980: Mykonos, Greece

Saints' Days celebrated, kissing icons, island life, a new mine and mineral

Santa Barbara is the Patron Saint of Miners and Gunpowder, as well as guarding other people who need protection from being blown up in their everyday work. Most of the older mines I have worked at or visited in the Catholic, Russian and Greek Orthodox countries have either a shrine or chapel dedicated to this illustrious lady, either at the mine or in a nearby village. I have seen shrines and altars dedicated to her in Austria, Chile, Mexico, Bolivia and Honduras. These were above ground in tiny chapels as in Greece, or statuettes at the mine entrance as in Portugal, where miners would cross themselves before going underground.

Sometimes the statues were located below ground in small niches carved out of the rock, or in large churches where side altars are dedicated to the celebrated saint. But, to me, the most memorable edifice was the tiny Greek Orthodox Church at the mine on the island of Mykonos where I worked for two years from 1980 to 1982.

The church was set on a barren outcrop of granite that looked down over the mine process plant, buildings, workshops and canteen. It was small, full with just fifteen people. The exterior walls were whitewashed in the traditional Greek style, with a pale blue wash covering the dome. The interior was decorated with a painting of the saint and a small altar upon which sat a silver framed *ikon*. Through the year, it was tended to by the mine foreman's wife who lived on the mine site. It was primarily used to celebrate the feast of Santa Barbara, the high Greek Holidays, or when some unfortunate miner was killed underground. During the two years prior to my arrival, four funerals for miners had taken place in the small, desolate church.

Each 4th December, a celebration was held here. Known locally as a *paniyiri*, it was a celebration of the saint's day, and with so many churches on the island, we were never short of *paniyiri* to attend, as all were welcome to the feast. Most of the churches were dedicated to Saint James the Patron Saint of Fishermen, and additionally, just to be sure of protection, Saint Nicholas who also acted as patron saint of sailors, fishermen and merchants. During the Easter period, most *paniyiri* featured the serving of extremely hot lamb soup from a cauldron in thin plastic cups which bulged in the middle from the heat. The soup was infused with rosemary and other herbs, and if you liked lamb, it was probably very nice. However, as neither Linda nor I were great fans of the soup, it was discreetly disposed of over the back of the low stone wall we sat on that surrounded the church. In the winter, the population of the island was less than a thousand souls, but many people came to celebrate Santa Barbara for the feasting, dancing and drinking. Buses that were normally used to transport the miners from the town to the mine, and tourists from the town to the beaches during the summer, were commandeered to bring people from the surrounding villages and Mykonos town to the mine. In addition, a special trip was made to bring the three surviving Orthodox monks from the monastery at the village of Ano Mera.

The mine was located on a bleak peninsula as far away as you could get from the discos and hotels of the town, which was actually only twelve miles away. December can be a cold month in Greece, even in the Cyclades, and often a keen wind would spring up that would last for days and days, driving people mad as the wind rattled the window panes, doors and shutters. My first Santa Barbara *paniyiri* turned out to be a chilly but sparkling day, and a lively northerly breeze blew in from the sea. To combat the cool wind, most folks wore brightly-coloured, warm, woollen Mykonian jackets, a speciality of the weavers of the island, or dark seafarers' peacoats and of course, the majority of men wore the ubiquitous Greek fisherman cap.

Much preparation had gone into the celebration with the best *bouzouki* band in town being brought from the village in the mine manager's Rover. The band consisted of an accordion, a couple of *bouzouki*, a *santouri* (a type of dulcimer), and a one-man percussion section beating all manner of tambourines, with a sort of fiddle leading most of the dance tunes.

To ensure all were well fed, 200 chickens and a couple of sheep were especially ordered from Georgio, the town butcher. The meat was brought to site in the mine's Toyota pickup, which also served to carry explosives from the storage magazine to the mine workings. During the winter, the island was supplied by two ferries from Syros and Piraeus that ran once a week, and one plane a week from Athens, and so the orders for the largesse were placed well in advance.

The amount of wine was never actually calculated but appeared as the 'normal' sum for Santa Barbara in the mine accounts. The number of chickens varied according to how many sheep could be bought for consumption. During the first year I attended the Santa Barbara celebration, we only had one sheep, but two the second year. The wine was always the best *retsina*, distilled locally, and when served chilled, it actually tasted very, very good. In addition, litre upon litre of white and red *domestica* was consumed, along with dark brown bottles of Fix beer. *Domestica* was a step up from store bought *retsina*, and amongst expats, the *Domestica* was renamed Domestos. The whole feast would also be topped off with shots of *ouzo*, sticky home-made *baklava* and Greek coffee.

This splendid social occasion was always preceded by a sort of Mass-type service and the blessing of the *ikon* of Santa Barbara in the tiny church. The priests of the monastery at Ano Mera performed the blessing. Priests could be an object of ridicule on the islands but when it came to the Blessing of the Saint, due reverence was afforded the black robed and bearded clerics. Whether or not the miners wanted to get into the church for the blessing I never knew, but as was typical for most *paniyiris* and important services in Greece, the church was packed with their wives and ladies from the town – the poor miners never got a look in.

After the blessing, the head priest from the monastery would exit the tiny building with the *ikon* of the Sainted Lady held high above his stovepipe hat. The *ikon* was a small painting of the saint holding a gold cup with rays of light emanating from within the cup. It was protected by a sheet of glass, all held in an ornate silver frame. On exiting the church, in an act of unprecedented co-ordination, all the miners, men of the villages and other hangers-on whipped off their caps as the priest held up the silver and gold *ikon* for all to see.

The removal of the headgear was quite an event. I had worked at the mine for almost five months before my first Santa Barbara, and had never seen the Mine Foreman's head exposed in this manner. Usually, Kyriakos was either covered with his beaten and dented miner's helmet or his greasy fisherman's cap.

The miners, management and others formed a single line along the path leading from the church toward the cantina where the celebrations were to be held. The head priest in his celebratory robes, accompanied by his two minions, then proceeded along the line of mining men and presented the *ikon* to each member of the assembled company to kiss. Father Georgio held the *ikon* forward to receive the kiss and uttered the blessing as his assistant liberally doused the kisser with Holy Water flicked with great aplomb from stalks of fresh basil. Father Georgio was old and had a long grey beard; he wore glasses of enormous thickness, and when reading from the sacred texts would take his spectacles off and hold the Bible within inches of his face whilst chanting the appropriate words into the Holy Book. The sounds of his mumblings were lost in the pages but everyone knew the responses by heart, so it didn't really matter.

A strict order for the kissing was maintained and I found myself third in line, ahead of people I felt were more important to the mine. Prior to my blessing were those of Tasos the Mine Manager and Vasilli the Mine Superintendent; after me came Stathis the Contract Manager and following him, Kyriakos the Mine Foreman, and Niko the Wash Plant Foreman. I was impressed that they should consider me so important, but I thought afterward I did represent the American owners of the mine and probably did have some contribution to the feast as I monitored the mine's budget and expenditures. George the accountant was not in the line-up, possibly because of his communist leanings.

The order and blessings carried on to the lowliest mechanic. When all had kissed the *ikon* and been blessed, the line broke up and we repaired to the cantina. Under normal circumstances, Nico's wife would provide meals at lunch time for thirty-five or so miners, but now the tables were pressed into service for more than a hundred souls.

But this was Santa Barbara, and at one end of the room the *bouzouki* band were tuning up. As we sat down to eat, they started to play. The tables were laden with home baked bread, cooked chickens roasted Greek-style in olive oil, accompanied by potatoes with rosemary, aubergines and squash, along with grilled portions of sheep. The ubiquitous *fasolakia* (green beans) were cooked in water with a little oil and flavoured with basil and thyme. Beans were about the only thing that would grow in the island's poor, thin soil, but as always they were delicious.

Toasts were drunk to one and all and the music, which began as a background accompaniment, grew louder and louder as people began to dance. Not fully knowing the steps to the dances, I was hauled out of my seat, protesting loudly, to dance with Linda for the Butchers' Dance. She had learnt it at a dance class and bravely pushed in the right direction and pulled on my handkerchief as required. I also attempted the *syrtaki* dance from *Zorba the Greek*.

"Zorba, teach me to dance!" I shouted.

Anthony Quinn would have been proud of me.

As we danced, the light drained from the sky, turning an already grey skyscape into one devoid of any colour. Rain began to accompany the darkening gloom, and condensation dewed on the windows of the cantina as the outside temperature fell. The first bus was designated to leave at 6pm, and much against Greek custom, it left on time, mostly filled with the miners' wives. It would return later to pick up those who chose to stay.

The band played on, and the miners stayed and danced until the early hours. Production quotas would not be met the next day.

Linda and I rode home with Vassili and Chrysanthi, squashed into the cab of the pickup truck, truly an all-purpose vehicle. Stathis had been designated to drive the band back to the town, but the head fixer, Antonis, drove them home, so Stathis rode with us in the back of the pickup and got a little wet..

The old Greek gods and Christian saints were honoured, and the Good Lady Santa Barbara watched over the mine and miners for the whole year with only a few accidents and no fatalities being recorded.

Easter was a very moving and special occasion especially at the culmination of the services when the priest entered the crypt, remerged with a lit candle and exclaimed,

"*Christós Anésti!*" Christ is risen.

There was a collective gasp from the congregation both inside the small church and the large crowd outside. It seemed as though most of the population of the town was there.

The flame from the priest's candle then lit those of the gathered faithful, who returned to their homes at midnight. The candle was carefully kept alight on the journey homeward and used to mark a cross on the lintel over the front door.

Another of the spectacular celebrations was the one that took place at Epiphany: the Blessing of the Waters. This took place on a small pier behind a little church in the town harbour.

Again, the priests were prominent in this celebration. The tradition is that a priest, after the customary repetition of prayers, throws a golden cross into the sea. The end of the pier is surrounded by brave young men and boys who are positioned in rowing boats and small fishing boats or *caïques* several yards from the end of the pier. The second the cross leaves the priest's hand, the divers jump into the freezing water to retrieve the 25cm cross.

After a few anxious, moments one of the youths appeared holding the cross high above his head in triumph.

Sensibly, the priest tied a long ribbon to the cross to slow its progress through the water and aid the divers in locating it. The lucky youth who captures the cross is hero for the day and treated to drinks and kisses from the girls.

There were so many festivals, and we attended quite a few, but nothing was ever as good as the feast of Santa Barbara.

8

LEAVING THE SUNSHINE

1981: Scotland

Snow, amateur dramatics, the arrival of Misty into our lives, developing a new mine

We'd left behind the sunshine of Greece to assist in the development of a new barite mine in Scotland, which the locals pronounced 'bayrities'. Barite is used in the drilling of oil wells, and as we were relatively close to the North Sea, the location was favourable for development.

Aberdeen Barite Company was a branch of the same company that owned the Greek mine where I had recently worked. They put us up on a full-board basis at the old and venerable Fisher's Hotel in Pitlochry. I was given a new Land Rover to drive, while other members of the crew had Jeeps, and the boss had a Range Rover.

Fisher's Hotel was very nice, but we needed something more long-term, and we found a farmhouse to rent. It was just outside of Aberfeldy and owned by a local farmer. It was a little isolated, and in the depths of winter, snow-clearing became an essential part of the Land Rover's duties. To create a snow plough, we fastened an old five-bar gate to the tow hitch on the back, slightly angling the top so it would push the snow to one side. For weight, we used Linda who clung on to the tow hitch as I slowly drove down the lane. Ploughing needed to be done to allow Linda to drive up and down the lane in her Ford Capri, and so that others had access to the farm.

Aberfeldy had six pub-hotels-bars, one of which was the Black Watch, as the village was the home of the Black Watch Regiment which was mustered in the Weem Cow Park in 1740.

The cricket club usually repaired to the Ailean Chraggan guest house restaurant and bar across the river; sometimes the cricketers met at the Breadalbane Arms.

The amateur dramatic club frequented another local hotel after rehearsals. We were an extremely talented bunch of thespians, winning Scotland wide acclaim and appearing at the Edinburgh Festival. Our forte was the Christmas pantomime, and we won prizes for the productions of *Aladdin* and *Oliver*.

Not having had a dog on Mykonos, we decided that as we were living in a farmhouse, it would be good to get a collie. One of the lads at the mine was married to the daughter of a local personality and sheep dog breeder called Alec Murray. One of his best bitches had produced a litter two months previously, and he was looking for homes for a couple of the pups.

The farmhouse was perched on a hill way above the valley along a pretty bumpy lane. Alec showed us Misty, a beautiful grey-white-and-black Merle Sky Collie. She came from a long line of champions that had won many, many prizes at sheepdog trials. Local folklore said her forebears had accompanied James Mackenzie, a famous sheep rustler in the 1850s, from Scotland to New Zealand. There is a statue of him and his dog in Fairlie on the South Island. So Misty was no ordinary dog.

Carefully, we bundled up Misty in a blanket, placing her in the back of the Range Rover which I'd borrowed from the boss as he was away for a few days. Misty had never been in a vehicle before and was violently sick all the way down the lane and back to the farm.

But she was never car sick again and loved to stand behind me on our Land Rover's back bench, sticking her head out of the window over my shoulder.

Alec had trained her, and even at that young age she would round up anything that moved, including our neighbours and our chickens. A truly wonderful dog.

The winters here were hard at the Foss Mine and in the valley.

One morning, I came down the farm track to find the 'wee postie, Tam' and his red van in the middle of the field next to the lane. He'd missed the track then driven further and further into the field. Fortunately, the ground was pretty hard and I'd put my snow chains on, so was able to rescue him. There must have been two foot of snow on the ground.

That winter was one of the worst in living memory with tens of feet of snow drifting and blocking the main road north over the pass at Killicrankie. The snow fell not only on the hills where the mine was located, but also in the valley and on the minor roads leading over the mountain pass to the mine.

A couple of days before Christmas, we closed the project for the holidays.

Our neighbours, the McTaggarts, lived about half a mile from our house and had invited us for Hogmanay. As the roads were unploughed, we set off across the fields to their house, together with our close neighbours the Robsons. They were small in stature, living a simple life in a semi-abandoned croft called 'Tomtewan', a couple of hundred yards up the track from our house. On the way back, we were able to follow our footsteps in the snow much like

King Wenceslas. After the party, there was a rising moon and Tony had brought a lantern. We set off for Lundin and Tomtewan like hobbits returning from Silverdale.

After the break, and after recovering from a rather drunken Hogmanay, I went up to the mine with a colleague. Before Christmas, we had a small, tracked, front-end loader working on upgrading the route to the mine, but the roads were still unploughed. Eventually, the county ploughed the road and we were able to cross the pass from the Tay to the Tummel Valley and gain access to the forestry gate at the bottom of the hill, which was where the track to the mine started. The Range Rover managed to get within a half mile of where the bulldozer had been left. As we crested the slope, the valley beyond was a flat plane of snow and no sign of the dozer.

Had it been stolen? Surely not! We slogged on through the deep snow which was frozen to a hard crust of ice, and as we approached the place where we had left the machine, we saw the very top of the exhaust pipe peeping out from a deep drift.

The machine was duly dug out by Alan Thompson, a contractor who had a JCB in his yard at Coshieville, back down the valley. The snowed-in machine was checked out, fired up and put to work. It took a full week of digging and moving snow to clear the track and reach the mine. In the interim, we walked there on the frozen crust, occasionally breaking through and ending up waist deep in powdery snow.

The not-so-glorious 12th

During the first summer we were there, one of the landowners whose land was close to the mine decided it would be good for all of us to get to know the moor ... and the fact that he had a really good grouse shoot that may have been compromised by the development of the mine. To show us how important the grouse were to the local economy, he organised a shoot for the staff from the project. Grouse is a challenge because the birds fly fast, making them particularly difficult to shoot.

There were no beaters and we did not stay in the butts, specially constructed shooting positions often built out of wood, stone and turf. Instead, we walked up with a small pack of gun dogs.

It must have been a bad year as our combined tally of birds was two grouse, one lost pheasant, and a very frightened and large tawny owl which sprang up out of the heather in front of me.

Fortunately, I am not a good shot with a 12-bore, especially fired in surprise, and missed the owl completely.

The game keeper remarked, "Aye, it's a good job you're no very good at this shooting, Mr Matthews, else the environmental people would have been after ye."

The village of Aberfeldy is on the River Tay and has a famous bridge, built by General Wade and designed by William Adam, one of Scotland's top architects at the time. It proved to be the single most expensive structure of the whole road network built by Wade throughout the Highlands, exceeding £4,000 on its completion in 1734 (about £500,000 today). The bridge formed the focus of the community, and it was also the finishing point of the Killin to Aberfeldy raft race.

So, it shouldn't have come as a surprise that the bridge became a contentious issue when we applied for planning permission to develop the mine.

Our plan was to use the local B-roads and the General's bridge to cross the river with our lorries carrying the barite on their way to Aberdeen. Objections were raised by many fearing the collapse of the bridge due to the increased weight and volume of traffic across it.

After studies and engineering inspections, we convinced the locals that the bridge would stand up to the traffic. During the measurements and surveys, we ran lorries with a load of ore across the bridge. Local observers accused us of not carrying a full load as they couldn't see anything, no mounds of earth or gravel. I explained that the density of the barite ore was such that a full lorry load about 30 tonnes would barely cover the bottom of the truck bed. During one of the regular town hall meetings we had with the villagers, I brought along a few kilos of the ore we were mining to show how dense it was and how a couple of feet in the bottom of the lorry could amount to a 30 tonne load.

An extraordinary deposit

The mine was a challenge. It was set high in the hills with a very complicated geology and difficult access. Prior to my arrival, a lot of exploration had been undertaken and the rough shape of the underground orebody outlined from the data generated. The barite actually could be found right at surface, and a tunnel was driven into the mountain following the outcrop. However, the orebody had been folded and formed into what may be best described as a series of ridges 10m apart that plunged at 30° into the hillside.

When it was formed in geological time, the barite was sandwiched between two layers of silica that exhaled in liquid form from a side vent of a volcano. First the silica came, then the barite, and then another layer of silica. This combination of silica-barite-silica encapsulated the barite and kept it whole in the orebody during the folding that took place subsequently. The entire package was enclosed in layered black schists.

It was amazing to see the men with their drilling machines drill through the schists which turned the lubricating waters black, then seeing and hearing the drill bit hit into the fine-grained quartz/silica which was incredibly hard and turned the water a light grey. Then the noise from the bit and drill would change, and the lubricating waters would turn a milky white, just like milk from a cow.

We used contractors to put the tunnel in place ensuring that they trained a crew of miners for us so that we could carry on production when they had completed the excavations. The contract miners were Irish and good at their job, but hard on the locals we had hired. They had some unorthodox methods to overcome various problems. My favourite was the use of a petrol soaked rag that Mick would set fire to and hold over the air intake of the diesel water pump in order to get it started on the freezing mornings. They would also use the rag trick to heat up the fuel tank of the Land Rover if the fuel had started to coagulate from the cold.

The contractors duly completed the driving of the tunnel and a decline tunnel, and went back across the Irish Sea. The village gave a sigh of relief, restocked the depleted supply of Bushmills Irish Whiskey, and stopped ordering vast quantities of Guinness from the suppliers.

The contractors did a good job and we were able to employ six local lads to carry on extending the tunnel. By now, I had become used to the strong Scottish accents and was able to understand when Billy the fitter said, "The effin' battry was effin' flat."

Geordie, who despite his nickname was a local and had been in the Merchant Marine, was a great fan of Misty and would feed her a part of his 'piece' (lunch) while she sat next to him at the table.

So progress was made, and we went ahead and sought planning permission to develop the deposit. It took several months to complete the necessary documentation and studies, but permission was granted some months later ... in record time. Then the demand for barite fell. We were to supply an associate company in Aberdeen with our amazingly pure barite, but due to a fall in the oil price, demand for our product fell, and the mine and we were placed on 'care and maintenance'.

It was just before Christmas when we were told by phone from Houston that we had to close the project. We had to lay off all of the miners, the secretary, and the draftsman (Linda). All were recompensed with a large turkey and four weeks' wages.

Care and maintenance was okay for six months or so, playing golf every other day, working the mine plan over and over, but then Linda and I decided we needed to go back to a warmer climate and dispense with wearing woolly clothes to bed.

I'd had the opportunity to work with a former colleague who had relocated from Scotland to Bolivia (more of this later), but I was also intrigued by the position of Development Assistant/Inspector of Mines to the Mines Department in the newly Independent Nation of Papua New Guinea (PNG).

After an interview in London, I was offered the job and we prepared to leave Scotland after three, fun-filled years. Our first job was researching how to ship our beautiful and highly intelligent dog Misty to PNG. Our investigations showed that regular animal charter flights flew from Heathrow to Australia where Misty could quarantine until we were able to fly her up to PNG. There were a few other dogs on the flight, but generally the flight was for horses.

We took her to a facility just outside of Cambridge, handed her over to the agents, and drove back to Aberfeldy with a tear in our eyes. Our departure was delayed by bureaucracy and we flew out to PNG six weeks behind Misty.

PNG proved to be one of the most exciting places we had ever lived but it was hard leaving behind good friends, as it always is.

∼

The Foss Mine was put into production in 1985.

9

THE ANDACABA LEAD, SILVER-ZINC MINE

April 1983: Bolivia

A Cornish beam engine found underground, dynamite for sale on the streets of Potosí, witches supermarket in La Paz, mountains made of silver

My ex-boss in Scotland, Ed Wardrop, had gone down to South America to buy tin, lead and silver concentrates for one of the big mining houses. Ed knew his stuff but wanted a second opinion on the workings and efficiency of a small underground mine. It turned out that he also wanted me to go there to work with him. The mine was situated in Bolivia in the south central portion of the Andes, south of La Paz, and south again of Potosí. Knowing that I had experience of mining tin veins which were usually less than a couple of metres wide and similar to those in Bolivia, Ed asked me to come for a visit.

As Bolivia was not on the normal travel agents' route, it took a bit of research by the local travel agent in Scotland to find where it was and who flew there. But within a couple of days, I was starting out from Edinburgh, then on to London and Madrid, (plus there was a stop somewhere in the Caribbean where we were on the ground for an hour or so), and then flew on to La Paz, arriving in the late afternoon.

The airport in La Paz is 4,061m (13,325ft) above sea level, and at the time, one was required to walk from the plane to the terminal building, then queue up to enter the customs and immigration hall. It's pretty high up, but unlike the airport in Quito, Ecuador, where there are signs stating, 'Warning! You are 3,500m above sea level. WALK do *not* run', no such sign existed in La Paz.

I was just about to enter the terminal building when I realised I had left my duty free behind. I ran back to the plane and up the steps, retrieved my duty free, ran back down and got halfway to the terminal, then suddenly realised that my heart was racing and that I could hardly breathe. At 4,061m the air is very thin and lacks sufficient oxygen for people from lower elevations to run and breathe. Fortunately, the queue to enter the terminal was slow moving, and I managed to get my breath back before facing the stern-looking Bolivian Customs squad. I used my French with a Spanish accent, adding an 'o' to all the words to get by. I paid the required fee (for what, I never knew), emerged with my suitcase and duty free, and was greeted by Ed.

Ed not only wanted me to look at the mine for him but also to consider becoming the mining company's rep in Bolivia as they planned to transfer Ed to Peru. That being the case, he wanted to give me the grand tour of La Paz and Potosí where he thought I could be based. Our schedule required that we leave La Paz next morning, so after a light Chinese meal that Ed thought would be easiest to digest, we topped the meal off with *mate*, a green tea made with leaves of the coca plant to help with the altitude sickness, and I went to bed. Despite the tea, during the night I developed full blown altitude sickness, manifested by a pounding headache.

Morning eventually came, and after tea, toast and more *mate*, we set off for Potosí and the Andacaba Mine.

Travelling south through the steep-sided valley which held La Paz, we emerged onto the Altiplano. It was flat and featureless but the road was in good condition, probably because it never rained there. It seemed as though the snow-capped mountains of Illimani which were both in front and behind us, never seemed to get closer – a feature of the clear, rarefied air which makes distant objects appear much closer than they really are.

At some point between La Paz and Potosí, we stopped at an *Aduana Interior*. This was a customs post, pretty much in the middle of nowhere. It consisted of a few buildings constructed of concrete blocks, and the official's room was furnished with a desk, filing cabinet and a phone. The buildings were painted white with a blue trim of which the Bolivians seem so fond. Its domain was marked by white painted rocks surrounding a flag pole where the national flag fluttered weakly in the cool mountain air.

We were subjected to the usual questions:

"What are you doing here? Where are you going? Can I please have 300 Bolivars for my tea?"

Fortunately, Ed had obtained the permits and other official looking papers required to travel from state to state. The two guardians of the Altiplano took the papers into their office and it seemed as though they needed to phone La Paz to verify our documents. Reluctantly, we also gave them our passports. After an hour of having documents scrutinised, verified and stamped, we went on our way.

Our route took us through Oruro, skirting Lake Poopó before turning east at Challapata. Lake Poopó sits 3,700m above sea level, is more salty than the sea and seems to be sloping to the east. After this, we turned left and entered the mountains where the road ran through areas of red rocks and again totally barren landscape with agriculture confined to the valley bottoms.

Eventually, we reached Potosí. It is an unremarkable city, much the same as most high-altitude towns in South America which all seem to reflect the colonial past, hosting several magnificent churches, statues of Simón Bolívar, and a poor quarter – not quite slums or *favelas*, but apparently where the less well-off lived. The National Mint of Bolivia was established here in 1572 to deal with the truly massive amount of silver extracted from the mines of the Cerro Rico; the current building was constructed in 1770. The mountain dominates the town, and all of the streets rising up from the town centre started and ended with the view of the mountain.

The streets were narrow with miniscule pavements, and the roads appeared to be paved with concrete hexagonal tiles. The buildings were made from brick, plastered over then whitewashed or painted a buff yellow or blue, with the occasional slogan *Viva la revolucíon* daubed on the side. Those facing the streets were mostly windowless, although occasionally, there was a barred window 2.5m from street level. The roofs, when not tiled, were red-painted corrugated iron. Gates into the yards of the houses were generally composed of thin sheets of iron plate with rebar welded on for strengthening.

Electrical wires and telephone cables formed a spider web with timber poles at the centre that surely should snap with the weight of the wires. Remarkably, they didn't.

Passing through the streets into the more commercial areas of the city, there were ladies in black cloaks and bowler hats selling sticks of dynamite. These were precisely arranged in small piles, neatly laid in a crisscross pattern. A few metres down the pavement, there were ladies of the same dress code selling lengths of safety fuse with detonators already attached.

Cerro Rico, 'mountain of riches', dominates the city. It has been mined for over 450 years, firstly by the Spaniards, then by the rich elite of Bolivia before the revolution, and then in its latter years by *cooperativos*. These are composed of groups of miners banded together to mine the ore, and ship it to the concentrators and smelters who would rob them blind for the privilege of turning their hard won ore into silver.

According to Inca legend, the silver-laden mountain was first worked by Huayna Capac, an Inca ruler of the late 1400s, but his workers abandoned the project when hearing a voice warning them not to take the silver as it was 'destined for other masters'.

When the Spanish found the silver deposits, they wasted little time in extracting the resources for themselves. In 1544, the reinvented mining town of Potosí began its rapid ascent into wealth and grandeur. It is still an important centre for mining with several tin mines operating nearby.

After a welcome rest in a hotel in town, the next morning we set off to the Andacaba Mine. Ed had been contacted by the owner with a view to soliciting a loan which would be paid back with concentrates containing tin, lead and silver, and we were to see if the mine was capable of producing the required amount of concentrates.

The mine was perched on the side of a mountain with the mill buildings running in a line down the slope. This was an excellent idea as all the steps of processing the ore were completed using gravity instead having to pump concentrates and fluids around the building. The buildings, although dilapidated, contained the essentials required to extract the valuable minerals from the ore.

One could only guess at when the mine was started. There were openings dotted all over the rocky mountainside where miners had followed the vein. Most of the entrances only had small piles of waste rock in front of them, indicating that the vein had petered out before too long. These were made more noticeable by the grey-coloured rock from within, contrasting with the light brown colour of the weathered rock at surface.

At some of the entrances, retaining walls were built to allow rails to be run out along the waste rock already tipped. At the end of the rail, small wagons from within the mine carrying ore or waste rock could tip their load away from the entrance. In some cases, the wagons tipped their load into small wooden holding bins. From here, roadways had been cut into the mountainside. Small trucks loaded from the bins and took their load down the hill to the processing plant.

Most of these workings were operated by 'tributors', miners who were not paid by the mine but who leased a portion of the mine from the owners. They were paid on the amount of ore they delivered to the processing plant and for the mineral content of the rock delivered. A difficult system to run properly, and always to the disadvantage of the miners.

Ed knew the Bolivian Mine Captain, and after introducing me, we donned overalls and other essential kit including hard hats and cap lamps, and set off into the main tunnel of the mine. The floor was uneven and laid with sleepers and rail; to the left hand side was a small drainage ditch that carried a trickle of water. After several hundred metres on the level, our guide disappeared into what seemed to be a small niche in the side of the tunnel. Ed and I followed him into a narrow passage, about 1.5m wide that sloped steeply downward. The passage was timbered underfoot with planks nailed to round timbers 15cm in diameter known as 'stulls'. These provided purchase for the planks and also helped to hold the left and right side of the opening apart. This area was a 'stope', an opening which once held the vein, mined out long ago. So under the timber footing was a mined-out void and when we looked up, we saw a set of stulls similar to those we were standing on, 30m above us. Who knew what was beneath us...

We reached the bottom of the slope and emerged into another level tunnel laid with railway track. It was uncertain as to where this level went, and we were told that this was the bottom of the mine. However, the Mine Captain said that he knew there was a rich vein underneath this area and they had sunk a 'winze' or shaft on the vein to a depth of some 25m, and were now developing it by drilling and blasting a horizontal tunnel.

We thought it would be worthwhile to see as the Mine Captain said that the vein was extremely rich. By now, the air had become quite stale and there was a slight mist created by the exhaust from the drilling machine we could hear below.

Rock drills are run on compressed air which has water droplets in it creating a mist; plus, the drill bit is lubricated with water, and an in-line device that supplies small amounts of lightweight oil to the air, all creating a sort of funky mist.

As the winze was only recently developed, the only way to reach the lower level was by a rickety homebuilt ladder made of bits of packing cases and smaller branches from the timber used for support. Otherwise, access could be gained by being lowered down into the bowels of the earth in a 44 gallon drum attached to a wire, which was in turn attached to a compressed air drum hoist. The wire looked like it had been salvaged from one of the electricity poles in Potosí.

The winch made a high-pitched screech as the operator opened the air valves to put the machine into operation as we were lowered into the dark hole one at a time. Ed went first, then me, and the Mine Captain went last.

On reaching the bottom, the drillers, seeing our presence, stopped work. As they did so, the small portable compressed air diaphragm pump began to operate. There was water from the drill and there was water seeping from the roof of the tunnel. When the drill was working, the pump stopped. The miners complained that when anyone came down in the skip, it took air way from their drills. The air here was a thick funk, a mixture of water vapour and lubricating oil issuing from the exhaust ports of the drilling machine or from the pump. The compressed air exhaust from the machines was the only ventilation.

Part of the problem was that the compressors situated at surface were old. In the rarefied atmosphere of the mountains, the compressors only operated at 50% efficiency.

We went to look at the face they were drilling. The vein was really rich, sparkling with galena, sphalerite, black jack, arsenopyrite and tin. We took a couple of samples for assay, knowing they would give very high values of lead, zinc, silver and tin. It's no wonder the Spanish colonised this country; almost every mountain had a treasure trove hidden within its depths.

Not wishing to disturb the drillers anymore, and not wanting to be further asphyxiated in the foul air made worse by the altitude, we decided to get back to the upper level and surface as soon as possible.

However, the Mine Captain wanted to show us an extraordinary tunnel that passed from one side of the mountain to the other, almost 3km long: *Túnel de Dom Fernando*. Reluctantly, after climbing out of the bowels of the earth, we entered the tunnel and set off toward the east side of the mountain. It was much larger than those in the mine proper, the rails and track in better shape.

About a third of the way through, we could see light coming from what must have been a shaft exiting at the surface. On reaching the pool of light, we found a large cavern had been hollowed out of the native rock. There, to our amazement were the essential components of a Cornish Beam Engine. I could clearly see the raised lettering on the casting: *Harvey's of Hayle*.

The mine Captain said in Spanish, "I thought you would be interested in seeing this."

Several years later, I was again asked to undertake a desktop review of the Andacaba mine and remembered fondly the Túnel of Dom Fernando.

On returning to Potosí, Ed took me through the Mercado Central, about the only place to buy your llama meat or fresh vegetables brought up from the lowlands. This also seemed to be the only place where one could shop for essentials, and I could not quite see Linda asking *el señor* the butcher for a nice piece of llama for a Sunday roast.

Oddly, Potosí also contained a brewery that made German-style lager. Apparently, the brewery was owned and run by Germans who fled at the end of the Second World War.

Potosí is still an important mining town, but as the rich silver veins were mined out long ago, tin is the metal of choice now.

Returning to La Paz, I stayed in a hotel close to the main square. It was an upmarket place; I was surprised to find the room was equipped with oxygen masks located above the bedhead. Ed left me to explore by myself, and as I was wandering in one of the streets behind the cathedral, I came across an area that was known as the Witches Supermarket, with several shops selling potions in medicinal type bottles, dried parts of animals, herbs, mushrooms and other bits and pieces one would need to create a spell or a love potion. But the most amazing items on offer were housed in glass jars, each containing the foetus of a llama. It was hard to imagine for what purpose one might use a pickled foetus.

Coincidentally, the musical group *Cacharpaya* were very popular at the time. They played mountain music on instruments some of which seemed to be made from endangered species, armadillo shells, condor wing bones and large conch type shells, the panpipes being the lead instrument. Nevertheless, the music has a certain quality that evokes feelings of the mountains and the lost civilisations.

I refrained from buying any llama foetuses, but did buy a small talisman as a souvenir of Bolivia. It is a silver model of the Tiwanakan god of abundance and prosperity, Ekeko. He is depicted as a small Bolivian peasant with all the goods he would need for life: a miner's gold pan, a woven rug, a bucket, an umbrella, a house, a pillow, a chair, set of panpipes, a shovel, a guitar, a table, a sandal, and a lariat which binds all the goods together. All this strapped to a small statue, some two inches high made of silver.

He has been all over the world with us, and always stands in a corner of the kitchen watching over us, keeping us safe.

I also bought a small wooden flute and a pair of cushion covers depicting one of the Aztec gods, El Tío, 'the Uncle' who rules over the mines, simultaneously offering protection and destruction if he is not fed.

The Braniff plane that took me on the first leg of the return trip from La Paz to Lima seemed to take a very long time to take off. The runway is over 4,000m long, and the plane barely made it before skimming over the surface of Lake Titicaca, and then climbing slowly over the Andes and down to Lima.

For some reason, the authorities in Lima took my passport and kept me in a windowless room for the two hours before my flight left for Madrid. My Spanish consisted of *'dos cervecas por favor'* and *'gracias'*, and I had no way of finding out why I had been detained.

A few minutes before take-off, I was escorted to the bottom of the steps and told to board the plane: a truly scary experience.

The flight made a stop in Bogota and then on to Madrid. From Madrid, I flew by British Airways to Gatwick, and on to Edinburgh.

Just twelve hours after leaving La Paz, I arrived back in Aberfeldy.

We didn't go to Bolivia, but the next year we moved to Papua New Guinea.

PART II
FAR FLUNG PLACES

Cornish Stamps, circa 1920, Misima Island, PNG

10

INTO THE TROPICS

1984-1989: Port Morseby, Papua New Guinea

Fun in the jungle, mountains, cannibals and gold, Inspector of Mines working for the government, horse races at Bomana in Port Moresby, Kiaps and Mining Wardens

In 1895, CAW Monckton left his native Australia to spend a tour of duty as a Resident Magistrate in the Colony of British New Guinea. The western half was known as Dutch New Guinea, now part of Indonesia; the eastern lower portion as British New Guinea; and the northern half of the eastern portion of the island, a German colony known as Kaiser-Wilhelmsland.

British New Guinea was declared a colony in 1888 and had been under British and Australian rule since 1884. There is a photographic record of Commodore James Erskine addressing a gathering of Papuan Chiefs on board *HMS Nelson* in Hood Bay and explaining to these worthy gentlemen the proclamation that made their country a protectorate of the mighty British Empire. If the Papuans had any idea of the might of the British Empire, I am sure they would have been impressed. Probably what impressed them more was the size of the vessel on which they had gathered and the clothes of the white men who spoke to them.

I made no such declaration of protection at the start of my contract to serve the government of Papua New Guinea, or PNG as it is better and more easily known. I had joined the country's Civil Service as an Inspector of Mines and began my duties in the capital city of Port Moresby about a century after Monckton. PNG must have been then, and probably still is now, one of the 'last frontiers' of western influence in the Pacific Rim.

Monckton made his passage to New Guinea on the sailing schooner *Myrtle*, leaving the Australian mainland from Cooktown in Queensland and making landfall in New Guinea at the island of Samarai. From there, he travelled up the southern coast to land, eventually, in the capital city of Port Moresby. His journey took at least six weeks, and along the way he was able to familiarise himself with the customs of the country and the expatriates who were heading north to seek their fortunes in the newly opened gold fields. Monckton was armed with £100 sterling and an outfit, in his words, "particularly unsuited to the tropics". But from his excellent account of his tour, he possessed an indefatigable sense of doing the right thing.

Our journey, commencing almost a century later, once begun, did not take quite as long as Monckton's but our departure had been delayed as the result of a bureaucratic hitch within the government. Each ministry was responsible for the recruitment of its own personnel, and the Department of Minerals and Energy (DME), having offered me the job of Inspector of Mines, and with me accepting the position, I expected to be able to take up my appointment on the contracted date of 1st September 1984. However, in the relevant ministries within the Independent State of Papua New Guinea, like all remnant colonial bureaucracies, the left hand knew not what the right hand was doing. After several visits to the PNG Consulate in London, we eventually left the UK in late October, flying from London to Singapore on a British Airways jumbo jet, rather than gently acclimatising to the ways of the country by travelling on a Pacific schooner.

There was a brief refuelling stop in Dubai and a three-hour layover in Singapore. From there, we flew by Air Niugini directly to Port Moresby. On board, we met our first Papuan ladies. The word 'papuan' is derived from the Portuguese explorer Jorge de Meneses who, when sighting the country named it *Ilhas dos Papuas*, 'land of the fuzzy-haired people'.

The Singapore to Moresby leg was one of the longest flights I have ever experienced. Perhaps not in the amount of time taken, but in anticipation and expectation, for we had little idea of what to expect from a country about which so little was known. The entire journey from the UK to PNG took 24 hours, and having landed at Moresby's Jacksons International Airport, we were met by Hussain, official meeter and greeter from the Mines Inspection Division at the Department of Minerals and Energy. Hussain was actually in charge of the department's diamond drilling operations. Not drilling for diamonds, but using a diamond-tipped drill bit to take core samples from below the Earth's surface. A very handy tool when looking for gold, but sadly not utilised nearly enough.

Our desire to go to Papua New Guinea stemmed from answering an advertisement placed in the *Mining Journal*, then a flimsy weekly periodical which was airmailed to the mining fraternity throughout the world. Now, as then, it informed of new mines, new projects, and the state of the mining industry as a whole. Possibly the most widely read portion of the magazine was the jobs section.

I had just resigned as project manager of the mine in central Scotland where we had spent three years bringing a small barite deposit to a production decision. Barite is used in the oil drilling industry, and the project's proximity to the North Sea oil fields made it an attractive development project for the company that employed me. However, as is often the case in the resource industry, the commodity sought was in a price decline and the mine had been put on hold. It's a very boring existence, looking after a closed mine. The decision not to proceed with the mine's development at that time prompted Linda and I to undertake a new challenge in what was known then, without a trace of political correctness, as 'third world'.

Our arrival in Moresby was uneventful, if somewhat tedious. All passengers of European origin spent hours queuing to pass through Immigration. I was staggered by the surly attitude of the local Immigration and Customs officials who seemed not to give a hoot that we had left our homeland to protect the lives and health of their brethren in the mines of Bougainville, Wau and Ok Tedi. I was, however, very impressed with the security measures adopted by the local customs officers. Their main concern was to prevent the importation of pornography, weapons and drugs.

To ensure none of this booty was hidden in our luggage, sniffer dogs were let loose to walk on the luggage as it made its circuitous way around a barely functioning baggage carousel. As we had been detained in Immigration for some time, and as it was at least 200 yards from the plane to the baggage hall, we arrived there at the same time as our luggage. It is quite an amazing sight to see a fully grown Alsatian dog leaping from suitcase to suitcase, occasionally stopping to pee on the better smelling leather bags.

No porn or drugs were found in our possessions and we passed out into the mass of black, grinning faces with teeth stained red by *buai* (betelnut) to find our escort.

Having accepted the position, we did our best to gather as much information about the country as we could. For some reason, there wasn't much. One of the main sources that we had always relied upon to at least give a global perspective of where a country was in relation to its neighbours, was our trusty *Reader's Digest Great World Atlas*. Published in 1975 (although not necessarily updated) and purchased in South Africa in 1977, it had only portions of maps of PNG: one segment appeared in the top left hand corner of the map for Australia, and the whole country did appear on another page as an insignificant part of the left-hand side of the map for the Pacific

Ocean. The western extremity appeared on the edge of the plate for 'The Far East'.

Undaunted, we tried the public library in Plymouth where we also met with limited success, but learned that PNG was home to the highly decorative Bird-of-paradise, and produced a lot of cardamom. Had we known that Hammond Innes, one of our favourite authors, had written an incisive and thrilling account of the riots that took place on Bougainville in the early seventies, or that the Australian author Jon Cleary had written an excellent account of the Coastwatchers who performed heroic deeds during the Second World War, we would have read these novels to at least give us a feel for the country.

We even went to Foyles bookshop in London to seek out larger scale maps. The gentleman who served us was uncertain but thought he had some aeronautical maps of the region, and led us into his cellar. There, in large 3 x 6ft drawers, lay aeronautical charts, full of expressions such as 'elevation believed not to exceed 12,000ft', 'area not surveyed', or 'last surveyed in 1914', and so on. I wondered whether or not we had made the right decision, given the lack of information available. *In A Sunburned Country* (published 2000), Bill Bryson comments at length on how difficult it was to find information on Australia and how little the affairs of the Australasian region are reported in the press of the western and northern hemispheres. It was even more the case for PNG nearly two decades earlier.

Since that time, we have been fortunate enough to find many fascinating and generally out of print books dealing with the 'early days' in New Guinea. These almost always refer to the period from the 1880s to the early 1950s. My favourite has to be *Black, White and Gold* (published 1976) and written by the Australian author Hank Nelson – a name that really does conjure up visions of a hoary prospector with sunburnt skin and a hat with corks suspended from the rim.

Nelson's book is closely followed by *Greatheart of Papua: James Chalmers* written in 1913 by W P Nairne. It's the story of one of those great Scottish missionaries who devoted their lives to bringing Christianity to the cannibals, only to be killed by them in what, even now, is one of the most remote parts of the Papuan coast. The cover is a painting depicting Chalmers striding ashore on a sandy beach in a white tropical suit complete with pith helmet. The caption reads *'They (the Natives) danced around him all the while'*.

Perhaps the most evocative title is *Patrol into Yesterday* by Jack Hides, written in 1936 and recounting his patrol into the central Highlands, starting from the Papuan coast, following rivers ever upward to the central range.

Chalmers was perhaps lucky that he did not contract and die from one of the many nasty tropical diseases that infest the Papuan coast to this day. The book has many black and white sketches with captions such as, *'When Chalmers took off his shoe there was a shout of surprise. For the natives of the region at that time had never seen western clothing and surmised he was taking off his foot.'* Or their dismay when, taking off his shirt, they thought he was peeling off his outer skin. There are many references in the recently developed folklore to white men removing certain parts of their clothing and astonishing the Nationals who had never seen such things before. These meetings between the colonialists and the local population are frequently referred to as 'first contact' and the expression has become the title of many books and documentaries.

Later during our stay, we heard the expression those that went to PNG were 'missionaries, mercenaries or misfits'. They should have added 'miners' to that phrase.

One first contact experience that is well documented was that experienced by Jim Taylor, an amazingly brave and intrepid explorer of the 1930s. In one report, he relates the horror expressed by a group of Highlanders who believed that his large wide leather belt was an extension of his penis.

Tribes in the Highlands generally sport the most amazing 'penis gourds'. Often long (depending on your status within the tribe) vegetable marrow-type gourds especially cultivated to give the required form and dimension, they are tied over the penis to 'protect and serve' according to the occasion. The gourds can be up to 2ft in length, and curl spectacularly from the appendage upward in an arc to nestle just at the breastbone. Thus, a white god whose penis was so long that he had to wrap it around his waist, buckle it and have its end trailing an inch or so below the buckle, would have been something to behold. One can imagine the shock and incredulity of the Nationals as the white god removed his 'penis' to take off his trousers.

To put this and other stories of the first contact tribes had with the twentieth century into perspective, one has to realise that these events took place in the 1930s when Papua New Guinea held the distinction of the country that carried more air freight than any other country in the world. These flights were to serve the alluvial gold mines at Wau. In certain parts of New Guinea, the Nationals' world was confined to what they could see in the next valley, and in the next valley they had no concept of the outside world. Smoke, and the sight of fires burning several hill tops far away, were thought to be the home of the ancestors.

These first contact experiences, in a somewhat modified form, possibly go on today; they certainly did in our time in PNG. We adventured into places where we were the first white people to have been seen by the majority of some tribes, and in many cases, the first white people other than missionaries they had seen in many a year.

The Australian Government managed its affairs through the Kiap System, a form of local government similar to that practised in other British Colonies. *Kiaps*, known formally as district officers and patrol officers, were travelling representatives of the British and Australian governments with wide-ranging authority in pre-independence PNG. Government representatives were still trying to contact tribes without the benefit of colonial rule into the early 1970s. The tribes, known to exist from third party contact, but who had never been inducted into the enfolding arms of colonialism, were to be told of the benefits of government and the fact that they could vote, be counted as part of the population, and possibly receive aid and benefits from organisations and people they could never conceive of.

One classic example of how savvy the local people of PNG could be was described to me by Warren Dutton, a Kiap based in Kiunga in the Western Province in the early 1970s. Warren is an Australian by birth who became a naturalised Papua New Guinean, and one of the first Members of Parliament for the Western Province where the Ok Tedi gold and copper mine is situated.

Warren told the tale of how he had been instructed by the colonial administrators in Port Moresby to mount a patrol from the provincial headquarters at Kiunga, and proceed downstream along the Fly River to the confluence with the Strickland, and on up to the area around Lake Murray. Here, he was to make contact with a tribe that had been heard of but not yet officially contacted by the government. Kiunga, at that time, would have consisted of literally a few huts made of bush materials, a trading post constructed of prefabricated materials brought in from Australia, and the government offices, again built of prefab material. Warren dutifully organised the patrol, complete with translators, affectionately known as 'talk turners', clerks to record the details of the tribe, and a medical officer.

The swamps of the Strickland basin are probably one of the most inhospitable warm climate regions of the world. Full of poisonous snakes, biting insects and plants festooned with thorns, a hard place to live. Studies conducted prior to the opening of the Porgera Mine in the late 1980s which is located in the mountains from which the Strickland flows, showed that the fish in the swamps were highly contaminated with mercury. A product of the mineralising system that formed the gold deposit at Porgera and Mount Kare, not from their subsequent mining. The tribe had been there since time began, and knew of the presence of white men and rumours of the government in far off places.

Warren tells of finally reaching the remote village, with his 'native' officers and 'talk turners' preceding him, calling out in the lingua franca, Tok Pisin also known as 'pidgin', and the local 'place talk' which is very specific to that area. PNG has over 850 different languages. Some are related where geographically close and referred to as 'place talk'.

"Do not be afraid, we are from the Government and are here to help you."

Possibly an oxymoron.

This may have calmed members of the about-to-be-contacted tribe. The village consisted of maybe ten to fifteen huts raised up on stilts above the swampy floor of the jungle. Ten or so of the elders stood at attention in the main clearing with their black palm bows and arrows held rigidly at their sides and naked except for each one of them wearing a pristine pair of white underpants, put on back to front.

The remarkably efficient 'bush telegraph' had warned the tribe of Warren's impending visit, and so as not to appear backward, the elders had designated a young member of the tribe to take wild pig meat, cassowary feathers and probably fish, south to Kiunga where he sold them for cash and purchased the Y-front underpants from the trade store. The ironic part of the story is that Warren's wife, a lady of Lebanese origin, owned and ran the trade store.

Moresby was, at the time of our arrival, blessed with three European style hotels: the Travel Lodge, the Davara, and the Islander. Hussain of the DME, after having located us at the airport, guided us to the parking lot and the official car, a white Toyota station wagon. Our bags had been collected by *buai*-chewing itinerants, and Hussain passed them a couple of *kina* as payment.

Nowadays, one travels on the equivalent of a super highway from the airport to down town, but the road on which we travelled took a circuitous route via the component villages that made up the National Capital District of Port Moresby. The roads and districts had strange sounding Papuan and Australian names. The main road into town was the Sir Hubert Murray Highway, a grand name for a road that was in parts two lanes and in parts a divided highway (dual carriageway), and was liberally sprinkled with pot holes that grew in size every rainy season.

Along the road, various landmarks were designated by the distance from the airport to the town centre. At Six Mile, the Ok Tedi Mining company had their local offices; from Six Mile, we travelled past the offices of the National Broadcasting Commission with their two English language services, one FM (Kalang) and one AM; on through Four Mile and Boroko, where the Brian Bell shopping centre was located; then on past Korobosea, where we were to later live; and then to crest the hill at Three Mile.

Rounding the corner at Korobosea, we were presented with a view to the southwest of the amazingly blue Pacific, and in the distance, the white fringe of breakers thrown up by the coral reef a few miles offshore. We were thrilled with the view, it was so *South Pacific*, with palm trees, bougainvillea, frangipani, hibiscus, huge rain trees, beautiful shades of blue in the sea, and a pleasantly warm climate.

From Three Mile Hill, the road winds down to Badili where South Pacific Brewery has its home and swings on round through the village of Koki. There was a local market where fish, shellfish and all manner of crustaceans were sold by local fishermen, and folk from the outlying districts would bring in corn, squash and greens for sale. There was also a traditional Motuan village at Koki, with houses made of native materials topped with sheets of corrugated iron raised on stilts up over the sea, very picturesque but not terribly practical for today's modern Papuan.

From Koki, the road splits and swings west along the palm fringed Ela Beach and passes the Davara Hotel which was to be our resting place for a few weeks until we were assigned a flat or town house. It was clean, had a swimming pool, and right across the road was the Returned Serviceman's Club, the library and the beach.

The other fork in the road headed north up over Lawes Road, cresting with a view of glimpses of the barren hills across the bay from the Yacht Club, then went on down to Konedobu, home of the Department of Minerals and Energy.

The hills were dotted with bungalows and houses built on stilts, all composed of fibre board and red-painted galvanised corrugated iron roofs. Cheap to build, but not too practical in the tropical heat. When it poured, you were deafened by the drumming of the rain on the roof. Most of the houses were in plots that had several palm and other native trees.

The day after our arrival, I was picked up by Hussain and taken to meet the staff at the DME. All but two or three were expats from either Australia or the UK, with the occasional Canadian doing good works. My boss at the Inspectorate was called Frank R, a small, bespectacled, pedantic 56 year old coal miner from Yorkshire, retired from the Coal Board. He had a sad demeanour, and one got the impression that he felt he had made a mistake in coming to PNG and that the local population were out to murder him. His second-in-command was a man called John T, a surly Scot, again a retiree from the Coal Board. They were affectionately known as 'Twaddlebottom'.

R and T were coalminers, a section of the mining community that we at Camborne believed were not equal to the rigours of hard rock miners. We mined by drilling and blasting metal and mineral deposits from granite hosts, schists and other solid rocks. Coal could be mined with a pick, and the seams of coal were sandwiched between easily mined limestone, sandstone and clays.

I was tasked with looking after the safety of the employees and miners at Ok Tedi, some of whom had never worn shoes let alone hard-toed safety boots and hard hats. Checking that the workers wore these items seemed to be more important to both of them (R and T) than reviewing the mine plans for the future or ensuring that proper blasting procedures and handling systems were in place.

However, I also met Vinnie Smith, an Australian who had been in PNG for years and loved the place. He was 'in country' well before Independence, and was mysteriously connected to the Lae riots, where legend had it that a white man was crucified back in the old days of colonial rule and 'cargo cult'.

Vinnie knew a lot about how the mining industry evolved in PNG and had been appointed the Head Mining Warden, in days gone by a very prestigious title and job. He was a large, imposing man and took no nonsense from the Twaddlebottoms who would try and impinge on his domain. He had a team of four Nationals (natives of PNG) who would conduct Warden's hearings in the villages where applications (Prospecting Authorities) had been made to explore for minerals. In the past, their main job was to settled disputes between the white miners and the local artisanal miners.

Vinnie was married to Little Rita a lovely lady of generous proportions who loved Aussie Rules Football and would listen to it on the AM radio from Queensland. When television came to Port Moresby in later years, Rita was able to watch her beloved games on EM TV, the one and only TV station.

Vinnie was on the Committee of the Bomana Race Course which was ten miles from the centre of Port Moresby. On Saturdays, we would drive out to Bomana to watch five or six races run on a small but adequate flat course. The viewing stand was a two-storey building with the upper level hosting a balcony, a bar and the public address system. It cost one Kina to mount the steps and enter the confines of the Jockey Club, about 25p.

Betting was allowed and Vinnie would always have a good tip on a local horse. There was also on-course betting with bookmakers that were all Chinese. You could even bet on races being run in Australia, and the commentary was broadcast over the public address system from one of the radio stations based in Queensland. The commentary would fade in and out, and several anxious moments were had by all betters, as the race finished in the hiss of static. The Aussie commentators were, in my opinion, the best in the world.

The Melbourne Cup, Australia's most prestigious race was broadcast every year and it was a very special day at Bomana. The expat ladies put on Ascot-style hats, and the men put on their safari suits (shorts with a light, short-sleeved jacket) that the bank johnnies wore. The important Nationals, or 'big men' as they were known, from the government often attended, some in national dress. One of them, John Kaputin, was ultimately my boss at the Ministry for Minerals and Energy.

After a spell of eight weeks or so in Port Moresby, familiarising myself with the PNG Mines Act, listening to Frank R and John T moan and argue, I was told we were to be stationed in the mining town of Tabubil where there was a newly developed copper—gold mine in the Western Province. Moresby had started to be fun with bush walks and trips to the nearby beaches, so it was a little bit of a disappointment to be transferred. We always went in groups to the beaches to deter the 'rascals' who would 'raid' the beaches occasionally, and steal all that was to be had.

Moresby was a very violent place. Just before we arrived, several white women had been gang-raped, and break-ins were a common occurrence perpetrated by gangs of Nationals who were inappropriately called 'rascals', a term which is more often used to describe naughty children. These were not 'naughty'; they were vicious gangs of young men who had come to the capital to seek work, or specifically to rob the whites of goods that they thought belonged to them.

The rascals would break into houses at night by smashing through the flimsy fibre board that most civil servants' houses were built from, steal, and if unopposed, sometimes assault the occupants. The police seemed helpless against these criminals, and even if caught and convicted, the prison at Bomana was so insecure that it was easy for them to break out and escape. In fact, a State of Emergency was declared in the capital just before our arrival because the government were losing control of the rascal situation.

Most private sector expat houses were surrounded by a 2m high diamond mesh fencing topped with razor wire. However, very few of the government-allocated housing had any form of security. Many had safe rooms, and if you were lucky, an alarm system connected to one of the private Security firms. Our town house in Korobosea, a suburb of Port Morseby, was in a small compound and had one old, rattling air-conditioner in the bedroom. The windows were louvered with holey mosquito screens.

We were all expats and looked out for each other, plus we had the 2m high fence, but unfortunately, there was no security system. And most people forgot to close the access gate to the compound.

The rascals' attitude was probably a hangover from the practice of cargo cult. In PNG, this is mostly associated with the arrival of the aeroplane in the 1930s when large pieces of mining machinery were flown to the alluvial goldfields in Wau, and seeing the supply planes land during the Second World War. The locals would see white men cut grass airstrips out of the jungle where the planes would land, and people and cargo would be unloaded. The Nationals believed that the delivery of goods came from the gods by way of the 'great silver bird'. To entice the plane to their village, in some areas they would cut away the grasses and jungle in the manner of an airstrip to imitate a runway. In some cases, they would construct wooden towers replicating the control towers they had seen in the proper airstrips.

In later years, as the colonial administration sought to contact tribes in the remoter portions of the country, exploring parties would be sent ahead and airstrips hacked from the jungle to enable planes to land and bring goods and services to the local populace.

Much of the travel undertaken in the country was still by plane in the period we were there as there were few roads, and no road from the south to the north of the island. Many of the people we met saw their first wheel on the bottom of an aeroplane.

Before moving to Tabubil, I made two trips by plane to the mine township and the Ok Tedi mine. This was with John T, and I was introduced to the senior management of the mine who were quite frankly amazed that the mine merited its own Inspector (as was I). John T and I sorted out the accommodation which was to be a three-bedroomed bungalow built on stilts or metal poles. As in all mining camps, there was a hierarchy associated with the allocation of housing. Ours was a B-house, and our neighbours included the mine doctor, Paul; the Treasurer; and the local police inspector, who was a National. We also had B-class furniture, which was fine. We were glad to leave the town house in Korobosea behind.

The Mine Manager, the Chief Executive and one or two top managers were housed in A-houses. Slightly larger, but the same general plan as the B-houses, and built on stilts, as were the C-houses where the foremen and tradesmen were housed. The contract workers, who were mostly from the Philippines, were housed in *dongas*, dormitory style single-storey portacabins. Others were accommodated in individual trailer-type static mobile homes. All of the accommodation was furnished according to the status of the occupant. Our B-house furniture included a TV.

Most of us gathered a few plants and occasionally orchids from the surrounding jungle to make the houses and streets more homely. The star of the plant show was the New Guinea impatiens which grew wild. Some of the orchids were quite rare and would put out beautiful sprays of flowers. They all grew well in the humid climate and the torrential rainfall, which was up to 3m a year.

The mining company had built a row of small offices for the government employees, the Customs officer, the Kiap, a representative from the Department of Primary Industries (Agriculture and Fish), and myself. It took for ever to get a telephone so that I could report to Port Moresby on my activities, and I had one chair and a small metal desk supplied by the Works Department in Moresby. I had to receive written instructions from Port Moresby by Telex which was located in the office of the manager of the mining company.

We had taken our three year old border collie, Misty, with us. Back in August, she had flown to Australia on a pet charter accompanied by an old English sheepdog called Rags. We did not see Misty again till Saint Andrew's night in late November. Because our departure from the UK had been delayed by six weeks, the Australian-imposed quarantine of three months was already halfway through, so we did not have too long to wait for Misty. She was shipped in a custom-built kennel which also served to take her up to Tabubil and back, and then on to Canada when we left PNG.

She was a beautiful dog with a fantastic temperament and probably the best Frisbee catcher in Papua New Guinea. She provided endless hours of entertainment for the locals and expats alike when we went walking along the shoreline at Ela beach after work. She seemed fine and suffered no physical trauma, however at the first major thunderstorm, of which there were many in Tabubil, she would run and hide in the space between the loo and the back wall and refuse to come out until things had quieted down. People said we were mad, but we would joke saying that she was a walking treasury as dogs' teeth are used as currency in certain parts of PNG.

The move to Ok Tedi

When we were initially transferred to Ok Tedi, we were told by the management that pets were not allowed on site. John T and I told them we were not obliged to follow their rules. It took a lot of persuasion and phone calls to get Misty on the plane to Tabubil.

As there were no pets allowed, the supermarket had no dog or cat food, so Misty existed on a diet of tinned fish, mostly mackerel, and rice, which happened to be the staple meal for many Papuans.

Ok Tedi was a remote location, only accessible by plane, and connected to the river port of Kiunga by a gravel road that was used by large trucks carrying hydrogen peroxide in 200 litre drums and cyanide in metal drums up to the mine. The hydrogen peroxide was used to destroy the cyanide that was used to recover the gold.

It was a pretty tough task being the Resident Inspector of Mines.

To my knowledge, no other mine in the world had a Resident Inspector. In addition, I was the senior representative of the country's 20% interest in the project. I had a duty to report back to Moresby on the progress being made on mining the rich gold cap of the huge deposit. It was also still in the construction phase with machinery and plant being installed to treat the copper ore that lay beneath the gold cap. The mine was mining 25,000 tonnes a day, and in 1988, it produced 6,182kg gold, 10,640kg silver, and 196,000 tonnes of copper concentrate. This generated about 7,000,000 Kina in revenues for the government and the landowners' royalty trust. At the time, 1 Kina =US $1. The number represented about 8% of the national revenue. In 1988, Australia was supplying A$52,855,000 per year in aid.

The landowners of the mining area were the Min tribe, and part of the proceeds from the royalties provided school supplies and to establish health centres. Another portion went to provide employment for the locals through small businesses. There was a community owned 'Gobble and Go' fast food joint, a pharmacy, the only and very well supplied supermarket (except for dog food), which bought the local produce, and was complete with wire baskets and trolleys. There was a farm funded by the royalties in the Highlands where cold weather vegetables were grown, including potatoes.

Linda ran the News Agency for the Min people, in association with the Business Development officer from the mining company. Here, you could buy all the normal things you would find in newsagents in Port Moresby or Cairns: *The Melbourne Age*, *Niugini News*, *Post Courier*, *Woman's Weekly* and so on. The *Post Courier* and *Niugini News* came in on the daily Dash-8 supply plane from Port Moresby. *The Age* and other Aussie papers came in usually a week late. The bestselling book was the Bible. Other books, like the *Atlas of the World*, and a book about the tenth anniversary of colonial rule which had a lot of pictures, were well thumbed by the locals, many of whom did not know how to read. But times were changing, and there was a primary school on site which taught both expat children and Nationals.

Not long after we arrived and to make things more difficult, I was told – by Telex – to close operations at the mine immediately. That afternoon, Walter Hannack, the designated Mine Manager and I went to the mine and stopped all mining operations.

It took six weeks for the dispute between the government and the consortium to be settled. Not a pleasant time for us as we were seen to be the cause of the closure which stopped everyone from going to work.

The dispute centred around the fact that the mine was not being developed according to the plan, and the PNG government believed that the consortium was mining the rich gold ore at the top of the mountain and not making any plans to mine the underlying copper-rich ore. The copper component would provide the treasury with income for many years to come, as did the Panguna Copper Mine at Bougainville. The government had invested some US$35 million in the project, and as a 20% owner felt it had the right to ensure the correct future of the mine.

OK Tedi Mining Limited (OTML) argued that there had been several setbacks which had delayed the progress of the mine, and they needed to mine the gold first to generate cash flow quickly to build the metallurgical plant to recover the copper.

I would often tour the mill building to see if all safety procedures were being followed and to see if the operation was running properly. I went to most areas, but no one except the gold room foreman was allowed into the gold concentrating room where two large shaking tables were housed. The ceiling of the room was an expanded metal grid which formed a viewing platform, and it was easy to see the gold table through the grid. The band of gold crossing the table was at least 50cm wide, the most I have ever seen in being treated. There were probably 70 ounces of gold an hour passing over the table. The amount of gold being mined was quite amazing.

One of the setbacks cited by the company, related to a huge landslide that took place in the area where the tailings dam was to be built. Construction in the area had just started with many acres of jungle uprooted and displaced, when the whole mass went sliding down the mountainside, a wave of earth 30ft high and over 800 yards long. The tailings project was abandoned as no other suitable site could be found in the mountains or valleys.

There were other reasons too, but a solution was proposed, accepted and everyone went back to work.

Misty, Linda and I overcame the initial difficulties and made great friends with the mining engineers, geologists and managers. We would regularly organise barbeques and parties, mostly on Sundays as the employees at the mine worked a six-day week. We would celebrate traditional occasions such as Bastille Day, ANZAC day, Saint George's, and a couple of strange ones such as Rhodesia Independence Day (when Rhodesia declared independence from Britain), Dingaansdag (the Battle of Blood River in South Africa), the opening of the Grouse Season on 12th August, and of course, Saint Piran's Day – the feast day for the patron saint of Cornwall.

Most of the parties were held beneath the B-houses because they were all on stilts, or on the very small terrace of the mobile home of a couple of the single men. Everyone would dress accordingly, berets and red scarves for Bastille Day, safari gear for the Rhodesian Independence Day, a safari with spears and rifles undertaken around the pillars of the house decorated with palm leaves and mock elephant dung (mud).

For the Glorious Twelfth, mock rifles were again improvised from broom handles and tennis racquets. A grouse was fashioned from several pairs of socks stuffed inside each other and a couple of 12" rulers strapped to the back of the 'bird'. One person was elected to beat the bushes and to put up the grouse by throwing the mock bird in the air. At which point all participants would shout, "Bang!" Misty would then retrieve the bird and we repeated the process as fine Scotch whisky was consumed to stave off the heat.

It may sound weird or even childish, but remember that we were far from home, there was nowhere to drive other than to the mine, and there was one TV channel which broadcast the US Airforce Forces Radio and TV services which included CNN. The service was, affectionately known as AFARTS. There was also a nightly movie broadcast from the mine office buildings.

Back in Port Moresby

After our mid-contract long leave, having circled the globe, I took up a new position with the government as Ok Tedi co-ordinator based in Port Moresby. The prior occupant of this position was a chap who had been a weather forecaster or 'meteorologist', as he liked to say, so as a mining engineer who had actually lived on the mine site for 14 months, I felt well qualified to take up the position.

We had an excellent team at the Mines Department at that time. Co-ordinators were appointed to liaise between the companies developing the gold mines and all the ministries and departments in the government. There was a Kiwi hydrologist who was the co-ordinator for the gold mine on the island of Lihir, located off the coast of the New Ireland Province in the Pacific Ocean; an American economist who was the co-ordinator for the Misima Mine, part of the Trobriand group of islands, and being run by Placer Gold, a company that had its roots in Papua New Guinea from the 1930s; a former Kiap handled the Porgera project, one of the toughest wildest areas of PNG; and last but not least, there was a lady environmentalist from the UK. We were all of similar age and got on well with each other, sharing our knowledge and skills to aid in the development of the mining industry of PNG.

In addition to the mining industry, an oil and gas deposit was being developed in the Highlands, and BHP was drilling on the north coast near Vanimo. The deposit in the Highlands was in an area first explored by Jack Hides in 1936, although limited exploration had been going on since 1911. A gas deposit was discovered when the Kuru-1 well blew out in 1956, and oil was discovered at Puri-1 in 1957. As I was the only one in the Mines Department who had any experience with oil and gas, I was appointed Inspector of

Petroleum. The government Geology Department was also involved in the exploration.

These were exciting times in PNG. In the Western Province, Ok Tedi was now producing at full capacity. On the island of Lihir, Kennecott Explorations Australia and its joint venture partner Niugini Mining Limited were developing what became an enormous gold mine. It was a unique deposit, in that the orebody was located in a recently extinct volcano. Much of the deposit was located at the bottom of the caldera which was still giving off heat, making the ground hot to walk on and the atmosphere like the interior of a sauna. At times, the diamond drillers had to construct steam blowout preventers and steam diverters as the drill rods would often intersect either boiling water or superheated steam when drilling.

The gold mine on the island of Misima was also being developed by Placer Dome, the same company that was developing the mine at Porgera.

Numerous other deposits were being developed and explored by junior mining companies. The majority of these were deposits known from exploration in the early part of the 20th century. The four co-ordinators had, I felt, played a significant role in helping these projects come to fruition.

Copper and gold mines are still in production at Porgera, Ok Tedi, Misima, Lihir, Simberi and Hidden Valley.

On moving back to Moresby, we had a challenge to get a suitable house. The Department had some control over who was accommodated where, and for a while, we were being housed in a small single-bedroomed bungalow at the crest of Lawes Road that overlooked the bay. It was quite an old structure with no security measures at all, which was a must-have in Moresby. There was a metre high diamond mesh fence that separated the front garden from the road. So our security was Misty and good sense. On the east side of the living room, the floor had separated from the fibreboard wall and we could see the hibiscus bushes that formed part of the boundary. The toilet had the most wonderful view down the hill to the sea and the reef beyond. It was a lovely little house but rather exposed. At times, especially for some reason on Sunday evenings, we felt as if we were back in the colonial era. At dusk, we would tune into an AM radio station broadcast from Cairns, Queensland, with the call sign 4QN4QY. As darkness fell, the signal would get better and we would listen to a programme of contemporary music accompanied by the singing of the crickets and buzz of the mosquitoes. The signal would at times fade in and out like the lapping of waves on the reef and beach.

After a couple of months, we were allocated a two-bedroomed house similar to the one we had in Tabubil, also on stilts, with a small laundry beneath the main floor. The advantage of having the laundry was that we employed a lovely local lady called Mary who was amazing. She would iron everything that moved and had a special method of folding socks.

This house had a security system. All the windows were alarm-wired, as was the door. In the corridor leading from the lounge to the bedrooms, the windows were louvered glass from ceiling to floor. Unfortunately, on occasion, Misty would happily walk along the corridor wagging her tail which would set off the alarm and bring the security team to our door. Even so, we had a break-in of sorts when a National was passing by, saw the door to the house was open, went in and stole some clothes and other items of small value. Mary was downstairs in the laundry, and on discovering this rascal in the master's house, took a broom to him and chased him down the road.

Our home also housed several nests of ants which lived behind the light switches and sockets, and would eat the plastic coverings of the wiring, causing electrical shorts. Not only that, but on one occasion, I put on a clean pair of underwear and had to remove them very quickly to run for the shower as the ants had got into the elastic of the waistband and the legs. Even though they were sugar ants, they had a nasty bite. Mary observed this incident and was laughing fit to burst. Shouting out, *"Anis, anis!"* Pidgin for ants.

When we left, Mary went to work for a good friend who told us that she cried for four days after we had gone. The norm being a two- or three-day weep.

I made several trips with the Department to some of the smaller gold projects, again most of which had been worked at the turn of the century, and each had remnants of the former workings. At Lakekamu, on the south coast on the river of the same name, there was a large dredge still floating on its manmade pond. In *Black, White and Gold*, Hank Nelson wrote, "Two ounces a day and dysentery," when describing the area.

On occasion, I was lucky enough to visit several of the south eastern islands projects: Fergusson, Normanby, Goodenough and Woodlark. I found old clay pipes that had belonged to the miners and discarded tin cans. In the north, on New Britain and New Ireland, it was common to find relics of World War Two. One incredible find was a Japanese rifle, wrapped by a vine and encapsulated in the trunk of a tree, which had grown since, and the rifle was now 5m up the tree.

At the time, Moresby was fun and more adventures were to be had. Linda had a job as a steel estimator, and we could afford a small sailing boat and went out on it or scuba diving with groups of friends most weekends.

As my contract was coming to an end and there was a need for entrepreneurs to assist in the development of the country's mineral wealth, I formed Melanesian (PNG) Mining Ltd. It was registered in the UK, and I set up shop advising companies on how to acquire Prospecting Authorities in PNG as well as helping with Wardens' hearings and providing geological services. Later on, I also had a contract from a group based in New Zealand to calculate the number of steel grinding balls that would be required for all the new projects coming on stream, but the first contract I won was to acquire a shelf company, Annapurna Pty Ltd, to hold a Prospecting Authority in New Britain. This was sponsored by the former General Manager of Ok Tedi with a group associated with buying the copper concentrates from the same mine. I had a 20% interest in Annapurna which was folded into a company called American Pacific Mining Ltd. It went on to greater things, acquiring a gold mine in Washington State and an exploration project in British Columbia.

The work went well and we enjoyed sailing in our 6m half-cabin-trailer-sailer and diving from our rigid hull inflatable. Overnight trips were made to nearby uninhabited small islands and diving on the numerous reefs. Linda became very competent at diving and taught me well. We would often get together with a group of friends and visit various places well out of Moresby.

Originally, Ok Tedi was planned to close in 2010. However, following an extensive community consultation process and revised mine plans, the mine life was extended to 2025. In 2013, Ok Tedi Mine Ltd became a state-owned enterprise when the government of PNG increased its direct ownership to 87.8%.

From the start of operations in 1984 to the end of 2018, Ok Tedi produced 4.83 million tonnes of copper, 14.8 million ounces of gold, and 32.7 million ounces of silver. And since 1984, OTML has contributed on average 7.4% of PNG's annual Gross Domestic Product which was around US$14 billion in 2010, reaching US$24 billion in 2020.

11

THE GOD MINER

May 1986, Enga Province, Papua New Guinea

Bulldozer in the bush, a letter from a would-be miner

Being one of the few mining engineers in the Co-ordination Department at the DME, Port Moresby, I was occasionally sent on missions to help artisanal National miners develop small alluvial gold deposits. On one such occasion, I was sent to visit the owners of the Kompiam Gold Deposit in the Enga Province.

The Highland province of Enga was well known for its gold deposits. In 1986, a Canadian company was developing the Porgera Mine, a huge gold deposit known since the late 1940s. The deposit was estimated to contain well in excess of five million ounces of gold; later it produced more than 14 million ounces. The Engan people had a fierce reputation, as do most of the Highland tribes, which made travel to the region an adventure, but also a little scary. The Engans also liked to war amongst themselves, attacking each other's villages, carrying off women and pigs, and killing the warrior menfolk. The disputes would often be over a small matter but took a long time to settle, with the victors demanding compensation, usually in the form of pigs, from the losing tribe.

The Highlanders also had a flair for business, often blocking the only road from Mount Hagen to the mine at Porgera, and then demanding 'compensation': compensation for what, no one quite knew, nor who was supposed to pay. They would demand one million Kina to reopen the road. As the majority of the people measured their wealth in kina shells or the number of pigs they owned, they really had little idea of what one million Kina was worth. However, it was a number they had often heard associated with the mine and it would have seemed appropriate. These claims were often settled for a modest amount by provision of pigs, actual kina shells, or currency. Kina shells were highly prized throughout the country and more so in the Highlands being a long way from the coast. These are beautiful mother-of-pearl shells, up to eight inches in diameter often crescent-shaped, used as currency and adornment. The modern Kina currency was introduced in 1975, replacing the Australian dollar.

In May of 1986, the Secretary for Minerals and Energy, my boss, had received a request from one of the Cabinet members, who was from the Kompiam area, to follow up on a letter he had received from the 'owner of the Kompiam God (sic) Mine'. 'God' was the way the locals pronounced gold.

The letter was penned by an unsophisticated hand but contained all the elements that might have been written to interest a speculative investor in a gold project in one of the wildest areas of the planet. The Secretary for Minerals and Energy, knowing of my keen interest in small-scale mining, instructed me to go there and meet with the God Miner, and assess the worth of the project.

As with all government departments, Minerals and Energy had a strict budget for travel which did not include quick trips to see hopeful National miners at the far end of the road. However, budgetary constraints were brushed aside, I was issued with plane tickets and ILPOCs (local purchase orders) for accommodation, and instructed to travel on TalAir to Mount Hagen and then on to Wabag.

I overnighted at the Plumes and Arrows Hotel close to the Mount Hagen airport. The hotel was a little like a fortress in the American Wild West, with high walls, watch towers and barbed wire surmounting the walls because it was often the object of disgruntled tribesmen seeking compensation, ostensibly because the expats had stolen the land the hotel was built on.

The flight out to Wabag was in a small Talair six-seater plane, with myself, the pilot and a Lutheran missionary returning to his church. It was a quick flight, and I sat next to the pilot. As usual, I was fascinated by a series of small tabs positioned to the left of the instrument panel. They were on a spring and clicked up or down. Each tab revealed an instruction in each position. The twelve tabs formed a checklist, and were designed to help the pilots remember important items, such as wheels down or wheels up, flaps up, flaps down: quite important really. Often the pilots would have a joke with the person in the co-pilot's seat and pretend to miss the wheels down tab. Not always a joke, as on several of the smaller grass strips in the Highlands, one could see a small plane off to the side of the runway with the propellers bent in a distinctive scalloped manner, a result of them hitting the ground with no wheels down.

Arriving safely, armed with my briefcase and a sports bag containing my overnight gear, I was met by the local Kiap with his government-issue Toyota pickup, and off we went on the Highlands Highway to Kompiam.

The Kiap could also act as magistrate, mediator, and provider of first aid and keeper of the peace. Arriving at his office, we were greeted by a group of *kanakas* (a term used by colonialists in the past to denote natives), some in semi-traditional dress, most in t-shirts, and a couple with 'ass grass' covering their front and back regions, and shorts from House Bilas, the great emporium that seemed to sell most of the clothing in PNG. The ass grass was composed of a dozen or so leaves about 12 inches long, overlapping to hide the rear and front essentials. One of the miners had a baseball cap with the New York Yankees logo; another one a traditional hat made from the fur of the Lesser Spotted Cuscus (a local tree-dwelling marsupial). None had any footwear, except the God Miner who was dressed in a leather jacket, jeans and cowboy boots.

After a few introductions, we set off in the Kiap's pickup heading off into the bush on an unmade dirt road. The Kiap and I were in the front cab with the talk turner who came along to translate the local lingo; the God Miner and four of his mates were in the back standing on the bed of the truck. The road was in reasonable shape and obviously had been put in using mechanical equipment. The vegetation was typical of the Highlands with vegetable patches cut out of the jungle that were bordered by *kunai* grass. On the ridges were *casuarina* and gum trees, along with various types of large palm trees and grasses. The elevation in this region is over 6,000ft, and the average daily temperature is around 22°C and varies little throughout the year. It can get chilly at night with the temps dropping to 15°C, and it rains a lot.

As we went through the villages, the God Miner would gleefully call out in pidgin from the back of the pickup, "Look at me, I am a big man. I have brought the man from the government to our mine!"

After a while, the road disintegrated into a track which, while not suitable for driving, was reasonable to walk on. All the men jumped out and we proceeded to hike through the bush. An unlikely crew we were: the Kiap was a Papua New Guinean from Mount Hagen; five Nationals; me, the Cornishman, now following a less well defined path through the jungle. One of the miners insisted on carrying my briefcase.

Off we went, initially uphill and then we crossed a ridge where the God Miner pointed out a 'rest house' where we could stay if we were delayed or lost – a bivouac, composed of bush material. I could almost see the fleas and other nasty insects jumping around.

I encouraged all concerned to hurry as I did not want to be in the bush overnight.

After descending the ridge on a narrow track, we came to a small river meandering its way through the *kunai* grass. It was very shallow and about 20ft wide with a gravel bottom. I have a photo of our motley crew trudging along the river bed with the lead man 100ft in advance, carrying my briefcase like some talisman that would deliver us to the gold mine.

The God Miner announced, "We are close."

Then, in the next bend of the river and behind a small clump of *kunai* grass, was a 1974 vintage D4D Caterpillar bulldozer. I was amazed, as was the Kiap. It looked to be in reasonable condition and still had its distinctive yellow paint. The miners pointed at it, gabbling away in place talk, and then arranged themselves in various poses on the machine for a photo to be taken so that the man from the government could show the people in Waigani that the mine was ready to go with a little investment. It was a mystery as to how the machine had got there. The last mile of the track we had come along had not been made by mechanical means, and the Kiap, who wasn't a local, didn't know either. The cab had a large metal ring which could have been a lifting point for a hook to lift the machine. We asked the God Miner how it came to be there and he said it was left by the white men who were there about five years ago.

There were no apparent workings in the vicinity that could have been made by the D4 but the miners said that this is where the mine is located. One could only assume that the D4 had been used to clear the *kunai* and other vegetation to expose the alluvial gravels that may well contain gold.

The briefcase now came into its own as I had a small, 6 inch diameter gold pan and several sample bags in it. The miners knew the purpose of a gold pan and were worried that I was taking their gold when I panned up some black sands from selected gravels and put them in the sample bag. I told them that the government would search the sample for gold and it would help convince them that the project was worth investing in.

With the samples in the briefcase and the gold pan safely stowed, we trudged back to the end of the road where we had left the Kiap's pickup. On the journey back to Kompiam, we dropped the mining gang off in their respective villages.

On reaching Kompiam, the Kiap took me to the Government Guest House which was a small bungalow with two bedrooms, a kitchen and bathroom. It was maintained by his wife, and was very clean. He said he would pick me up in an hour to take me to the club for some *kai* 'food', and a beer or two.

The samples were assayed and had at least some gold in them; perhaps not enough to encourage investment.

However, during subsequent years, I found reports from reliable sources that a large nugget of platinum was discovered in the river four miles northeast of Kompiam. Did the God Miner know something we didn't?

The letter from the God Miner to the government

> Report about Kompiam God Mine, Koyakam
> I estimate to get 6000 Kina for bank loan
> To start the project:

<u>Equipment</u>

- (8) Machine *8 D6 Caterpillar bulldozers*
- (1) Generor *generator*
- (1) Air compress *air compressor*
- (40) SepAEDS 300 Pigba Karma *40 spades and 300 long crow bars*
- God Bottles 300 *gold bottles* [*empty vaccine bottles mostly from penicillin vials*]
- (4) Track Isusa *4x4 Isuzu pickup*

- (2) Car *2 cars*
- new house
- 300 hundred Labours to work *300 labourers*
- (10) Driver *10 drivers*
- White man *white man*
- Dissilions 400 Drams *400 drums of diesel*

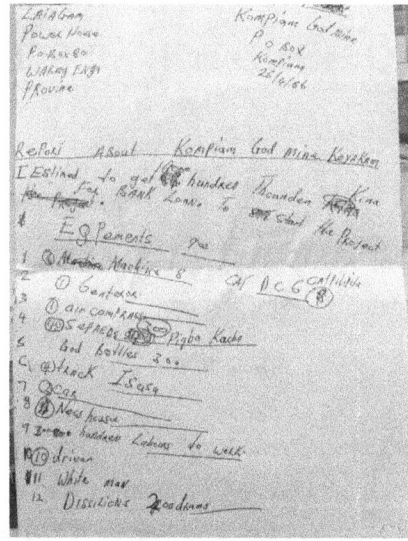

Letter from the God Miner

The God Miner

12

WORKING FOR MYSELF

1987: PNG

Melanesian Mining, prospecting in the mountains and islands, holidays on forgotten islands,
a true gold rush.

In 1987, my three-year contract with the government of PNG was complete. I had worked as an Inspector of Mines at the Ok Tedi gold and copper mine, and latterly as the Ok Tedi Co-ordinator, acting as a liaison officer between the mining company Ok Tedi Mining Limited (OTML) and the various government departments that were involved in the mine. At the time, there were three large gold mines and several smaller ones being developed throughout the country. I had been involved in all of them.

However, at the end of the contract with the government, we were enjoying life so much that Linda and I formed our own company and decided to stay in Port Moresby. Linda was employed as a steel estimator, and I started a consultancy helping offshore companies acquire mining and exploration licences in PNG. When I was with the government, I was also appointed Head Inspector of Petroleum, so I also had a few small jobs with the oil companies. A couple of discoveries of a gas field and some smaller oil discoveries brought a few of the larger oil companies to PNG.

I had a small office in downtown Port Moresby, and would travel around the mainland and offshore islands meeting the local council leaders and assisting companies in their application for mineral licences, known as Prospecting Authorities.

We also had our own Prospecting Authorities in various parts of the country: one in New Britain, one near Madang, one covering an area around Milne Bay, and one a hundred miles southwest of Moresby in the Oro Province near a small village called Keveri. There were no roads to Keveri, and the nearest grass airstrip was fifty miles away. The nearest surfaced road ended at Kupiano, then the road became a track and went on to Bomguina where there was a Kiap station, and a little further on to Abau and a Seventh-day Adventist Mission.

There are alluvial gold deposits throughout PNG, and a few of them were under licence to junior mining companies from Australia and Canada, who had to enter into joint ventures with the local communities as most alluvial mining was reserved for the Nationals.

There were known to be small alluvial gold deposits at Keveri, and we had permission from the landowners in the area to prospect and carry out some minor test work on the Prospecting Authority we had been granted. We were hoping to find a large copper-gold deposit similar to that at Ok Tedi in the mountains. To give us some direction as to the most likely area to host a deposit, we started prospecting in the Keveri valley.

I had identified the area as being of interest by reading several of the books written by prospectors and explorers about PNG: *Up From South – A Prospector in New Guinea 1931-1937* by Jack O'Neill,

Savage Patrol by J G Hides (1936), and *Black, White and Gold* by Hank Nelson.

Nelson relates that Frank Pryke and his brother Dan worked the Keveri in 1903. At the end of a ten-month expedition, he is said to have banked 256 ounces of gold. Pryke and his brothers were famous prospectors and miners, and travelled all around the south coast and southerly islands prospecting and mining for gold.

Nelson also details how violent the locals were in the Keveri Valley. In the early 1900s, they raided coastal villages and those several days march away, killing many. Even though several were arrested and jailed for murder, they continued raiding right up to the 1930s. The violence finally ceased around 1940 when many of the locals received the word of God and gave up their largely animist relation of *puripuri* (sorcery), killing, dances and songs. Most of them moved to one of the coastal mission stations. Charles Abel was a renowned missionary from the London Missionary Society, and it was his two sons, Cecil and Russell, who brought about the conversions.

Abel founded the Kwato Mission on the small island of the same name in 1890, and also introduced cricket to PNG. Kwato later began to play cricket against other teams, particularly Samarai where 'the classic formality of English cricket' was observed with white clothing, pads, caps and a scoreboard, imitated exactly.

Other missionaries arrived and there are still several operating in PNG.

Given the history of the area, we were quite anxious to ensure the local populace, now down to just a few hundred people, were happy with what we were doing. We employed two local helpers for the geologist, and made a couple of visits to the local Seventh-day Adventist Mission to explain our plan; if a deposit was discovered, all would benefit.

I really wanted to prospect the area as I believed there was a greater potential for a larger copper and gold deposit close to the alluvial gold area. The Keveri lay in a valley 3,800ft above sea level, bounded by Mount Clarence (6,330ft), Mount Obree (10,260ft), and

Mount Suckling (12,100ft). The ranges associated with these mountains made it a little difficult to get a helicopter into the area.

Helicopter pilots in PNG were a fearless breed, many having flown in the Vietnam War, and quite willing to take on new challenges. Our plan was to test the alluvial gravels using gold pans, washing four pounds of gravel at a time, which would be a very labour intensive operation. To speed things up, we planned to fly a cement mixer into the valley. The mixer would wash the gravels and the gold, if there was any, would rest in the bottom bowl of the mixer. It seemed a good idea at the time.

Our consulting geologist, David Lindley, had been in PNG for over fifteen years and knew the geology, the people, and how to operate in remote locations. Accordingly, we assembled our equipment on the coast at the Mission station: fuel, tents, food (tinned fish and rice) and, importantly, several tubes of Pringles crisps. And a brand new cement mixer.

The chopper flew down from Moresby, and took David and his crew of three into the valley and dropped them off. With help from the locals the cement mixer was slung beneath the chopper and delivered to David along with fuel and the rest of the supplies.

David spent a week prospecting, washing the gravels and panning. On his return to Moresby, he brought two of his faithful assistants with him because they had never been to Moresby before, so it was a treat for them to see the big city.

Our office was on the fifth floor of the only multi-storey office building downtown, and there was a small lift. David told me that his men were a little reluctant to get inside the small box. The doors closed and the lift ascended so slowly, you would not know it was moving. When the lift reached our floor the doors opened and the two men were amazed. The hallway they had seen when the doors closed had changed into a different room. David opened the door to our office and ushered them inside. One went to the window and let out a cry of amazement – he had never been that high before. They jabbered away in place talk and refused to move more than two feet from the door.

The campaign had gone well and they had recovered a few grains of gold. Geological knowledge told him that the source was not far from where we were prospecting. I suppose the few small flakes were worth only a few Kina but it was a success – we had a property with gold!

I still have the pieces of the gold recovered. It is a beautiful colour, and one is in the shape of a wishbone, about ½" long and 1/8" wide.

There were a lot of alluvial gold deposits in PNG, one of the largest was in the Morobe Province centred round the towns of Bululo and Wau. In 1931, Papua New Guinea set a world record for the amount of air cargo carried: 3,947 tonnes of freight, and 2,607 passengers. Most of the cargo was comprised of mining equipment, including large dredges that had been broken down for reassembly in the gold fields; and most of the passengers were miners headed to the gold field. The discovery of gold in the Bulolo Valley saw a rush of aircraft and pilots to Lae, flying equipment and supplies in, gold out, and passengers both ways.

Dredges are floating mineral processing operations. The material treated is mined by scooping material from the bottom of a pond or lake with a chain of large buckets attached to a boom that is lowered into the water. The buckets, driven down by a motor, dig out material which is brought back to the deck of the dredge along the boom. Usually, there is already a river on which the dredge is initially positioned. There are a lot of moving parts, the buckets can weigh up to a ton and the floatation pontoons are large. In PNG, there were few roads to the goldfields and sometimes none at all, so air transport was the only way to get the machinery in to the areas.

In 1932, a Junkers aircraft transported a 1,100 tonne gold dredge to Bulolo. Two years later, Guinea Airways had carried some 7,000 tonnes of cargo, including drilling machinery, hydroelectric plant and additional dredges. A few of the dredges can still be seen in various locations because when the mining was finished, there would be no use for them and they are too complex to dismantle.

In 1988, we sold the Keveri Prospecting Authority to a friend who, unfortunately, did not follow up on the potential. I was correct in thinking there was a larger deposit nearby. Today in 2022, I see that a small Australian outfit is developing a copper/gold porphyry in the mountains around the valley.

The Last Great Gold Rush

In 1987, Conzinc Riotinto of Australia (CRA) a large mining company, was drilling for gold in the Highland Province near Mount Kare. The mountain itself is 9,200ft high and sits in the serrated mountains of the Muller Range and Central Range that separates the north of the island from the south. It was a relatively unpopulated area as the climate was damp and harsh, and the soil too poor for cultivation. But the region was known for its gold mines.

Mount Kare is fifteen miles southwest of Barrick Gold Corporation's Porgera operation, a mine which went into production in 1991 and has produced in excess of 14 million ounces of gold. Porgera took many years to get into production and had been through the hands of several mining companies before Barrick placed the underground mine into operation.

In the early days, I had been to Porgera as the Inspector of Mines, travelling in a small plane that left from Mount Hagen carrying six passengers. One of the passengers was a Papuan lady carefully holding a piglet on her lap: pigs are a form of money in PNG. For some reason, we did not land at the normal landing strip next to the village but an alternate grass strip to the south where the pilot said we were to drop off some cargo.

As we landed and came to a stop, a wild looking older white man rushed to the plane and started ushering all six of the passengers out of the small plane.

"Quickly! Quickly!" he said in a strong German accent. "The

Inspector of Mines is coming and we have to unload the cargo as fast as we can."

This was Rudy who had been with the project since the 1970s, and I later found out that the cargo turned out to be a box of detonators.

For geologists reading this, you will see that the Mount Kare discovery is an epithermal mineral deposit comprising a folded and faulted sequence of meta-sediments that have been intruded locally by gabbroic and mafic-porphyry dykes. For the non-geologist, layers of mud cooked and turned into rock, then pushed into zigzag shapes, then injected with silica and quartz and gold. A dog's breakfast of jumbled up rock.

In late 1987, CRA had taken up a Prospecting Authority in the area. While prospecting, their geologists discovered an outcrop of gold mineralisation near the uninhabited Kare Puga marshland. They also found evidence of alluvial gold. Much of the gold was in the form of small nuggets, and it seems that the deposit was exposed as a result of a massive landslide.

The geologists took a Christmas break before starting full-scale drilling operations, but when they returned, they found a gold rush under way. Through 1988 and 1989, Nationals from all over the country worked the gold. We were told of people without tools pushing their hands down into the soft clays and mud and feeling with their fingers for the nuggets. Others having managed to procure crowbars, shovels and gold pans worked the area in a haphazard fashion. At the height of the rush, there were around 7,000 miners digging away.

It was unusual in that the gold was in nugget form but had not travelled very far from the source vein. This helped preserve the texture of the gold and there were remarkable museum-quality specimens being gathered by locals from the soft clay and weathered rock of the landslide.

The traditional landowners of the area fought hard to keep others out, but ordinary National folk were hiring helicopters to drop them near the discovery. Extraordinary prices were being paid for essential items. I knew of one National, a Mining Warden, who went to the diggings and said that a box of matches was fetching 2 Kina (about US$2) when they were 25¢ a box elsewhere. A chicken was fetching 10 Kina, (normally 2 Kina), and a tin of fish could fetch up to 5 Kina (normally 1 Kina). Shovels were at a premium, and helicopter pilots were taking payment in gold nuggets.

At one point, the locals shut down the drilling operations as they believed the geologists were sucking up the gold from the earth through the drill pipes.

People selling gold nuggets appeared in Moresby. There was a small smelter operation at Six Mile near the airport where the gold could be refined. Much of the Kare gold graded in the region of 15 to 18 carats. A friend of mine had an office at Six Mile and would buy some of the better quality nuggets which fetch a premium over the pure gold price.

One day during the height of the rush, two Nationals dressed in ragged shorts and T-shirts came into my office in Moresby carrying an eight-ounce sized coffee jar filled with gold nuggets of varying sizes. They were not from the Highlands, a people with a very distinct appearance, but looked like people from the north coast which meant they had bought them or been early at the diggings, because after a while the local landowners stopped others from joining the rush.

They stood by my desk, placed the jar on the table, and said, "How much?"

I quoted a price lower than the morning quote in the newspaper, and discounting the price again as the gold would probably only be at most 16 carats and would fetch less than the 24 carat full value. I also told them that I would not be able to pay them now as I did not have sufficient cash in the office.

They also knew the latest gold price but not the value of the nuggets, and turned down my offer. I directed them to my friend at Six Mile who had more money. However, I did take out a couple of the nuggets to view and picked out a beautiful teardrop-shaped nugget that weighed just close to an ounce. I offered the full gold price which they accepted. It now adorns the neck of Linda and worn on special occasions.

From my friend at Six Mile, I also bought a Mount Kare nugget shaped like an eagle in soaring flight with crystalline gold on one of the wing like-surfaces. It is very rare to see crystalline gold, and the nugget is worth four times the actual gold value.

The deposit was eventually mined commercially, but it took quite a while to sort out the ownership as the Mount Kare area lay astride two provinces – Enga and the Southern Highlands – with no boundary marking the border. Eventually, the Special Mining Lease was granted to the Mount Kare Alluvial Mining Pty Ltd, 49% of whose equity was held by the Kare Puga Development Corp Pty Ltd, representing 6,000 landowners from both provinces; and 51% held by Pacific Minerals, a CRA subsidiary of the company who made the discovery.

Samarai Christmas 1986 and 1987

The island of Samarai is located offshore from the PNG peninsula which forms one of the arms of Milne Bay. In the late 1800s and the mid part of the 20th century, Samurai was an important trading base and coaling station for the trade between Australia and China. It is separated from the mainland by a body of water known as the China Straight, about ¾ mile across and four miles long, which funnels water from the Coral Sea through the Straight and into the Solomon Sea.

We had first heard of Samarai from a couple of expats, husband and wife friends, who had worked in the government for several years. As they had been in PNG for some time they knew many of the more interesting, remoter, but accessible places to visit.

I had been in the area recently as I'd attended a Wardens hearing for a Prospecting Authority I had recently applied for on behalf of Melanesian Mining, our recently formed company.

Mining Wardens hearings were always held when a company had applied for permission to explore for minerals in a specific area. After due notice was published and the Kiap at the nearest Government Station had been informed, the local landowners and tribe would assemble either at the Kiap station or church. It seemed possibly superfluous to publish these applications in the newspaper as few of the locals could read. The main use for the *Nuigini News* was as cigarette paper. The locals would roll up a six inch long tube of the paper, fill it with raw tobacco and set fire to it. Probably better than chewing betel nut.

At the hearings, the locals would either voice their support for the project or address their concerns to the Mining Warden who was an employee of the Department of Minerals and Energy and always attended the hearing. In addition, a representative of the company that had applied for the prospecting permit would attend. There were not many objections as most knew that the development and even exploration activities would help the economy of the area. In all of the Wardens hearings I attended, the main point of discussion was about education. They all wanted to ensure that development would include educational facilities for the children. Of secondary importance was the establishment of an Aid Station to offer basic health and first aid services.

To get to the village, the Warden and I flew to Milne Bay airport on a scheduled flight. At the airport we met with John Wild who ran a private air service to the remoter islands and villages. Mostly, he serviced the coastal areas and had a small four-seater float plane. On this occasion, it was just myself and the Assistant Warden, Isiah, who was local to the area and so could communicate in place talk and pidgin.

We flew out of Alotau and off to Suao village some thirty miles across the peninsula from the airport. All went well, and we landed on the lagoon which was flat calm and had plenty of room to land, the reef being some 800 yards from the palm tree-lined pearly white sandy beach.

The hearing took longer than normal and the wind had sprung up and was blowing onshore from the reef. The tide had come in too, and waves were breaking over the reef, creating a significant chop in the lagoon. John made a few signals to hurry me up, and I then signalled Isiah. We closed the hearing and jumped on to the plane, which was bobbing quite vigorously and tugging at its mooring rope.

John fired up the single engine, ran through the pre-flight checks at a rapid speed, and we headed into the wind and the choppy waters. Spray was obscuring the windshield as the floats lifted and then banged down onto the surface of the lagoon. This happened again and again until we lifted clear but only for a brief period and then banged down again before skimming over the tops of the waves. This time we stayed a couple of feet above the churning waters of the reef. Slowly gaining height, we headed for Milne Bay. Isiah had turned a whiter shade of pale, and John was grinning at me. Always a sure sign that the daredevil knew he just had a close shave. Quite an adventure.

The Alotau peninsula and Samarai had captured our imaginations, and a friend knew of a guest house run by a lovely couple on the island, we thought it would make a fun spot to spend Christmas. We managed to get through on the telephone and booked a five-night stay with Wallace and Jenny, owners of the guest house.

To get to our holiday destination, we flew from Moresby on the small independent airline Talair down to Milne Bay airport, and took a taxi to the pier. Friends had arranged for a National boatman named Richard Tanaka to pick us up at the pier at Alotau to take us to the island. He turned up late and took on extra passengers, two young ladies who lived on the mainland opposite Samarai. The vessel was known locally as a banana boat, a fibreglass narrow hull about 25ft long and 3½ft wide. Richard had mounted a 50hp outboard motor on the transom, but there were enough seats for all of us.

We left just before dusk, but after ten minutes, Richard remembered he had also arranged to pick up another three passengers from Alotau. So he headed back to shore and we picked up an expat Aussie, his National wife and their eight year old daughter. They were going to his wife's family home for Christmas in the village Loani on the peninsula.

We set off again at a great lick into the starlit velvet night, and the wake from the motor churned up a fantastic plume of phosphorescence in the inky black sea. The moon rose, and the bright lunar light glinted on the sea, silhouetting the hilly jungle-clad hills to our right. As we sped through the waters, I was reminded of the Paul Simon song *Under African Skies* and the lyric,

> *Joseph's face was black as night*
> *The pale yellow moon shone in his eyes.*

Richard's skin was a light brown, his eyes inherited from his Japanese father.

As is often the case in PNG, the weather changed very quickly and the light from the moon was extinguished by clouds. And then it rained, with tropical intensity. Fortunately, Richard had a large tarpaulin, and we all sheltered beneath it as we sped across the strengthening chop. The expat and his wife had a couple of packets of biscuits which we shared. The rain eased at last and Richard throttled down; apparently, we were low on fuel. Somehow, out of the intense darkness and seemingly impenetrable tropical rainforest, he guided his boat to a small wooden pier. After a lot of shouting, a light appeared in the window of a shack stationed just up from the pier. With more shouting and laughter, he refuelled and we carried on.

We dropped off the expat and his family at their village, followed by the two girls complete with their Christmas cake at the next village, and then on to Samarai. It was now well after 10pm and we were supposed to have landed several hours earlier. As we approached the skeletal jetties and loading docks, we could see two people standing on the only serviceable pier holding a hurricane lamp and an electric torch.

These beacons were held by Wallace and Jenny, our hosts and keepers of the Kinanale Guest House. Richard helped us with our luggage, and after greeting Wallace and Jenny, we followed them back through the mostly abandoned buildings to their guest house. Even in the darkness of the night, there was a sense of things forgotten, of times before, of dilapidation and of former grandeur. All these feelings were reinforced in the morning, and it felt a little like the setting for a Somerset Maugham story.

At one time, these islands were the home to cannibals, actually not that long ago, the last cases in this area are reported to have been in the 1970s. Wallace was from the island and had worked in the electricity generating station. We noticed that he had lost his right arm below the elbow, and that's when he told us his grandfather was a cannibal. He would joke about having been brought up by his tribe as a 'larder boy', and they only took a small piece of him and left the rest as he was not ready. In fact, he had lost it in an accident at work in the generating station. Jenny was an Australian who had come up from the south as a Registered Nurse, and they had two very pretty daughters.

Jenny and Wallace, these wonderful people, took us into their family and we had Christmas dinner with them. Wallace, with a strange sense of humour, told stories of cannibal raids by his people to capture larder boys. These poor boys would be kept and fed and eaten at a later date.

The next day, we spent some time wandering around the abandoned wooden buildings and wharfs. Most were still in a reasonable state with verandas that covered the sidewalks in Australian colonial style. The wharfs had been rendered unusable during the Second World War as the Australians and Allies were worried that Samarai would provide a perfect place for the Japanese to launch an invasion of Australia. They were only partially repaired later.

In the Burns Philp warehouse, there was nothing valuable but we found old bills of ladings and invoices from the 1960s. One scrap of paper was the Firearms' Register from 1955. Another document had all the telegraph-teletype codes for ports around the nearby islands. It also had phrases from Bentley's Complete Phrase Code and a list of codes to be used: YAAPR, *regret cannot agree*; YABAB, *Catalina*; YAAXZ, *airmail*. The book claims to have nearly 1,000 million code combinations.

Walking along the overgrown streets, it wasn't hard to imagine what a hub of activity the island must have been when it was the administrative capital of Milne Bay in times gone by. With the docks in operation, miners coming up from south heading to the gold fields on the islands in the Louisiade Archipelago or further afield on the south coast. Island-hopping copra traders, the colonial civil servants, missionaries, and the always present swindlers. Many would have gathered at the Golden Fleece Hotel or the cricket club. There was a fairly substantial church with slanted tin roof gables and a steeple. We went there for the Christmas carol service.

There was a walk of about a mile that circled the island, lined with *casuarina* and huge mango trees laden with fruit, as well as giant fruit bats feasting on the bounty. There was a cricket pitch but no clubhouse and no team. On the boundary we saw a monument raised by public subscription to Christopher Robinson. The inscription at the base reads, *His aim was to make New Guinea a good country for white men.*

Perhaps a little dramatic but it should be remembered that in 1901 James Chalmers, a missionary from Scotland, his friend Reverend Oliver Tompkins, and ten students from the missionary school, were invited to visit by native islanders, then killed and cannibalised. Robinson died in 1904 after serving just one year as Acting Administrator.

The Memorial, according to old reports, was financed and erected by 'citizens of Samarai', mainly the European miners in the early 1900s, who were working gold mines on the nearby Sudest, Woodlark and Misima Islands. Robinson committed suicide after being severely censured for an incident when he was leading a party of police to arrest the possible murderers of Chalmers, described in the book, *Great Heart of Papua*.

We went snorkelling on the far side of the island where there was a fair amount of coral but only a few fish. Wallace told us that we should go over to Bonarua Hili Hili Island because there were a lot of fish ... and sharks. We saved that experience for another time.

The last excitement we had in PNG was when we had our 'Go finish' party – an expression used for when a contract or job had been completed and the expat would leave the country. There turned out to be three of these: one at the house of the Minister of Mines, one at the swimming pool of the New Zealand Trade Commissioner (with plenty of Marlborough Sauvignon Blanc), and one at the house of a great friend who always threw Linda in the pool.

From the tropics, we were off to British Columbia. The only similarity being that it rained a lot in both places.

And as they say in pidgin, "Em Tasol." *That's all, folks!*

13

DOLLY VARDEN MINE

June–September 1989: Dolly Varden Mine, Alice Arm, Northern British Columbia, Canada

A prospector's dream of a silver mine, abandoned mining camps from the 1930s, the remote coast of British Columbia, native fishermen, white line fever, wolverines and bears

The Vancouver Stock Exchange was on fire early in 1989. Fortunes were being made by stock promoters on sometimes worthless ventures, and occasionally – and only very occasionally – one of the well-known promoters would make a big hit, finding a massive gold deposit. The stock would go wild, trading large volumes as the promoters sold their 'penny stock' and investors would buy into the play.

This would cause a big staking rush with people inventing geographical trends and staking claims along lines between two known discoveries where they hoped further deposits could be located. As well as those promoting trends, there were the 'closeology' pundits who would stake or acquire land as close to the discovery as possible, telling investors that they could see the drill rigs of the new discovery from the land they had acquired. Those claims that obviously had no potential at all were labelled by most as 'moose pasture'.

Promoters would seek money from unwary investors while waxing lyrical about the merits of their claims. A typical pitch would be, "Our property lies right on trend between the Golden Dagger and the Silver Dragon mines. These are past producers of millions of tons of gold and silver ore. The geology seems to be epithermal in nature and we think we can find the bonanza zone."

The more savvy investors would ask, "How close to these past producers is your Lucky Chance property and exactly how much gold did either of them produce?"

The promoter replies, "Good question. Production records are unclear as the mines were operated in the 1890s, but we have compiled a set of aerial photos of the claims and we can clearly see the trend encompassing both mines and our Lucky Chance claims from a height of 25 miles. We are very excited about this property and are looking to raise $1,500,000 to initiate exploration, undertake target definition and cover ongoing costs. Our geologists have studied all the available data and now can say that this really could be epithermal."

Here follows a translation of the promoter's spiel: "We have very little idea about the geology but the mention of epithermal gold gets the punters excited. We don't know how much gold was produced or how we will proceed. The money will be used to pay my salary, my wife's salary as Corporate Secretary, purchase a few maps and coloured pencils, and pay for a very small drilling programme. There will be enough money for a road trip to Europe to promote the deal over there which will be undertaken by my wife and I; we will engage a graduate geologist for peanuts and then we raise more money."

So there was money to be made as the type of properties similar to the Lucky Chance (with little chance of success) were being funded by speculators anxious not to miss out.

The Dolly Varden was somewhat different as it was itself an old producer of silver, and within a few miles there were several small mines that produced moderate amounts of silver and copper ore. The ore was sent to the old smelter at Anyox which was just around the bay.

Even before Canada was officially a country, the area now known as the Golden Triangle was a hub for prospectors looking to strike it rich. In 1861, Alexander 'Buck' Choquette struck gold at the confluence of the Stikine and Anuk Rivers, kick-starting the Stikine Gold Rush. More than 800 prospectors left Victoria on Vancouver Island to go to the Stikine in search of gold.

A few short years later, an even more significant rush would occur just to the north in the Cassiar region – it's where British Columbia's biggest ever gold nugget, weighing in at 73 ounces, would be found. The Atlin Gold Rush, an offshoot of the world famous Klondike Gold Rush, would also occur just north of the Triangle.

What stoked the flames of the newest gold rush in the Golden Triangle was that recently, after drilling 109 diamond drill holes, two very small exploration companies, Stikine Resources and Calpine Resources finally intersected exceptional gold values in the discovery hole at Eskay Creek. The assays from samples from the drill core that intersected the vein recorded almost an ounce of gold and silver across a distance of 208m. The values of 27.2g per tonne of gold and 30.2g per tonne of silver would yield a metal value of over $1,000 per tonne when mined and treated. These were exceptional values and this set the shares of the smallest companies with gold properties in the area listed on the Junior Stock exchanges soaring. Eskay would go on to become Canada's highest-grade gold mine and the world's fifth largest silver producer, with production well in excess of 3 million ounces of gold and 160 million ounces of silver.

Even though the Dolly was a silver mine, our geologists had a theory that the old timers had missed the gold values which were deeper and parallel to the silver vein. We had great hopes that Dolly would get similar results to those at Eskay.

The project was located in northwest British Columbia at the head of the Alice Arm inlet, very close to the tip of the Alaska panhandle which defines the border between Canada and the US on the Pacific west coast. The area had a grand mining history and was at the base of the Golden Triangle. Back at the beginning of the century, the area was a hot spot for mining development with the smelter at Anyox taking ore and concentrates from the nearby small- to medium-sized mining operations. The mine and smelter had shut down in 1935 and the town was abandoned, with all of the industrial infrastructure being removed in the early 1940s.

The nearest habitation to the project was the now abandoned, once busy town of Alice Arm which consisted of a collection of mostly derelict timber cabins, probably built in the early 1900s. A few survived. On the opposite shore of the Alice Arm Inlet stood the modern mining town of Kitsault, home of the AMAX large open cast molybdenum mine.

Kitsault was established in 1979 to house the management, workers and support personnel for the mine, and designed for 1,200 residents, with a shopping mall, restaurant, swimming pool and bowling alley. In 1982, however, prices for molybdenum crashed and the entire community was evacuated after just 18 months of residence.

Even though the mine was closed, there was a full-time caretaker who lived on the property with his wife. He was from Yorkshire and was quite an amiable chap despite living fifty miles from the nearest human settlement. He mowed lawns, ensured the company houses were in good order and generally looked after the place. He had a small flat-bottomed ferry boat which we often used to ship supplies and a couple of vehicles across the Arm. He also had the key to the massive padlock and gate that prevented casual visitors from entering the town from the logging roads.

The area had a lot of snow every year which pretty much cut them off from the world between October and May. During the winter months, supplies were flown in by float plane from Prince Rupert. Perhaps the compensation was living in the wonderful, pristine, coastal rain forest; the halibut and salmon fishing in the Arm; watching the fish eagles and the bears gorge themselves on the spawning salmon and generally being away from it all.

Dolly Varden had exactly the same geological characteristics as a huge gold strike at the Stikine project made by a famous mining promoter called Murray Pezim (1921-1998). Son of a butcher in Toronto, he became one of the wealthiest men in Vancouver. The Dolly was only 122 miles from the strike at Stikine (close in promoter's terms), and our two promoters bought and leased the claims covering the Dolly as soon as the Stikine discovery was announced. Shares in the company were quickly sold to fund the exploration programme, and the wheels set in motion to again rediscover the silver and gold at the old mine. I was working for a group who invested a lot of money, and I was appointed Project Manager to ensure their dollars were spent wisely. The plan was to establish a base camp at Alice Arm in early May, and then locate an exploration camp close to the old mine where we would be conducting exploration and drilling holes to discover untold wealth. Hmm.

The remote location proved a real challenge. The nearest town and airport of any size was Smithers, some 100 miles northeast as the crow flies. Smithers was serviced by Canadian Airlines from Vancouver, regularly carrying miners, loggers and prospectors to the north. There were a couple of motels and a bar where scantily clad young ladies performed strange gymnastics around a chromium pole.

Road access from Smithers to Dolly was along the Yellowhead Highway that led to Terrace and then turning north at Kitwanga on to the Stewart–Cassiar Highway. About fifty miles further on at Cranberry Junction, the path left the paved highway and headed west on gravel-topped, single-lane logging roads: quite a dangerous road. Here, the rule was, give way to logging trucks loaded with huge, old-growth conifers heading outward to the highway. Sometimes they could only fit three or four trunks onto a 30-tonne trailer.

Failure to give way would result in your pickup being pushed into the bush. The loggers driving the trucks would warn other truckers on their CB radios that a couple of pickups were on the way in and to look out for them. We had no CB radio so were somewhat cautious when driving.

The road crossed over the Stikine River on a rattling Bailey bridge (a type of portable truss bridge, developed in the Second World War), then left the main logging route, entering onto the Kitsault mine road, heading for the foothills of the Kshadin Peak, the snow covered Illiance Mountain, and the permanent ice fields of Lavender Peak.

Luckily, as manager of the project, I was usually able to get a ride back to Smithers on the helicopter that was permanently stationed at the camp, and there were several unusual sights to see along the way. At Morristown, First Nation Indians used long poles to hook salmon that leapt from the water attempting to scale the rocky falls on their way to their breeding grounds, and at Kitwanga, there was a collection of totem poles next to a small Russian orthodox church. This was also the location of the nearest store. Much to the delight of our loggers and assistants when on their way out for a break, the store sold beer. We ran a dry camp and so this was the first opportunity for them to taste the amber liquid after a dry stint. The drillers were not subject to the dry camp rule but complied most of the time. Occasionally, their boss would fly in with his helicopter and then forget to carry out the bottle of Scotch he brought with him.

After Kitwanga and further up the road on the Cassiar Highway, I experienced a sight that I shall never forget. Hanging over the tailgate of a highway maintenance pickup truck was a man with a small paintbrush in his right hand and in his left a small can of white paint. The pickup was travelling at about 15mph. At regular intervals, the intrepid man painted a thin white line down the middle of the road; some five miles behind him, a purpose-built vehicle was following the white line and at predetermined intervals sprayed the road with the permanent centre road markings.

The Dolly Varden Mine was discovered in 1910, and the town of Alice Arm thrived until 1935 when the mine closed. During that time, it produced 1,403,209 ounces of silver from over a million tons of ore.

The deposit was discovered in an unusual way by a syndicate of four prospectors. The dead uncle of Ole Pearson, one of the four original prospectors, came to Ole in a dream one night while he was prospecting up the Kitsault River with his partners. The uncle told Ole that he would come across a large white boulder further up river, and there he would find a high grade vein of silver and that he would start a fabulously rich mine and would never need to work again. The uncle told Ole he was to call the mine the Dolly Varden after the heroine of the novel *Barnaby Rudge* by Charles Dickens.

Stories like these keep prospectors searching for minerals in remote areas all over the world.

There was not much left of Alice Arm, the town that served the miners and prospectors. The once grand Alice Arm Hotel stood alone in the swampy fields beyond the town's streets. It had a strong list to port and looked like it would surely collapse at the next winter's first heavy snow. As there was no accommodation in the town, we relied on the main resident who had acquired several of the old cabins, and rented them out to hunters and fishermen. He was affectionately known as, Vince I-will-invoice-you-later Brown. The other permanent resident was an old prospector called Wilf who delighted in having company for coffee, tea, beer or a barbeque. There were a couple of families who had cabins and who came in the summer for the fishing. Wilf lived there from snow melt to first snow. He was the personification of a grizzled prospector, slightly hunched from looking at the ground for signs of ore, a white straggly beard and clothed in a fleecy tartan shirt and dungarees. The cabins were arranged in a grid pattern, the east–west roads named 1st Avenue and 2nd Avenue; the north–south streets being the Kitsault Valley Road and Victoria Street.

On a visit to the area with Linda and her cousin Herbert, we stayed in number 5678 Kitsault Road, one of the cabins owned by Vince. He also owned cabin number 1234 and a cabin designated number nine. In fact, he owned most of the town and, he liked to think, everything in it. One day, we noticed an old oven rack lying in the weeds and decided to make a small barbeque with it.

Vince came along while we were grilling and said, "I see you found that; keep it for now and I will invoice you later."

He never did. However, he did invoice the company for use of the old Post office and Station House built on the old wharf. He also charged for a couple of hundred gallons of very old diesel that would have ruined an engine if you tried to run it in your pickup. We decided we could use it in the oil stoves that were to heat the tents at the camp when the weather would inevitably get colder.

Cabin 5678 held a few surprises. I stayed there a couple of times by myself, eschewing the company of the crew in old Station House, and discovered that behind the flimsy plywood panelling some enterprising prospector had attempted to insulate the cavity between the ply-board and the log exterior with mining magazines from the 1920s.

They made really interesting reading, headlining discoveries close to areas that were still being mined. The adverts for mining machinery included names such as Ingersoll Rand and Denver Mining, both of which are still around.

Vince showed us one of the other cabins on Victoria Street where brown bears had tried to get inside after some food left behind by careless visitors. There were claw marks reaching up over eight feet to the eaves of the cabin roof. The area was popular with bears for the fishing in the shallows and flats of the Kitsault River where large numbers of salmon headed upstream to spawn every year. It was an amazing sight to see the large bears chasing the salmon through the winding channels. Ospreys and fish eagles could be seen plucking salmon from the water, and flying off with the fish frantically wriggling in the eagles' vice-like grip.

Working with a group of experienced geologists, we quickly identified a suitable site to build the small camp. The camp was to be situated some sixteen miles upriver from Alice Arm, and initially we took over the old Station House and former Post Office where the steamers would dock, to house the team while the camp was being built. The railway track which had run from Alice Arm to the Dolly Varden mine site was passable by pickup truck in most places, and provided at least some access to the old workings along the valley and close to the camp. However, time and successive snow melts that produced the icy blue melt water had eaten away at the supports for several of the bridges that crossed the rushing streams. We were able to repair some of them but we were still ten miles from the mine and campsite. Helicopter time was expensive, so getting supplies and drill equipment nearer to the camp lowered the costs a little. Because the season was so short with the snow melting in May and the first heavy snowfall usually expected in early September, there was no time to lose.

As the area was so remote, no commercial logging had taken place for at least fifty years when the mine and railway closed, so there were magnificent stands of conifers lining the valley bottoms and sides. These proved to be both a problem and a blessing. The area we selected for the camp was close to the tree line and was a rocky crag that had a few mature conifers in place.

The trees had to be felled so that a helipad for the chopper and store for its fuel could be constructed. Our faithful team of loggers quickly felled the trees and we used the stumps as the foundation for the helipad. We reused some of the timber staves that had formed the settling tanks in which the ore from the old Dolly Varden Mine had been processed. The leaching process used cyanide to recover the silver from the finely ground rock produced by the processing plant. The settling tanks stored the cyanide and rock mixture extracting most of the silver which, after treatment, was contained in a solution. This was further treated in different tanks to recover the silver as a precipitate. The tanks were made of beautifully shaped 40ft lengths of redwood. Fortunately, they had no trace of silver or cyanide remaining. The crew cut the staves into suitable lengths and then we slung them beneath the chopper up to the campsite.

In ten days, we had constructed a camp which consisted of six four-man tents, a shower block, a canteen and cook shack, and an office tent. Almost all of the timber for the camp was flown up by the chopper from Kitsault. Ingeniously, the carpenters built the base framework and floors for the tent frames in the storage and laydown yard in Kitsualt. Then they attached a long piece of plywood to the back end to act as a rudder, slung the frame beneath the chopper and flew the frames up to the campsite.

After some exploration on the ground and much discussion between the geologists, the promoters, the drillers and occasionally the cook, the first drill pad was located and the heli-rig slung beneath the chopper and gently laid on the platform constructed by the logging crew. The sense of excitement grew. Would we hit the bonanza silver and gold mineralisation in the first hole? Would we at least see some encouraging signs that the gold and silver were nearby? At this point, no one believed we would not encounter at least signs that would give us encouragement and point us in the right direction.

I went to watch the start as the hollow tubular drill rod with its diamond tipped circular drill bit spun round and round and slowly advanced in to the rock, lubricated with special chemicals and water. The bit generated fine rock cuttings that came back to the surface so one could at least tell the colour of the rock that was being drilled through. Black meant sulphides such as pyrite or sphalerite, which we were hoping for; pure white meant just quartz. After the hole had advanced ten feet, the driller dropped a tool into the drill pipe. The tool was connected to a wire which fastened onto a tube within the drill rod. This was known as a 'core barrel' and contained a 9ft length of rock which was drawn back to surface on the wire.

The core barrel was carefully picked up by the driller, and the circular length of rock was placed into a specially constructed wooden box with partitions which neatly held the core. Each core box held about 16ft of core, and at the end of each shift, there were seven or so core boxes on which plywood lids were nailed and then airlifted by chopper to the campsite. Each hole was designed to intersect what was hoped to be a significant structure containing mineralisation. As the holes neared the target, the geologist sat on the rig monitoring progress. As soon as the core was pulled and placed in the core box, the geologist pounced on it, examining each centimetre for signs of mineralisation. This would consist of quartz of a certain type, minerals that sparkle, minerals of colour, and minerals of green or blue or red. We all wanted to see free gold in the core, a very unusual sight ... but it was not to be. The problem with drilling for gold is that it is nearly always entrained with or associated with other minerals, so when looking at the core you may see flashes of pyrite ('Fools' gold'), or sphalerite, or even galena which carries silver with lead, but rarely will one see pure gold. The amount of gold will only be determined by sampling the core and submitting it for assay.

Only once have I ever seen free gold in a drill core, and only once seen free gold underground in many years of exploring and mining for the yellow metal.

To get the samples to the assay laboratory, the core was split along its length with a rock saw. Careful measurements were taken to determine the position of the rock in the core boxes and thus its position beneath the surface. The interesting looking portions of the core were placed in tough, secure bags, labelled and sent by the fastest means possible to the assay lab in Vancouver.

Assaying is really the only way to tell what metal values are in the core. Thus we were always anxiously awaiting the results. On a couple of occasions, we could see signs of mineralisation, a flash of pyrite or was it gold? With over ten years' experience and looking at over thousands of metres of drill core that contain gold, I still could not say with any certainty if a particular section of core contained any gold.

On one occasion, we actually drilled into a small silver vein. It was hosted in pyrargyrite, a mineral that flashes red when first exposed to sunlight. Side by side with the pyrargyrite was a tiny vein of native silver. The assay was spectacular.

Rumours abounded in the Stock Exchange. Somehow the word got out that we had a good intersection. Had the drillers said something? The stock rose 50% in three days. The promoters were on the radio telephone, which was an open line, asking questions: *Does it look good? What is the associated mineralisation?* And so on, seeking a clue as to whether or not they should buy more stock or sell their holdings.

Eventually, we put a secret code in place to describe the mineralisation we had seen and made a rule that no assay results were to be reported or talked about except on a secure landline.

The drilling went on through the short summer. We were far enough north to see the Northern Lights and read the newspaper at 11pm without need for a light. We also had staked and acquired claims in the surrounding area and employed a seasoned 'bush' geologist with a lot of experience to prospect the claims.

Gerry the geologist was to be dropped off by helicopter in the chosen area with three days' worth of food, fluids (mostly water), a small two-man pup tent and a radio. He was also supplied with a fit young man to do the grunt work. Having pored over maps, shaky satellite images and old geological reports, Gerry, John and I jumped into the chopper with Jack the pilot, and headed for the Lavender Ice field. It was only a ten minute ride but would have taken a couple of days to hike there from the nearest road. Our route crossed steep sided valleys cloaked in slide alder and massive conifers, skirted ice fields and crossed the source of the Kitsault River which seemed to be leaking from the melting ice field. As we got close to the drop-off point, we disturbed a pack of what I thought were wolves that ran off across the ice field trying to get away from the noise of the helicopter. They turned out to be a pack of wolverines, and we veered away from them, not wishing to alert them to the fact that a couple of tasty meals were about to be deposited in their hunting area.

Mist and low cloud was always a problem for the helicopter, visibility being the only reliable navigation tool (at that time) in these remote areas. If the pilot couldn't see the required distance, he couldn't fly. The guys would be isolated if the weather closed in, so we carefully chose the time for them to go exploring.

Initially, the wait for the assay results was a lengthy procedure until we got a satellite phone and were able to connect a fax to the unit and receive the results first hand. Again, to maintain confidentiality, we had to call the lab to get them to call us and send the results while we cleared the line and made sure only those who were authorised got to see them. As it turned out, we seldom had any results that were of any consequence, and toward the end of the summer, the decision was made to shut down the programme and clear the site.

It was a timely decision. As was predicted by the locals, the first snow started to fly in late September. All of the camp gear, tents, stoves, freezer unit, timber bases for the tents and every other item of equipment had to be shipped off site. Several of the bulkier items went to Vince who promised to keep them safe (for a small fee) until we returned. The more valuable items – generators, chain saw, rock saws, Pionjar samplers, shovels, spades and the invaluable Pulaski fire fighters tool – were shipped off to our expediters store in Smithers.

Even though the assay results were in and the camp cleared away, the work went on. All the data had to be reviewed, analysed, computer models created, reports written and all the bills paid. The geologists were proposing new theories as to the location of the 'bonanza high-grade areas', trying to convince the investors that they should employ them next year as the analysis of the results showed new targets.

The stock price fell to pennies. Some people bought at the high for the year and several sold at the low of the year; others bought low and sold high. I leave it to the reader to deduce if those who sold at the high are on their yachts in the Cayman Islands or those that didn't are still looking for the bonanza high grade gold zones.

I had made my recommendations not to spend any more than the $1,000,000 already spent at Dolly, and was instead given the task of upgrading and modernising the El Mochito lead-zinc- silver mine in central Honduras.

Over the years, several junior exploration companies have taken options on the claims from the Dolly Varden Company, only to break their pick searching for the bonanza high grade gold and silver.

Note: the use of 'tonne' and 'ton' reflects the fact that the Imperial system was used in Canada until April 1975, subsequent to which the metric system was in place and all tonnages reported as tonnes.

14

THE LION IN SINALOA

1993: Sinaloa, Mexico

Colonial style hotel, barricaded villas, Copper Canyon

In February of 1993, I was asked to accompany a team of mining engineers on a visit to the Santo Tomás copper property in the Mexican State of Sinaloa. The Santo Tomás project is situated in the Sierra Madre Occidental, about 20km east as the crow flies from the town of Choix, which had evolved in the last few years as a construction town providing accommodation for crews working on a nearby hydroelectric project. It was also a growing centre for the drug trade.

Choix is not the easiest place in the world to get to, and as we had come from Tucson, the most efficient means of getting the highly paid consulting engineers to the site was by hiring a small private plane in Hermosillo. From there, we flew down to the town of El Fuerte which had a landing strip of sorts, an option not available to Choix. Part of the plan was to fly over the mining project to get a bird's-eye view of the possible difficulties in establishing a road to the site.

El Fuerte is a typical small rural town in the semi-desert region of northern Sinaloa, famed for being the birthplace of the legendary Zorro. It still exhibits remnants of the Spanish colonial era, boasting an impressive central square or plaza, containing the ubiquitous grand Catholic Church and colonial style municipal buildings forming three sides of the plaza. Later, in 1996, I was to spend a summer in Spain and noted the similarity and conformity of the plaza plans to that in El Fuerte. The format had obviously been carried from the Andalusian plains to these remote regions of Mexico.

One side of the plaza harboured the best accommodation in northern Sinaloa (possibly the only accommodation other than the trailer camp at Choix), an 18th century hostelry with what appeared to be furniture made in the same era as the hotel. It formed a square around a garden festooned with bougainvillea, cactus and semi tropical plants. The rooms were enormous, with high ceilings and double doors of castle-like proportions, and a large covered cloister ran around the upper level of the internal garden. Large sideboards of dark wood stood at intervals along the interior walls of the cloister, and upon investigation were found to house the linen for the hotel. To make the place feel even more Spanish, halberds and suits of armour (doubtless from Toledo), lined the walls. Whilst initially finding it odd that such a grand hotel should exist in such an out of the way location, I later realised that El Fuerte is located at the bottom of the Copper Canyon Railway which winds its way from the Pacific across the coastal plains, from Los Mochis through El Fuerte, and enters the canyon to emerge in the state of Chihuahua at Batopilas. Along the way, the track climbs 1,000m and passes through some of the most spectacular and rugged scenery in the world. El Fuerte is not an obvious commencement or ending point, but is considered by some *the* place to start from.

The rest of the town is unimpressive, consisting in the main of small single-storey shacks with television aerials poking out of the roofs, and a few streets of grander brick-built houses which appear to be mini prisons, but are, in fact, protected from the outside world by gates and grilles of wrought iron. These fortresses are purported to be the homes of minor local drug lords.

After inspecting the project from the air, a site visit was necessary, and next morning, six of us crammed into a four-wheel drive single cab Toyota. With only room for three in the cab, the rest of us rode in the bed of the truck, not a pleasant experience in the broiling heat of the Sonoran Desert sun.

The road from El Furte to Choix was paved and sealed, but also had an abundance of small canyons known as potholes. My travelling companions made themselves comfortable with their backs against the cab of the truck, and I faced the front, leaning back against the tailgate. I was therefore the only one able to have a view forward, and was the first and only one to see the beast.

In a small cage on the side of the road, was a fully grown African lion complete with mane and tail. The cage looked like a typical circus cage and measured some 4 x 3m and 2m high. But what an earth was it doing there?

I shouted at the others to look, but by the time I had their attention we had passed the lion and the cage.

Was it an advertisement for an upcoming circus? As we went on to Choix and further west, I looked for signs of a circus. There were none.

There was no circus in town.

Had the circus just left and they would come back for it later?

Who fed it and where did they get the meat? Someone suggested later that it was possibly a pet for a drug lord, or perhaps a disposal unit for non-compliant henchmen.

Sometimes I think on the fate of the lion.

PART III
USA

Linda claims Tom Thumb peak for Cornwall! Scottsdale, USA

Scottsdale's Got Me

Scottsdale's got me, it won't let go
The weather is great and there ain't no snow.
I got a hot lady with a real fast car
She's a rodeo queen I met in a bar.

She's looking at me like I'm a fool
I wanna go back to somewhere cool.
My head is aching and so is my heart
I wanna leave here but I can't bear to part

With my horses my fast red car
And my Rodeo queen from the Westworld bar.

I gotta a nice house with a swimming pool
Two cutting horses and an arena, too.
My friends they all wear western gear
And only ever drink that ice cold beer.

Everyone tells me that it's a dry heat
But I'm gonna end up like a piece of dried meat.
I'm sure I'm going to die in this desert heat
I really wanna leave here but I can't bear to part

With my horses my red fast car
And my Rodeo queen from the Westworld bar.

Sunday's we go up to Greasewood Flats
To see the Harley riders, they're real cool cats.
Drink a few beers and listen to the band
Just relaxing in this warm desert land.

My ex-wife called me from New York State
She's got six foot of snow outside her gate.

It's the middle of April and twenty below
I'll just stay here I don't want to go

Away from my horses my red fast car
Or my rodeo queen from the Westworld bar.

© Alan F Matthews

15

THE EARLY DAYS OF KERNOW RESOURCES AND DEVELOPMENTS LTD

1994: Arivaca and Joutel

Tales of hidden treasure in the Arizona desert,
a discovery in Quebec,
arsenic laden water in Nevada,
stock quotes at Tim Horton's coffee shop in Newfoundland

Arivaca, Maricopa County, Arizona

In 1994, the company I was working for decided that I was far too talented and much too intelligent to work with them. To avoid any embarrassment to them I decided to leave and form my own company and list it on the Vancouver Stock Exchange (VSE). I had passed the Canadian Securities Institute Course known as the Brokers exam in 1990 and had a good idea on how the Exchange worked. It was an excellent venue to raise money for exploration and development of mining projects. Many people had made a lot of money backing what are known as junior mining companies when the company discovered a significant deposit. These companies had very small market capitalisations and often very little cash. However, their share price would rocket by hundreds of percent when they made a new discovery and the junior was bought out by a major mining company, giving the shareholders an enormous profit.

This was before one of the most spectacular rises in a junior called Bre-X rocked the Exchanges and the junior market. The share price rose from tens of cents to over $280.00 in the space of twelve months. The company's property was in Indonesia, and the rise was followed by a huge crash which left many people unwilling and possibly unable to invest in the mining market.

I decided that I would stick closer to home, and as we were living in Tucson, I made plans to acquire a set of Mining Claims south of us near the small settlement of Arivaca which is west of I-19, the freeway that leads from the Mexican border to Tucson. The Interstate was signposted in kilometres and was the conduit for illegal immigrants travelling north from the Mexican border town of Nogales.

There was not much between Tucson and Nogales, but just after the exit from I-19 to Arivaca at Amado, there was a restaurant-bar called the Longhorn Grill and Saloon. It was housed in a large, single-storey, whitewashed building constructed as the head of a Texas Longhorn cow. The horns extended about 20ft either side of the head and framed the entrance.

Arivaca did not have a lot to recommend it apart from the MH Mobile Home Park and a bakery that was famed for its sourdough bread.

I had obtained information about the area from my previous employer, with geological maps and assays from several small veins at surface that showed there was the potential of discovering a small gold deposit on the property. The claims were known as the Yellow Iron group of claims. Yellow Iron, according to folklore, is the translation of what the Chiricahua Apaches called gold (cited in the book *Blood Brother* by Elliot Arnold, 1947). At one time, the claims were held by a prospector who lived just outside of Arivaca. After a couple of calls, he agreed to meet and take me through the plans and data that he had. He lived in a trailer home (a large caravan or mobile home) on the way into the town. In the yard, there was an International Harvester Travelall car with cream and brown paintwork: the quintessential classic American touring car, this one dating from the early 1970s and was synonymous with road trips and the wide open spaces of the West.

From his bearing, I guessed he was ex-military, possibly a Vietnam vet as he had a Thai wife and was wearing army fatigues. Linda and I were served cups of green tea by his wife. I think it was the first time I had tasted green tea. JD had a good knowledge of geology and small mines, and we talked for a couple of hours. Towards the end of the discussion, he started to tell me about a hidden cave high in the mountains out toward Baboquivari where, in the late 1800s, a couple of old prospectors had hidden sacks of silver balls from the fabled *Planches de Plata* mine, the location of which has varied over the years, depending on which legend is being quoted.

JD offered to take us to the cave next time we came, but only after we agreed to several conditions which seemed too onerous. I told him I would think about it and promised not to tell anyone.

Subsequently, I found references to the mine on several websites and in books, and there are a few similar legends about the deposits. I'd say the exact location is unknown, but no mention of hidden sacks of silver.

The Yellow Iron claims were quite close to the Mexico US border and at one time Linda completed an endurance race on horseback which passed close to the claims, so we knew a little about the area.

Before staking them, I sampled several of the claims, and the assays confirmed the presence of gold in the rocks. A couple of weeks later, with a good friend and consulting geologist, I staked ten claims covering an area of 200 acres. This was the first mining asset for Kernow Resources and Developments Inc, an American company that we formed to acquire mining claims and projects in the US. The projects were used to raise money on the VSE for further development and exploration. The company also provided a vehicle for us to maintain our visa status in the USA as I would work for the company I had just incorporated. Our original visa was dependent on the employer who no longer required my valuable services.

Much later in the journey across the mining world, I consulted for a company heavily involved in the tungsten business, a rare metal which was used at the time for the filament in lightbulbs. Just to the west of the Yellow Iron claims was an area containing tungsten that was held by General Electric. Their claims covered thousands upon thousands of acres and probably covered the location of the *Planchas de Plata*.

Joutel, Quebec, Canada

While Arivaca seemed to be a good bet to me, those with more knowledge of the VSE suggested that we take up further claims and projects. I had knowledge from various sources of an area open for staking close to the Agnico Eagle gold mine in the township of Joutel in north central Quebec.

The area we wanted was a small block of some twenty claims covering approximately 320ha, and it was to be acquired for Kernow Resources and Developments Limited, our Canadian parent company.

After writing out the complete name a multitude of times, I wished I had given the company a simpler and shorter name: 'We Seek Gold,' or some such direct name.

One of the tricks of getting brokers and mining analysts interested is to acquire a property next to a known mine or project that had great potential. The Joutel claims bordered the claims of the

Agnico Eagle mine. In addition, there was a whole town built a few kilometres away to house workers for that mine and the Joutel Copper Mine 3.5km to the southeast, not forgetting the Poirier Mine that produced Copper and Gold 3.5km to the west. I hoped the proximity would catch the jaundiced eye of the broking community.

By the time we started our exploration programme, the town was pretty much unoccupied as the mines for which it was built had closed. By 1988, it was a modern day ghost town with only a few occupants. Typically Canadian, it had a wonderful ice hockey rink, a school and a well-equipped hospital. I once spent the night there in what remained of the single men's quarters. There were a couple of caretakers who only spoke French, and a team of drillers working for a different company. Actually, the French was Québécois which is pretty difficult to understand, even for the French.

After listing Kernow on the VSE, now known as 'KRD' by its trading symbol, we spent our first $100,000 on drilling the Joutel and, yes we intersected a mineral system with high grade copper, silver and zinc. Brilliant! That was in the December of 1995. The assays were excellent and the stock price tripled for a week after we had announced the assay results. Of course, I couldn't sell any of my shares as I was bound by an escrow agreement which prevented me selling any stock for twelve months after listing.

The excitement was huge. My geologist, Gaetan, who lived in the mining town of Rouyn-Noranda, and had helped me acquire the claims, supervised the first round of drilling. He told the local geological and mining fraternity that we had made a new discovery. The core from the diamond drilling was showing that we had intersected the same type of mineralisation as that of the Poirier and Joutel mines. I was thrilled, this was amazing! My first drill hole in my first public company had hit a rich seam of copper and silver. From the style of the mineralisation, we could see it was a type of deposit called a volcanogenic massive sulphide (VMS): the same as the other three nearby mines.

For a while, we were the talk of the town at the Très Forche restaurant and the Tim Hortons coffee joint in Rouyn. The Prospectors and Development Association of Canada (PDAC) were due to hold their annual conference in Toronto in March, and if we could ensure the team of drillers worked quickly, we could have the results and assays from the drill holes at the conference. This would help us visit the Toronto stockbrokers and, hopefully, we would be able to raise significant monies to carry on drilling and developing the property.

Back in Scottsdale, Arizona, where our offices were now located, I spent a lot of time on the phone rounding up investors to provide financing to drill the next set of holes. My financial partner and I also spent time on the phone encouraging shareholders to buy more shares. The funds were raised and we started to drill in mid-January. We were lucky to get a drill team as much of the work undertaken in that part of Quebec can only be done when the ground has frozen, and drillers were hard to find. But both Gaetan and I had connections, and after the Christmas break, the drills started turning on 12th January.

Having missed the first round of drilling, I really wanted to see the drill core as it came out of the hole and so flew up from Phoenix where it was a balmy 24°C to Rouyn where it was a cool -24 °C. The motel where I was staying had power outlets to enable guests to plug in their cars so as to keep the battery from freezing. It's amazing how practical people can be in cold climates. I, on the other hand, was not.

The drillers had an accommodation site not too far from the project which consisted of a group of portacabins where their crews could get fed, sleep and relax between the twelve hour shifts in the bone freezing cold. A lot of the exploration drilling in Northern Quebec takes place in mid-winter because much of the ground being explored was semi-swamp and access was easier to gain in winter across the frozen ground. The drillers did not seem to be bothered by the cold and constructed a small canvas shelter around the drilling rig which held in the heat from the diesel engine block.

I really wanted to see the rig in operation, so Gaetan and I rented a snowmobile to cross the frozen ground along tracks made by the drillers, and set off from the road camp at 3pm, just before dark. Prior to leaving, Gaetan asked if I was going to go out with the clothes I had on, which were my warmest. My upper body was wrapped in pullovers and a down thermal jacket, plus a woolly hat with a Union Jack on it – not so good for Northern Quebec – but I was like the characters in the cartoon *Wallace and Gromit*: I had the wrong trousers.

"Mr Alan," said Gaetan, "if you only wear those jeans you will be f***ing frozen."

Gaetan lent me a pair of insulated trousers, and so we went off to the rig on the snowmobile in the gathering gloom.

It was cold: very, very cold. I had been in the cold in Scotland and the flat plains of Northern Germany but nothing compared to this.

When we arrived, the drillers were pulling the core from the core catcher which was steaming and hot from the friction of the bit biting through the hard rock and laying it in the core box.

Unfortunately, the core was plain-looking greenstone with a few specks of iron pyrite.

But Gaetan was encouraged and said, "We are getting close to the orebody," which he firmly believed was there.

After freezing in the cramped canvas shelter for thirty minutes, we decided to go back to the portacabin camp. The camp was also icy cold, and after a hot dinner, I went to sleep in the bunk I had been allocated along with most of the clothes I had in my backpack.

The core was sent off to the assay lab and the results came in. They were okay, but nothing to match the high grade assays intersections we had from Hole KRD 1. Undaunted, we carried on drilling and using geophysical methods to try and locate Gaetan's orebody which was proving elusive. As spring came, we stopped work, demobilised the drill rig and moved our efforts to the great state of Nevada. We did raise more money to drill again at Joutel, but we never found the orebody. I guess we caught the tail of the tiger and were sensible enough to let it go and not spend more money chasing it.

Dyke Hot Springs and the Shawnee

The American geologist who helped us to stake the Yellow Iron claims said he had another couple of projects which were available for acquisition. The Dyke Hot Springs was close to the border between Nevada and Idaho near the town of Denio (population 47) with a gas station and one motel that had a very small casino. It is a very remote place.

The second project he offered was known as the Shawnee, beyond the Black Rock desert on the eastern slopes of the Jackson Mountains. Although it was a desert, it also snowed and the winds from the east froze all liquids in their path. When drilling, we took our water supply from a well on an old ranch where the rancher grew alfalfa. The well water was a little brackish, and for curiosity we had it analysed to see if it contained any of the elements that would indicate proximity to a gold deposit. One of these was arsenic. The water contained far in excess of the allowed concentrations of arsenic for any domestic purposes other than washing your car. I thought of the old practise of feeding horses small amounts of arsenic to make their coats gleam before selling, and wondered about the health of the cows and horses that were fed the alfalfa from the huge field.

Shawnee was forty miles from the municipality of Winnemucca where decent accommodation could be found. Winnemucca was advertised as 'City of Paved Streets' on a huge billboard on US Route 95 approximately ten miles to the north. The main street was wide enough to turn your wagon around, and probably at one time hosted the pioneers travelling west on the Emigrant Trail. It was the seat of Humboldt County and housed the local Bureau of Land Management and the County Administrative offices where you filed your Mineral Claims and paid the annual fees to hold the claims.

A large mining company had explored and drilled the Shawnee

a couple of years before we acquired the property. We bought their information and used their data to site new drill holes to obtain maximum knowledge and ensure good results. We had to spend a specific amount of money on the project and have an independent geologist recommend further work to use it as a property suitable for listing purposes.

We drilled three holes and intersected the vein we knew to be there. The results were interesting but not spectacular, but the results along with some prospecting and a geophysical survey we had recently completed allowed the independent geologist to recommend further work.

Sachem Bay Claim I and Voisey's Bay

Even with what I believed to be excellent exploration properties, I was still having difficulty in getting a broker to sponsor our listing on the Vancouver Exchange. Fortunately, another one of those rare discoveries that ignites the junior market took place: a story of a modern day prospector looking for diamonds and instead found one of the largest nickel deposits in Canada from the last sample taken during the day.

It is known as the Voisey's Bay discovery, the site of a large open cast mine, and is located in northern Labrador. The discovery sparked a staking rush. In Labrador, it was possible to 'Paper Stake', so instead of having to go out into the field and pound wooden stakes into the ground, a person can go to the Recorder's office in St John's and define the area one wishes to explore, pay the appropriate fees, comply with all the requirements, and the mineral rights to that area of land are then yours. One claim measures 500 x 500m or 25 ha (about 61 acres). A mineral claim grants the exclusive right to explore for all minerals. The owner must then expend a certain amount on each claim each year.

I had a contact who had staked an area of ground very close to the discovery and was prepared to sell the claim to me for cash and shares in the company. After consultation with my lawyer and the stockbroker with whom I was working, we bought the property for Kernow. By now, our treasury was severely depleted, but I put more money into the company as the broker had assured me the listing was an assured thing and when the stock listed, it would fly.

The listing took place in May 1995, and Kernow Resources and Developments Limited became a publicly listed company. The stock price had a moderate increase and the brokers sold their shares, but as mentioned earlier, I was unable to sell any of my own stock. It was a very proud moment for me as I had done much of the report writing, getting the accounts audited and marketing the idea by myself, ably supported by Linda.

We spent a lot of money in Labrador but also received a reasonable amount of money by Joint Venturing the property to other juniors looking to get in on the area play. I spent quite a few days in helicopters flying over the claims, prospecting with a JV partner. There were many companies competing for helicopter time, geologists, aeroplanes to fly aerial surveys and field assistants to help the geologists.

Goose Bay was the nearest airport to the Voisey's Bay discovery so hotels there were at a premium. The Tim Hortons coffee house installed an electronic Stock Market ticker that recorded the trades of the companies involved in exploring in the area in real time. A real boom town where its prior claim to fame was being the closest airport to the one in Shannon, Ireland. Oh, and being a NATO air force base.

Toward the end of the hysteria, the brokers and traders became somewhat jaded. Companies were putting out news releases saying they had flown a geophysical airborne survey over their claims and had found a distinct anomaly in the data showing where it may be likely to find a deposit of whatever was the flavour of the month.

One broker commented, "Anomalies are like assholes. Everybody has one."

Eventually, the market quietened down, no other deposits were found and the Inuit went back to their quiet way of life. It took nine years for the Voisey's Bay mine to be permitted and Inco to start mining the deposit, providing employment to many locals.

Just after we had unsuccessfully drilled our main claim at Voisey's, the stock market was a little sceptical of area plays, so I decided that we should try to acquire a more substantial project and to negotiate the acquisition of the Jales gold Mine in Portugal.

However, that is not the end of the adventures of Kernow Resources and Developments Limited.

16

THE COPPER GIANT PROSPECT

2015: Pima County, Arizona, February

*Looking for new projects and minerals,
stopped by the Border Patrol, hanging out in Snoopy's brother's town in
California*

About a hundred miles west of Tucson, three miles south of Ajo and close to the now closed New Cornelia copper mine, lies the Copper Giant mineral deposit. It was probably named 'Giant' to entice investors. Usually, 'giant' ore deposits are in the hundreds of millions of tonnes; I doubted if this one was of that size but it deserved a visit. Mexican miners called the site Ajo, perhaps influenced by an O'odham Native American name for the area – *au-auho* – for the red pigment they obtained from the ore-rich rocks. Even though it's not a giant deposit, it's interesting because it is known as an 'exotic' copper deposit. The operations in the New Cornelia area commenced in the mid-1800s, and copper concentrates were shipped to Swansea, Wales, in the 1850s. That sounds like a long way, but this area was part of Mexico until the Gadsden Purchase of

1854, and there were no railroads and no nearby smelters. Also, it may have been easier to get the concentrate to the Colorado River which went quite a way north at one time, than to transport it by muletrain wagons back into the States. Later, railroads were built to transport materials and mules became redundant, although there are a couple of gold-mining ghost towns like Oatman in Arizona that have a few wild *burros* wandering around.

But back to New Cornelia: the high transportation costs and the loss of a concentrate-bearing ship off Cape Horn forced the mine to close until operations restarted in the early 1900s.

Ajo, like many towns in southwest US and in particular those in Arizona, relied solely on copper mining to sustain the economy. The closing of the mine in 1983 threw many people out of work and the only remaining employment, in most cases, was for clean-up operations of the closed pit and waste dumps. Main Street was a reflection of how the town was in the 60s and 70s: independent department stores with large plate glass windows, bars with flashing neon signs offering cocktails, mom and pop hardware stores, now no longer operating, a couple converted to antique stores. Most of the establishments were housed in early 1920s-style redbrick buildings. There was also a plaza with several Spanish Colonial Revival buildings.

As mentioned, the Copper Giant is an exotic copper deposit. These are generally formed of high-grade copper ores composed of chrysocolla, chalcocite, malachite, and azurite. They are very colourful minerals with vibrant blues and greens. This type of deposit is relatively easy to mine and treat with low capital expenditures which makes them attractive to small mining companies. This was also an area for specimen collectors and may well have been a place to collect the rare bluish green copper mineral ajoite.

On the property, we could see where old timers had mined the ores and treated them with acid to recover the oxide coppers. They'd dissolve the copper ore in acid and then precipitate the copper onto now rusty pieces of iron contained in wooden and sometimes concrete tanks lined with pitch. This was an easy way of mining and treating copper, and during the Great Depression and between the World Wars, prospectors and small mining groups would find and treat the ores. They wouldn't have made much money, just scraping out a living in those hard times. The remnants of their operations are scattered throughout the deserts of Arizona and Sonora in Mexico. Most of these places were abandoned and never visited again. The dry desert atmosphere preserved the shacks and some of the equipment that was too big to cart away, and sometimes just beneath the surface, you'll find small personal items such as a shaving brush or a medicine bottle. Often, the mines had grand names such as 'Copper Queen', 'Copperopolis' to the northeast, and this one, the 'Copper Giant'.

Pretty quickly we decided that the property was not of any use to our company. The Copper Giant held evidence that the deposit could be reasonably extensive, but the land was close to the Organ Pipe National Forest and a possible host for the protected and rare desert tortoise. These factors, combined with its remote location would make it difficult to obtain operating permits. Logistics would also have been difficult, trucking acid and supplies several hundred miles to the site.

To mix business with pleasure and to make the trip worthwhile, we knew that out in the scrubby desert southwest of Ajo there is a deposit of fluorescent calcite. When exposed to ultra-violet light, this mineral glows an acid green and a lurid orange. Certain types of calcite will normally fluoresce a pretty pink to reddish colour. So minerals from here are highly collectable and unusual.

The site where the minerals occur is located between Lime Hill and the Growler Mica Mine. Lime Hill is noticeable from quite a distance as it is a brilliant white – and the only hill in the area. This portion of desert is in fact a very wide flat dry river bed. The vegetation consists of widely scattered creosote bushes, *cholla* cactus, a few organ pipe cacti, the occasional mesquite tree, none of which grow more than 12ft in height, along with twisted and stunted Palo Verde trees. The guide book *Minerals, Fossils, and Fluorescents of Arizona* (Neil R Bearce, 2006) suggests that to reach Lime Hill from

Ajo, one should take Bates Well Road south for seven miles and then turn west at John the Baptist Junction. After that, the road deteriorates and it follows one of the abraded channels of the dry river.

I was driving quite slowly and had lost sight of the John the Baptist Mountains – not really mountains but small hills – and Lime Hill had vanished too, so I stopped and rolled down the window, trying to get my bearings,

To my shock and amazement a Border Patrol agent appeared next to me.

"What the hell are you guys doing out here and why didn't you stop when I signalled? I've been behind you since the junction at Bates Well Road."

"I'm sorry, officer. I didn't see you."

He was fully rigged with pistol, pepper spray, handcuffs and other stuff that American cops have on their belts. With the broad brimmed hat and the sunglasses, he looked a pretty mean dude.

"Surely you must have seen the lights flashing?"

"Sorry, no," I replied. "We were concentrating on finding the track to Lime Hill."

"So what the hell are you doing here?"

I explained we were looking for the Growler Mine to see if we could find some fluorescent calcite. By the way, it's now about 110°F and we have the dogs with us, panting in the back of the Jeep.

He seemed sceptical, and so we showed him the book *Minerals, Fossils, and Fluorescents of Arizona* which we were using to locate the deposit. It didn't make much difference. He was still amazed that we were in the area.

"Don't you know this is a bad place to be?" he said. "This area is one of the main drug and immigration smuggling corridors in the southwest US. Drug runners and people traffickers would not hesitate to shoot you on sight if you came across them."

He told us that the Border Patrol and other units were also conducting exercises in the area to catch illegal aliens, and had set up a semi-permanent camp nearby.

Over 300 illegal immigrants die every year in this small area of Arizona. The desert is a brutal place to be at any time of year, with temperatures in the summer months reaching 120°F. Without shade and water, dehydration and death come quickly.

Heeding his advice, we turned around and headed back to Ajo, then north to the King of Arizona Wilderness area and the famous King of Arizona gold mine.

After three days in the desert sun, I was looking at a riverbed but no river. So, the story it told was of a river that had once flowed but was now no more. It made me sad to think it was dead and gone. (I'm paraphrasing *A Horse with No Name* by the group America, but it seems apt.)

September 1998

During our first stay in Arizona, we visited another copper oxide/exotic copper prospect, north and slightly west of Ajo. It was called Chuckwalla Wash and was close to the town of Needles, California, a city that owed its possible moment of fame to the Schultz cartoon character Snoopy whose brother Spike lived there. He sported a wide brimmed Mexican hat and a *Viva Zapata* moustache. Odd for a dog to wear a hat, but in the world of cartoons no holds are barred, a little like prospecting and the people in the junior mining business. In the UK, this is the AIM (the international market for growing companies trading on the London Stock Exchange), and in the US the 'pink sheets'. They are sometimes run by unscrupulous promoters who exaggerate the value of the stock and the potential contained in mostly worthless mining claims. Not me, of course, but Bre-x Minerals was a huge scam. The majority of the companies are run by honest people raising money to explore for minerals. My company raised about £4,000,000 over ten years, and explored all over the US, Canada and Portugal with moderate success.

Initially, I was not going to bother looking at the project as it was in California which is a state where it is very difficult to obtain permission to develop a mine when faced with a hostile group of county commissioners and environmental groups who will stoop very low to derail a project.

I do have an example of that.

The state had told the powers that be in Riverside County to grant permission to a mining company so they could go ahead and start a gold mine. This enraged the environmental protection groups so much that they undertook yet another assessment and survey of the fauna and plants in the area of the mine.

Strangely, and to everyone's amazement, they discovered the Three Banded Mohave snail. Apparently, it was one of the great discoveries of all environmental time. The area was in the process of being declared a reserved habitat when one of the mining company's employees, whilst discussing the matter with the desert protection people, happened to notice that the bands on the snail were flaking off. It was reportedly a hoax and the bands had been painted onto the snail's shell. In any event, the mine was put on hold for several years. This, of course, may be a miner's tale.

Chuckwalla was between the Dead Mountains Wilderness and the Mojave National Preserve, and was accessed from State Route 95 which went north to Searchlight, Nevada. The property was pure desert with very little vegetation, and what existed was confined to dry river beds and the occasional seep marked by a stunted mesquite. As usual, there was an abundance of *cholla* (jumping) cactus, but the seep was dry and dying. The prospect contained a lot of shallow pits and a few old workings. You could see where the old timers had built basic acid tanks and gathered together scrap iron on which to precipitate the copper solutions. The mineralisation was also sparse and not that interesting, and even though the county commissioners in San Bernardino County were more favourable to mine development, the prospect seemed a little too hard to handle.

Interestingly, there were a couple of old unpaved tracks that crossed the property, running parallel to Interstate 40, the highway that travels west from the green and rolling hills of North Carolina to the

'American dream' lands of Southern California. During the Depression, these tracks had been populated by folk going west to start a new life in the California sunshine, much as another wave of emigrants had done back in the 1800s. I had heard of similar routes that ran west across Nevada, where sometimes one could find pieces of household furniture such as dressers or wardrobes that just became too much of a burden for the wagons and were abandoned on the side of the road. Here in California, we came across a couple of carcasses of old Ford motor cars with all of the moveable parts stripped out, a few Bentwood chairs and an old mangle: an incredibly poignant reminder of the struggles some people went through to achieve the American Dream.

It's amazing to think that having come west from Oklahoma or Kansas you would have to abandon probably your only asset in a desert, and then walk onward to the coast. The temperatures here reach 115°F during the summer months, and it gets really cold at nights from autumn to late spring.

So after the assessment of the property, we went back to Needles. The city lies on the western banks of the Colorado River which, at this point, still seems like a viable river. A few hundred miles south, after being sucked almost dry by irrigation pumps, the river drains what little is left of its waters into the Mexican deserts. Apart from the fact that Snoopy's brother lives close by, there is not a lot to Needles.

Although, it does have a Best Western Motel next to a place called the Buffalo Bar, frequented by the type of people who you vow not to make eye contact with and hope that they are not staying in the motel. There were a few of these playing pool, and from the way they drank and swaggered, one could tell they were ex-service men who had been trained in martial arts, and therefore best avoided.

In addition, there were a few Native Americans slumped over the bar, with the widest bottoms you ever did see, what you might call a seat-hider backside. They were also getting drunk.

After a glass of dry white wine which tasted like sherry (really?

in a Bar in Needles?), and a vodka on the rocks (which seemed safer), we went to the Chinese restaurant, had some plum wine, and retired to the Best Western, bypassing the bar.

It was only 110 miles to the Vegas Strip, and 50 miles to London Bridge at Lake Havasu – I can't think why we didn't go there to spend the night.

Next morning, we headed back to Tucson and took the backroads which are sometimes quite scenic. Firstly, we picked up I-40 that heads east to northern Arizona, then turned south at the Pilot gas station where the world's worst coffee sits in a percolator all day only to be drunk by the unsuspecting tourist.

Now, we were heading south on Arizona State Route 95. The highway runs parallel to the Colorado Valley and passes through some amazing landscape, including a Copper Canyon lesser known than the Mexican version, before entering the flat lands. The highway goes on through the resort of Lake Havasu City, a spot where college students and wannabe college students come for spring break and water fun. Stay clear of Havasu during spring break

To make the journey a little more interesting, we decided to again follow the backroads using SR-72. We passed such delightful places as the Lone Cactus Egg Farm, and Bouse, where there is a Sherman tank on display in the town centre. That's not quite as whimsical as it sounds because Camp Bouse was the home of the 9th Tank Group. Oh, and there was also a cement tank that was made into a swimming pool by the town's founder ... and not much else.

We were headed for US Route 60. Many of the backroads in Arizona follow old tracks, in some cases from the Spanish colonial era. They were easy to build, simply by grading and filling a few dry washes with run-off pipes, then adding a seal of normal tarmac coating and gravel. In a lot of areas the road surface contains a network of cracks that have been filled by tar. The resulting image is as if the road surface has a bad case of varicose veins. These roads are not well travelled or maintained, and many of the roads crossing the desert have the same malady.

After passing through Vicksburg, we came to the town of Hope. There is not a lot here either. We travelled this way so I could get a picture of me standing next to the sign on the city limits, which states: "You are now beyond Hope."

The name was inspired by the community's optimism for increased business after merchants visited the town. Today, it consists of one RV Park, one gas station, one store selling antiques, and one church.

From Hope, we went east to Salome then turned south east to join I-10 into Phoenix.

There are many quirky place names in Arizona, such as, Why, Love, Bagdad (yes, spelled like that), Date, Lake Montezuma, and Show Low. All have a story behind them. The town of Show Low is named because the land on which it is situated was won in a poker game where the winner had the lowest hand. In southern New Mexico there is a city called Truth or Consequences. The city changed its name in the 1950s from Hot Springs as the result of a radio show contest.

Alongside Interstate 8, there is a stretch of highway that passes from Gila Bend to Smurr, Theba, Piedra, Tarton, Sentenial, Stanwix and Aztec (not far from Mohawk).

Unusual, but probably not as strange as passing from Trengilly Wartha through Constantine and on to Gweek.

17

STANTON, YAVAPAI COUNTY, CENTRAL ARIZONA

2015: Arizona

Racing the storm back to the main road,
gold nuggets as big as potatoes,
yet another deposit discovered by a mule,
the surprise at Santo Domingo Wash, visit to a ghost town

The old Arizona mining town of Stanton can be approached from two ways: from the north, Prescott via Skull Valley and Kirkland; or by following State Route 89 and travelling 20 miles northeast from Wickenburg.

We approached from Kirkland having spent the weekend in the high cool pines of Prescott, escaping the 115° F heat in Scottsdale. Stanton sits beneath the escarpment that hosts Yarnell and Peeples Valley, the topography and vegetation totally different from the country surrounding Stanton. From Wickenburg heading to Congress, the countryside is flat, scrubby desert and as you approach the escarpment that rises up to Yarnell and Prescott, you can see where the highway winds through the granite boulders and outcrop, up over the hill. Halfway up is the monument to the Granite Mountain Firefighters who tragically lost their lives in the Yarnell Hill wildfire of 2013.

The town was originally a stagecoach stop known as Antelope Station, and was later renamed after the businessman and crook, Chuck Stanton, who took over the town in the 1870s. It's located a few miles south of Rich Hill.

From the Memorial rest area halfway up the hill looking to the southwest, you can see the dry river beds, washes, *arroyos* (streams) and *barrancas* (gorges) that run from the escarpment out onto the dry desert flats. Some are hundreds of feet across; other juvenile tributaries are less wide but have steep banks that are difficult to negotiate. All are heading toward the Hassayampa River which flows south toward Mexico but never reaches there, being swallowed up in the Sonoran Desert.

The area below the escarpment only gets a few inches of rain a year, and the heat can be extreme with summer temperatures reaching 125°F in the shade, although there's very little of that. Plant life consists of wiry, green-barked *palo verde* trees with tiny leaves, creosote bushes, not much more than 4ft in height, the occasional *saguaro* and the ubiquitous *cholla* cactus. From the escarpment, you can look down to the plain which stretches back to Phoenix. Above the escarpment and after the Main Street of Yarnell, the climate becomes more temperate with grass and pine trees growing in the area of Peeples Valley. Here, there are farms with white post and rail fencing and horses in the meadows.

Turning off the highway close to the town of Congress, the road to Stanton becomes dirt and gravel although reasonably well maintained. Stanton has changed quite a bit in character over the years from being a rip roaring gold mining camp of the 1880s that boasted a saloon, an 'opera house', a jail, and an assay office. It has taken on various guises over the years until the present day where it now hosts the winter RV park of the Lost Dutchman's Mining Association (LDMA – named for the famous gold mine, lost for 125 years and recently rediscovered).

Stanton had a fearsome reputation in 1892. For example, a Prescott newspaper reported that the residents of Stanton, "drink blood, eat fried rattlesnakes and fight mountain lions."

In the late 1950s, *The Saturday Evening Post* purchased the ten-acre town and then gave it away during a radio jingle contest. In the 1970s, it was a hideout for hippies who, according to local report, tore down several of the historic buildings for firewood. The LDMA has restored a few of the town's original buildings, including Chuck Stanton's store, an old saloon and dancehall, and a hotel. The town jail is also standing, and work has been done to restore the town's pioneer cemeteries.

The RV's in Lost Dutchman Park are owned by serious and amateur gold prospectors. Beyond Stanton out on the gently sloping plains that are cut by the dry riverbeds, both amateur gold prospectors and 'snowbirds' establish themselves either singly or in groups of three or four RVs in the flat, dry desert. Most of the snowbirds are from the north looking to escape the cold winters of the Dakotas, Montana, and Canada. The snowbirds not only roost in Stanton or on the plains of the Hassayampa but they are scattered throughout the old placer mining areas of southern Arizona. In the winter months, the town of Quartzite on the border between Arizona and California hosts thousands of the snowbirds in and around the city, hunkering down on public and BLM land. Some staked placer mining claims which allow them to camp on the 20-acre claim and park their RVs, wash and dig for placer gold. Some are moderately successful, some do little except barbeque, drink cold beer and bask in the winter sunshine. A few who know what they are doing and use the right equipment pull up small but valuable nuggets.

In Yavapai County many were inspired by the tales of the Potato Patch located on the side of Rich Hill, a few miles north of Stanton. Legend had it that the gold nuggets on the hill were as big as small potatoes. The belief of many – and not too far from the truth – was that during the rainy seasons over the millennia, gold nuggets and particles that form gold dust would wash from the hills and settle in the washes out on the desert plains.

On occasion, we would buy a few nuggets from prospectors as an investment and to display for their beauty – but nothing to match the nugget bought in Papua New Guinea.

Rich Hill was found by a group of prospectors searching for gold in 1863. Led by a frontiersman named Pauline Weaver (real name Powell Weaver), the explorers were camped along Antelope Creek when one of the group chased after a runaway *burro*.

After climbing to the top of what would become known as Rich Hill, Alvaro the mule master tripped over a pile of gold nuggets that were, "As big as potatoes."

Soon after, Pauline Weaver and a friend found another pile of gold on top of nearby Antelope Hill. Weaver said that gold was so plentiful in the area that he could pop nuggets out of the ground with a knife, and that one acre yielded nearly $500,000 in gold.

I think if it wasn't for wandering *burros*, many of the richest gold and silver deposits in the western US would have gone undiscovered.

After walking around the main street of Stanton, we had a look in the graveyard noting several Cornish surnames including Tregonning and Penrose, we decided to head back to Phoenix. Rather than go via Route 89 and down to Wickenburg, I decided to traverse the Hassayampa River Canyon Wilderness and join Highway 89 beyond Wickenburg. I knew there were dirt tracks heading south and east.

As we drove further from Stanton, we passed small groups of RVs belonging to prospecting snowbirds circled like pioneer wagons next to the dry stream beds.

I also noticed that large thunder clouds were building on the escarpment behind and to the northeast of us, and as we proceeded east, the roads started to deteriorate. I knew we would have to cross Weaver Creek in the next five miles, and later the Hassayampa a little further on. Normally, this wouldn't have been a problem but as the thunder clouds grew, we could see sheets of rain starting to fall on the cliffs. The rain would very quickly run into the washes and soon after initially wetting the stream and river bottoms, the waters would coalesce, and rivulets would grow and join the normally dry beds, flowing rapidly toward where we were traversing the plains.

Crossing Weaver Creek was a challenge as it had steep sides and the track had not been maintained that year. Making my way slowly into the dry bottom in our four-wheel drive, I drove across, studiously keeping to the beaten path. The wash was about 200 yards wide and deviation from the beaten path could have led us into one of the deep sand beds that were so difficult to get out of.

Having crossed the bed of the wash, the track on the far side was in reasonable shape. We proceeded east-southeast still looking at the rain clouds anxiously. Perhaps a decision to try and cross the area at this time of year when it received its small amount of rain which could turn the dry washes into raging torrents was not a good idea.

The craziness of this was reinforced when large rain drops began to fall and we had not yet made the Hassayampa. It would have not been a good idea to turn back, so off we went. We drove at a faster pace than we had done prior to crossing Weaver Creek, not worrying so much about the rocks in the road and the creosote bushes scratching the sides of the car.

We made the Hassayampa quickly, and the banks of this major wash were easier to get down than those at Weaver Creek. However, the wash is about 400 yards wide at that point and we could see that water had started to infiltrate some of the smaller braids of the channel. In a low gear, we crossed and made it to safety. It was almost as if the rain gods had simply wished to give us a stern warning, because the rain stopped as we crested the high bank.

After ten miles of relatively good dirt road, we joined the Phoenix-Wickenburg Highway, breathed a sigh of relief and stopped across from Hassayampa River Preserve Park at the Texaco gas station for coffee.

The area around Wickenburg and east toward the Hieroglyph

and Bradshaw Mountains is incredibly rich in minerals. South of Wickenburg in the Vulture Mountains is the famed Vulture gold mine which still operates as a tourist mine and occasionally produces a little gold. To add to the riches of the Vulture Mountains there are several prospects containing the now much sought after lithium. In the seventies, rubidium and other radioactive minerals were looked for and found there, but not in economic quantities at the time.

Most of the mines were small prospects but several warranted the hardiest of miners, packing construction and mining equipment into the remote areas, either by old jalopy style trucks of the 1930s, or *burros* for the small miner in the early days. From the 1960s, flatbed trucks were used, and in the 70s F250 pickups; you can often find worn out mule shoes, old wheel rims with the tyres disintegrating, and occasionally the shell of a 1960s flatbed with every conceivable movable part removed, the remaining carcass peppered with bullet holes looking like it had been in a Rambo film.

Prospecting in the area was relatively easy as all the old mines and showings had at least the remnants of a track leading to them. In the digital age, finding these mines is a little easier with the mapping systems showing topography, and because it takes many, many years for tracks to return to their former state and for vegetation to grow over disturbed areas.

Other signs of mineralisation could be found by looking for the efforts of the Spanish Conquistadors who roamed these desert hills venturing north from Mexico, searching for the famed City of Gold or Eldorado. Occasionally, in more remote areas, you can find workings, adits, tunnels and some shafts. These were close to flat areas where the ore dug from the tunnels was crushed with stone hammers or *metates* and then milled in an *arrastra*, a circle made of flat granite flagstone on which the hand crushed ore was spread and milled by a large circle of stone rotated around the dressing floor. The millstone was attached by a wooden spoke to a central vertical pole which was in turn hitched to a mule which walked round and round the circle, causing the millstone to rotate and crushed the ore to a fine powder. The gold, if there was any, was recovered by washing in steel prospector pans. The Spanish prospectors would use a hollowed-out cow horn to check the gold content of the crushed rock. They would take a sample of the powdered rock, place it in the horn and half fill the horn with water. Then, by gently rocking the curved horn and washing away the waste rock over the lip, the gold would be revealed. If there was any gold present, it would be visible as dust or extremely small particles known as 'colour'.

Unfortunately, the days of discovering potato-sized gold nuggets just below the surface are long gone in the West. However, as we have seen, there are areas of the world where indigenous peoples still find such treasures buried in the mud of landslides.

18

SHAWNEE

Late 1990s: Humboldt County, Nevada

A slice of life in a small town in Nevada

Two fat men sit at the bar. Their rear ends overlap the barstools, they are in their early thirties. Probably, they were once linebackers for the local high school football team, now truck drivers for the local mining company. Their official title is 'heavy equipment operator', and they drive trucks, big trucks, 230-ton trucks, but they don't get paid on the size of truck they drive. They sit all day and drive their trucks and their butts get bigger. They are from around here. They grew up back when things were better and the price of gold was higher, and their fathers earned good money working in the open cast mines. Now, they earn just enough above minimum wage, plus health benefits to make them feel good, so it isn't so bad.

Back when they were in high school and athletes, they kicked a whole lot of butt against the Winnemucca Wildcats and Fallon Falcons. Now the muscle has gone to waste, their Levis are doublewide, so are their trailer homes, so are their wives. It's a

Friday night in Shawnee, small town Nevada and the lads are out on the prowl in the Sagebrush Casino and Motel.

Times have changed: mining is a dirty word back east, mines are closing and their skills are commonplace. They cannot move, they are boxed in.

"Ain't no call for miners in Warshington or California, what with them damn greenies, and all. They 'bout shut us down."

They are not the only ones under pressure from the slowdown in the mining industry. My company relies on its existence by raising funds through the junior mining sector of the Vancouver Stock Exchange, using those funds wisely to explore and hopefully make a big discovery to sell to the major mining companies to develop a mine.

However, the miners at the bar have to carry on; they have the wife, the kids, and the payments on the trailer home.

They look around the bar in desperation, "God damn, it's Friday night. There's got to be some action here soon."

They have cashed their pay-cheques at Rayley's the local supermarket, paid for the groceries for the last two weeks, and now have a little left to spend. They'll take a turn at the Blackjack table, drink a few beers, maybe cheat on the wife, but it's a small town.

"Hey, some guy in here last week won $2,000 on that table over there. Don't tell me it can't be done, just have to have the right cards. The dealer has to be on a losing streak, then you got to hit her hard and keep on hitting her hard."

Jolene, the dealer stands at the Blackjack table, bored to tears. Two of her old high school friends are out on the town. The female parallel of the two miners, blown out to triple-X size. Intermittently, the gals play $2 hands sipping their free rum and cokes, losing more often than not, screaming in fake girlish joy when they win.

"Shit, Jolene, can't you deal us some real cards?"

Jolene smiles, draws on her generic cigarette and asks if they want to play one more hand. The girls call for another drink and discuss the situation.

The Sagebrush is the only motel and only casino in Shawnee. It has two Blackjack tables, no Roulette or Faro wheel, but it does have the normal compliment of dollar, quarter and nickel slots. The old ladies of the blue-rinse brigade monopolise the nickel slots. The Sagebrush has a deal with retirement clubs and associations, and busses the old folks in from surrounding states. They get a good room rate, breakfast and a coupon book full of two-for-one bets on the Blackjack table, 'a dollar off your dinner in the Fireside Lounge and restaurant,' and the best of all, a free dollar roll of nickels.

The bar is long and inlaid with dollar and quarter video poker machines that will eat up your $20 roll of quarters faster than a high speed internet connection. There are a few regulars, a couple of strangers, a couple of younger women out for a drink without the kids, and the two fat guys. A group of four Californians stand out like a Pinyon pine tree on the desert horizon. They smoke like chimneys and drink Martinis, straight up with a twist. They talk loudly of success in the internet equity market, the money they have made, and how they like to come over the state line to Nevada for a hassle free smoke and a few drinks.

Behind the bar is a huge mirror rescued from the Silver Dollar Bar in Mill City – a crumbling ghost town three miles down the road where ore from the surrounding silver mines was treated during the boom times of the 1880s. Mill City is now only a collection of trailer homes, a few wooden shacks and a general store; the Silver Dollar was knocked down in the forties. The mirror is magnificent, reflecting the past and present of Nevada. Things haven't changed much in the last 100 years or so: mining, gambling and home to desperados, the mirror still reflects these images.

The two fat girls decide to play another hand. They put down their $2 chips, the cards flash like lightning from the deck in Jolene's hand. One girl has a seven showing, the other a three.

"For fucks sake, Jolene, deal some goddam cards we can play with. You skinny bitches are all the same."

Jolene is showing a king.

The first girl looks at her hidden card, "A nine, that and my seven makes sixteen, what the hell use is that?"

She pushes the cards away from her. Jolene sneaks a look at her hidden card. She asks the girls if they want another card and without waiting for an answer flips over her cards, now showing her king and a six, she draws from the pack, a ten, bust. Her quick delicate hands pay the girls their winnings, smiles and waits for them to play again.

"*She-it!* We won!"

Jolene smiles enigmatically. She knows they would have hit the sixteen and lost. She says she is going on a break and shutting the table unless they want to play some more. If they want to play some more she will call over Sherrie to take care of them. The girls decide to wait until Jolene comes back from break. Sherrie is another skinny bitch and the girls wander over to the bar.

The girls take their meagre winnings and decide to join the blue-rinse ladies who are using their $1.00 worth of free nickels for a chance to hit the daily jackpot. The ladies carry their winnings and playing money from machine to machine in quart-sized plastic drinks cups. At 25¢ a spin for five lines, it seems like a good deal. For a while, the two girls do okay but inevitably the 'plays available' message shows '1', so they have one more chance. They pull the arm of the one-armed bandit together and … win or lose it was a good night out. Let's hope the girls don't end up as blue-rinsers.

The two strangers are drillers. They work for Bill Hanson Drilling Company. Bill owns two rigs that drill for gold on behalf of junior mining companies. Bill takes shares and promises in return for payment. Some time back, one of the Penny Stocks he took as payment for the drill job struck it big, not here in Nevada, but in some foreign place whose name ended with a 'stan'. He's been living on the proceeds of the sale of the shares for a while now. He pays the drillers in cash. He knows they can't pay the bills with Stock Certificates. If the shares of my company he has taken as payment hit and we get some good gold numbers, the share price will rocket and he will cash in then. But the market is tough and he owns a lot of paper of Penny Stock that rarely trades.

The drillers are tough-looking, dark skinned guys. Probably with some Mexican or Native American blood.

Drilling is a dirty, greasy job, and most of the guys seemed to take pride in getting cleaned up for dinner and for the after-dinner activities that may be found in Nevada.

These drillers have cleaned up nicely and have just finished the all-you-can-eat rib-eye special in the Fireside Lounge and Restaurant, complete with salad, coffee and dessert, all for just $6.99. Clean they are, but a smell of diesel and drilling grease lingers around them. Bill just paid them and their rooms are covered, so they have a little money to gamble with. But the Sagebrush is such a hokey joint they think they'll maybe wait awhile until they can get into Winnemucca or Fallon.

Two of the other men at the bar are the owners of the mining claim where the drillers are working. One is an Englishman who hails from Cornwall and who has a company listed on the Vancouver Stock Exchange, the other an American from Minnesota, a geologist who sold the Englishman the claim. He also gets some work out of the sale, supervising the drillers and sitting on the rig ensuring the job goes smoothly, logging the core and generally calling the shots. He has a lot of experience and will know when they have hit the ore zone. They talk endlessly of epithermal systems, high level mineralising fluids and bonanza grades. The days of bonanza grades have gone, but that's what made the Hursts, Mackays and the other mining kings of Nevada rich. Mackay was a Scot born in the proverbial humble cottage. He ended up controlling the telecommunications cables across the Pacific and then, as one does, became a mining magnate owning a railroad. He was one of four 'Silver Kings' that extracted over $8 billion in silver from the Comstock Lode, Virginia City not too far from Shawnee.

The days when miners could find hundreds of ounces of silver and tens of ounces of gold for every ton of ore are over. There are most definitely a few deposits still to be found, but five holes out in the hills of Shawnee have about as much chance of striking the mother lode as the fat girls of winning the $5 million accumulator prize on the slots.

The Californians get louder; more Martinis, more tales of Venture Capitalists throwing money at their start-up companies. The pall of smoke from the fat cigars and cigarettes gathers around their heads and gets thicker.

The Englishman comments to his geologist that it's been the Californians and the internet that has sucked all the speculative money out of the mining market.

"No one wants to take a gamble on a junior mining stock any more, all the money is going into this internet stuff."

They were three holes into the five-hole drill programme: the first two holes missed the target, hit water and cost a bomb to seal the holes. The water was rancid, full of sulphur, arsenic and smelly. They both took comfort in the fact that the condition of the water means that they are getting closer to the target. The third hole hit the vein and they are waiting for the assays from the samples of the core that were sent to the laboratory in Reno. The lab will determine the percentage of copper and hopefully the amount of gold and silver in the rock.

The Englishman gets up and asks at the reception, "Is there a fax for me?"

The receptionist checks the fax machine next to the cash register. "No" she says, "I told you, I'll come and get you if anything comes in."

"Brent," he says to his buddy, "I'm sure those assays will come in tonight. Let's go play a little Blackjack."

At the same time, two of the Californians decide to hit the table. The two fat girls see there is action and move on over. The two miners decide that there is no point in trying to cheat on the wife tonight and decide to risk a little money. The Englishman and the geologist drift away to play the slots. There is only room for six at the table.

Jolene comes back from her break, opens the table and two new decks of cards; she shuffles and deals. The game goes up and down, back and forth, the Californians betting twenty-five bucks a go, the miners five, the two fat girls stick to their two-dollar bets. Jolene is fast, the Californians drop a couple of hundred in the first quarter of an hour, the rest of the table stays even.

Another half-hour goes by, the Californians have dropped a couple of grand. What is anybody doing with that sort of money in a hick town in Nevada on Saturday night?

"Come on, Miles," one of them says, "enough is enough. Let's go down to Reno and find us a craps table."

The other reluctantly gets up to leave. "Damn! I hate leaving money in a hole like this."

"That gal's too sharp for my money!"

"She got ya, Miles. The cards ain't with ya. Let's go".

They leave the table, round up their two friends from the bar who pay the bar bill with a hundred and leave the change, all of ten bucks, and head out the door.

A conversation breaks out between the players about the 'Geeks from California' – none of the statements or opinions are complimentary. Jolene gets no tip but is glad to see the back of the high rollers.

The Englishman and his geologist take the Californians' place at the table, and Jolene slows down the pace of the cards. The house is covered for tonight; she's just killing time.

The evening drags on, the fat girls get so drunk that the barman cuts them off, a rare occurrence in Nevada. They leave, swaying out back to the parking lot, two huge mounds of flesh hugging each other as they make their way to the old Ford they have parked outside.

"What do people do for a living in this place?" the Englishman asks, almost to himself and his geologist.

One of the miners overhears and says, "Those two are on Social Security; most of the people here are. Else they work at the mine or Rayley's."

God, what a life.

The miners leave, the drillers go to bed. They have to be up at six to get to site and start the drill for the last hole. Now it's about 11.30pm. Brent and I wait for the fax to come in.

The bells and whistles on the slots have stopped; the blue hairs have gone to bed, clutching their plastic super-sized mugs of nickels to their ample bosoms. Now it's relatively quiet and you can hear the song on the juke box,

"Some gotta win, some gotta loose,
Good time Charlie's got the Blues."

The bar is closing down, the regulars are gone. The cashiers are counting the bills left behind by the Californians, the Fireside Lounge and restaurant is closed. If you want coffee, you'll have to get it from the bar.

Bill Hanson walks in and he has a paper in his hand, a big smile on his face.

Jolene greets him, "Hi, boss. Watcha grinning at? Is that the tab for tonight's takings?"

"No, Jolene," he says in a slow ponderous voice. "This one here's for the Limey."

The geologist perks up. "Hey, Bill, do you own a piece of this place?"

"Sure I do. Don't think I could stay alive living off the peanuts you prospectors pay for drill holes, do ya?"

"Hey, Bill," says the Englishman. "What you got there?"

"Just a fax with the results from the Acme Analytical Laboratory for sample numbers 3-001 to 3-015."

"Hey! Those are the results from hole three," says the geologist.

"Sure are, you better take a look at them."

Bill has had a look, the assays are good but not great, but they will allow the Englishman and his partner to raise another swag of dough to go drill some more holes, and Bill is pretty much assured to get the work.

To the Englishman, the assays are great, so he and the geologist decide to have one more drink. Bill slopes off with Jolene.

Bill's had a good night and his share of the Sagebrush is starting to pay dividends. A few more nights with the internet geeks from California and things will work out fine. The Englishman got some numbers and his stock will trade a little on Monday on the hopes of a big discovery.

Jolene knows that Bill is going to take care of her and she can get the hell out of this small town, move to Vegas and get in with the high rollers.

For the miners, they saw a little action. Maybe the Englishman and his geologist will find another mine here, life will go on. The fat gals went back to their trailer homes drunk but happy.

The Englishman and his geologist make plans about the next drilling programme and curse the high-tech stocks. But what the heck, the geeks are so loose with their money, it's all going to get back into the economy one way or another.

"Tell me this though," says the Englishman to the geologist.

"How the heck does Bill keep going?"

"Oh," says the geo, "you know the Vancouver Stock Exchange: one day the penny stock will hit a big hole, the share price will rocket and Bill will cash in his shares or chips, depends on how you see it."

This was the first time I had drilled the Shawnee project which was located near the town of Denio in northern Nevada, and I liked to be on site for such an important occasion. There was only one motel in town, and that's where I and my geologist and the drillers stayed while the work on the project was being undertaken.

As usual I liked to record what I saw, and the above is a reflection of what could be seen in small town Nevada during the bust part of a mining cycle.

19

MINA

1992: Mineral County Nevada

Dry as dust in Nevada, copper prospects from long ago, lingering
remnants of a frontier town on the plains,
and oxide copper in the hills.

Straddling highway US 95 in central Nevada lies the small settlement of Mina. US 95 runs from the junction of I-80 and US 95 at Fernly, and on down to Las Vegas. Mina lies beyond the submarine nuclear weapon storage facility at Henderson and south of Walker Lake whose banks are formed of alluvial terraces that step down to the receding lake showing the water drop over geological and modern time. The next town, Tonopah is 70 miles to the south.

The lowering of the lake level has left boat ramps barely reaching the receding water. Mina is a few miles beyond the timber loadout chute at Luning where the Santa Fe Railroad ran in the early 1900s. The railroad now goes no further than Henderson and is only currently used to ship naval munitions to the coast in California. In the early 1900s and up until the 1950s, Mina hosted a small but vigorous mining community with ore from various mines being shipped from the railroad siding to smelters throughout the West. The defunct railroad timber loadout chute is still standing, but there are only a few single-storey buildings stretched out along the highway. There is not even a casino or a bar with quarter slots.

But in Mina you can park your RV at the Sunrise Valley RV Park, get a room at Sue's Motel and fill your water bowser for your drill rig just along the highway. You can get a burger at the Socorro Burger Bar where they serve Nevada-Mex burgers with, when the wind is blowing in the right direction, a liberal helping of sandy magnesia soda dust from the nearby dry lakes. It's a very small town, but a prospector called Tom Evans lived there and he had, in the past, provided good leads to mineral properties located in the hills and mountains to the east and west of the long Soda Spring Valley. The Soda Spring Valley is flat, one of those places on earth where you can see into tomorrow and beyond. It's located between Pilot Peak to the east of Mina and Thunder Mountain range to the west. Both areas rich in minerals with potential for small and not so small copper mines.

Mina was named after Fermina Sarras who was born in Nicaragua and immigrated to America in 1867. She was a prospector and a remarkable lady, venturing into the Central Nevada desert alone; her hard work and tenacity made her into a highly successful miner and she became known as the Copper Queen.

My business partner Bob and I were looking at an area with the same name; most likely named for Fermina. She had staked a lot of claims in the area in the late 1800s, and as a true entrepreneur, sold them using some of the money to invest in other businesses, the cash flow from which would fund further exploration and prospecting.

We'd been sent details of a copper oxide property located at the east of Mina on Longshot Ridge. The area could be accessed from above the New York Canyon along a rough dirt trail. Bob also had details of another property, a buried porphyry copper orebody, in the flats east of Mina, not far from the canyon.

We drove out to the deposit to where it outcropped in the form of a very small hill in the middle of the otherwise flat valley bottom. Amazingly, beneath the small pinnacle of granite type rock there was known to be a massive copper deposit of some 800 million tonnes – the tonnage defined by drilling. There was a very old shed in which there were thousands of metres of drill core drilled by one of the major mining companies ten or so years earlier. The copper grade was probably too low for economic development at the time of drilling but the copper price was rising, making the deposit interesting.

Just a little west of the area where the copper deposit lay buried were faint traces of an old frontier town. You could just make out the path of Main Street by the lack of sagebrush in a straight line through the desert. Left and right of Main Street were the outlines of collapsed timber framed buildings. Scratching around in one of these, I came across a broken mirror and the remains of what could have been a barber's chair. And then I found an old copper talcum powder tin with a silver top which when polished at home still gleamed in the sunlight. The dry conditions had preserved the collapsed wood and other remnants of the town, as there was no moisture in the dry desert atmosphere to allow rust to form. It was probably deserted in the 1930s.

Many of the mining camps and settlements that sprang up in the western states after the end of the Civil War were temporary. Structures with false fronts posed as grand edifices above shops, hardware stores and barbers. The larger towns had hotels on the second floors of saloons. Most of the accommodations for miners and labourers were tents raised over wooden platforms about 12ft square, with planking on the side up to a couple of feet above the floor. Unfortunately, these were canvas tents and were extremely flammable. Most tents had a pot belly stove in them, so fires were a common occurrence, some caused by drunken miners or

Chinamen passed out from opium, according to local reports. If one of the fires got out of control, it could start to burn the rest of the town. On occasion, a fire would be set by a preacher dismayed at the lack of morals and general heathen ways practised by the miners and whores.

The other property we were looking at was known as Long Shot Ridge and was a copper oxide deposit located in the hills east of the buried porphyry that we had looked at earlier. We were dropped off by Tom, our local prospector, and we arranged to meet back at the Copper Queen site, Bob and I set off to assess the property and do a little prospecting as we went.

As is often the case, we got involved with figuring out the geology of Longshot. There were abundant outcrops of rocks containing copper oxide minerals such as the blue of azurite and the green coating of malachite. That's the benefit of prospecting in a dry desert environment, being able to see the rocks and geology. In other situations you have to dig into the soil cover and strip away vegetation to see the geology. We had a theory that the mineralisation on the ridge would probably extend down in to the valley in a canyon parallel to the road we came up in New York Canyon.

Following signs of mineralisation, we headed to the west along a dry drainage that headed downward to the valley. The gully had sparse vegetation of sagebrush and spindly bunches of cheat grass. The canyon got steeper and we really had to scramble, slipping and sliding on the gravel and small rocks, and there were a couple of spots where we had to slide down smooth limestone slopes. Suddenly, the canyon ended in what would have been a geological fault, some 100ft above the floor of the valley. There was a goat or sheep track on the face of the wall and that seemed to be the only way down. Neither of us was sure if there was time to go back to the top of the canyon, or if we could even get back up those places where we had slid down the rock face.

Following the sheep trail, we passed the point of no return – defined by being able to go down sheer slopes easily enough but with no way of going back up if the path stopped and ended in another sheer cliff. Eventually, we reached the bottom of the crag and walked across the desert in the gathering gloom, glad to see Tom waiting by the core shack.

"Hi, guys, I guess that was quite the adventure. I have been watching you two for half an hour or so through my field glasses and wondering if you were going to make it or if I was going to have to call out the Mountain Rescue to get you out of the gully."

Bob and I looked slightly sheepish knowing we had taken a risk we had not needed to take.

So we thanked Tom for his help, went back to Mina, picked up the hire car and headed down Highway 95 to spend the night in Goldfield.

Both deposits are still there, waiting to be developed.

PART IV
PORTUGAL AND THE EAST

Underground at Gralheira, Portugal

20

THE RUSH FOR LITHIUM

2015 forward: Arizona to Spain to Portugal

The Green Revolution, and my part in the quest for a metal with half the density of water to save the world

In mid-2015, the rush for lithium was gathering pace. All the Canadian junior mining exploration companies were raising money on the back of the anticipated demand for lithium for batteries to power Elon Musk's electric vehicles. Large vehicle manufacturers such as Ford and Volkswagen were rushing to make deals with small exploration companies that had claims with the potential to host the lightest metal. Lithium in its elemental form is soft, silvery and light, with a density about half that of water. It's the lightest metal on the periodic table.

The rush was not just for lithium but also so-called battery metals such as cobalt, nickel, and the old favourite, copper. Encouraged by the flood of money that levitated junior mining stocks in a sea of liquidity that seemed to be pouring from the pockets of speculators, promoters, prospectors and investors alike, including myself, started the search for properties that might contain interesting quantities of lithium. It can be found almost anywhere, including seawater. But as usual, the trick was to find it in sufficient quantities to make it worthwhile extracting.

The stock promoters picked up on the enthusiasm, and as the Green Revolution started turning in earnest, I put together a portfolio of prospective properties that could host the metal. I did a great deal of research using the internet and searching the files of the Arizona Geological Society, and it was fairly easy to identify occurrences and deposits in Arizona. As usual, stockbrokers in the know suddenly became experts on lithium.

"Well, of course you have to have spodumene in the mix."

Or...

"It's way too difficult to treat the micas, petalite and lepidolite, and as for the clay hectorite, forget it."

It's doubtful many of them knew what mica was.

Some of them bothered to find out that a larger proportion of the world's production came from brines pumped from relatively shallow zones and springs beneath the Earth's crust. Nearly all of these producing facilities are located in South America in what is known as the Lithium Triangle made up of an area encompassing parts of Chile, Argentina and Bolivia. All of the deposits there are located beneath salt lakes or *playas* (dry lakes) at high altitude in the Andes. The brines are pumped up from bore holes and piped to large settling ponds. Then the brines containing the lithium salts evaporate in the sunshine (also aided by the high altitude). As the brines dry out, they leave a white crust rich in lithium salts which is harvested and sent for further processing. Most of the processing is done in China which has almost 80% of the world's lithium ion battery manufacturing capacity.

Deep within the granites of Cornwall, there are hot-water brines that contain lithium, but we don't have either the altitude or sunshine to evaporate the brines to harvest the lithium salts. However, work is underway to devise a process to recover the lithium from our brines that does not require high altitude or sunshine!

Living in Arizona at the time and being familiar the rules regarding the acquisition of exploration land in the Western United States, and after a great deal of research, I went out exploring for lithium. Much was being made of the minor brine production from a few wells in the Clayton Valley in southern Nevada. It was easier to raise money on the potential of near term production promised by the easily extractable lithium rich brines. If your project was in the vicinity of producing properties, it became easier still. So dried up old lakes became a primary target.

Arizona was known to host lithium occurrences in various places up and down the state. Close to Wilcox in the south, there is a *playa* with the requisite characteristics to host lithium brines. In fact, at one time several ponds were constructed to harvest potassium salts in Wilcox. The altitude of the *playa* (around 5,000ft) and the desert climate gave it a high priority for exploration.

To the north of the state up in the Ponderosa pine country, during my research I noted several claims were located near Snowflake, a ski village, that ostensibly hosted the light metal. The company that owned the claims had, at one time, staked fifteen mining claims over an area of some 300 acres.

I decided to have a look at these claims as the offices of the company that owned them were very close to where we lived which would make possible negotiations simpler. I had a very nice trip with the dogs, but on inspection of the ground and geology of the claims, it showed that the lithium must have melted with the Snowflake. As is often the case, the claims were part of a scam used to fleece the unwary investor and the 'offices' were an accommodation address in a small strip mall – the company had long gone. The values from the samples I took showed that I was correct: not a trace of lithium.

To the north of Phoenix and beyond the Western-themed town of Wickenburg was the Lucky Mica deposit. It was located at the base of the rugged peak of Vulture Mountain. The area contained typical desert vegetation with the occasional *saguaro* cactus, spiny *cholla*, and creosote bushes. Any disturbance of the surface would remain visible for years in the dry desert climate, and I could see clearly the trenches and cuts in the ground made by the old prospectors as they searched for minerals decades ago. The deposit was discovered and partially developed during the uranium boom of the 1960s for the rubidium content in the rocks. The deposit also contained significant amounts of lithium which was not seen as an economic metal in the sixties. As a radioactive element, rubidium was at a premium during the uranium boom, and is the prevalent mineral at Lucky Mica.

Fifty miles northeast of Lucky Mica and at the base of the Wickenburg Mountains and in the headwaters of the usually dry San Bernardino river bed there are several quarries which were producing phosphate rock up until the 1970s. Geological reports noted high lithium content from production records. These deposits were associated with hard rock pegmatites. The deposits are the result of very slow cooling of magma and consist of the components of granite: mica, feldspar and quartz. The Lucky Mica contained large crystals of mica and spodumene – one of the minerals that contained lithium. It also contained petalite, another lithium-bearing mica.

The country in the area of the San Bernardino wash was pretty rugged and a four-wheel drive was essential to move around. Once I made it down into the broad, hard packed sand river bottom, it was easy to drive up and down carefully as the wash only ran with water in the height of the rainy season.

As I rounded a sharp bend while travelling up the wash, I came across a mine dump and what appeared to be a processing mill made of sheets of corrugated iron. The whole structure was clinging onto the barren side of the river bank rising a hundred feet above the valley floor.

Parking the Jeep, I wandered around the mill building which had been stripped of all the movable equipment except for a crusher embedded into the hillside and probably too heavy to cart away. I estimated the age of the buildings as pre-Second World War or just after. It was difficult to see what it was they were mining for. I went up through the mill and found a track leading off into the hills. Not wishing to leave the Jeep, I went back and found the track leading away from the mill. It could be a little scary out in the desert with most prospectors and some small illegal miners defending what they believed were their claims, and their right to defend the claims by shooting unwary claim-jumpers or just folk that had wandered off the beaten path.

The track led to a small open pit at the bottom of which was an adit (tunnel). Again, there was very little sign of what the old timers were searching for. After a good look around, I found a vein of pegmatite and sampled it along with pieces from previously hand-sorted piles of ore. I later discovered that this was the Red Cloud Mine, and they were mining phosphates used in the production of fertilisers. The pegmatites always contained large crystals of feldspar, quartz and mica so it was fairly easy to sample.

Quite encouraged by what I had seen, I checked with the records office at the Bureau of Land Management and State Land Records to see if the ground was free to claim. The BLM manages the federal government's nearly 700 million acres (2,800,000km^2) of subsurface mineral estate (mineral rights) located beneath federal, state and a few areas of private lands severed from their surface rights.

The assays came back from the lab and they were exceptional, running up to 3.0% lithium more than double the amount needed for economic development. I could not find records of anyone having staked the area either in the BLM or State records, so I went back out a week later. To my dismay, I found several recently placed sets of claim posts over the areas I was looking at. Even more disappointing, I discovered that the claims were staked by the US subsidiary of an Australian company. The Aussies were all over the western US, Canada and Iberia, acquiring ground and raising money to develop the claims.

However, I did a little research and found that the ground and mineral rights at the Lucky Mica, to the west of the Red Cloud were available for acquisition. So I hired a team to stake the claims. I decided on staking twenty claims, each claim encompassing twenty acres. My stakers went off armed with a map I had put together, accurately defining the areas I wanted to acquire. The stakes were wooden posts of a proscribed size. Each post was positioned to define the four corners of the claim, and a stake is also placed in the centre of the claim. Attached to this post was a small screw top plastic bottle into which was placed the location notice that gave the staker the mineral rights to the claim.

Subsequently, the staker, a US citizen would assign the claim to my company. We spent quite a bit of money exploring and sampling the claims and unfortunately the lithium values did not match those of the reports from the Arizona State Geological Archives.

Over the years, throughout Nevada and Arizona, I had found many staking centre posts with tobacco tins nailed to the post with the original claim notice inside: most were the Prince Albert brand. A few of the old claim posts and notices were from the 1930s when a lot of desperate men went west to seek their fortunes by staking a mining claim and trying to work it for the minerals that may have been present. Very few were truly successful, although most managed to scrape up enough product to send a few dollars home and buy supplies for a month or so. A hard life, but you have to think it was better than relying on the government to look after you and your family.

In the centre of the state and close to Prescott is a quarry known as Lyles Deposit. It's on State Route 96 heading west from Kirkland Junction towards Skull Valley and Bagdad. It was the only known hectorite deposit in Arizona, a clay containing lithium. It was being mined by an old timer who could not be bothered to negotiate with anyone for a deal. There was one other known deposit in western US located in the small town of Hector in California.

The old timer's reluctance to deal with anyone was unfortunate as the lithium values in the quarry were spectacular. He was selling the untreated clay to an oil well service company as drilling mud – totally ignoring the lithium value. As it turns out, it wasn't that unusual for miners to ignore the lithium contained in their product; companies mining feldspar in Portugal failed to realise the value of the lithium. There are rumours that they knew about the content but failed to record any income from its add-on value.

Back in the US, the Lucky Mica was now in the hands of a company of which I was a director, and it was drilled with moderate success. Unfortunately, the lithium grades were not encouraging enough to spend further money.

It's not just the western US that hosts lithium deposits; Portugal probably contains Western Europe's largest lithium resources. Having left the US and armed with my knowledge of both the geology of Portugal and the deposits of the US, I applied for an exploration licence in Portugal just south of the headwaters of the Douro River in an area of pegmatites that were known to contain lithium in the correct type of mica.

Unlike the United States, the acquisition of minerals in Portugal was not an easy process, with many layers of bureaucracy to be peeled aside, such as dealing with archaeologists, environmentalists, village committees, the mayor's office of the town nearest the area under application, and the government department that approved the application. Even when approved, the paperwork continued, with a requirement to submit annual reports, cataloguing the work and cost completed on the licence area.

Unfortunately, the Portuguese government was so overwhelmed with applications to explore and mine lithium, the department that handled them imposed a moratorium on new submissions and refused to accept any requests for the exploration. In most Latin countries, the state owns the mineral rights over the entire country and will grant the right to explore for minerals; if found and proven economically viable, they will grant a lease to mine any of the mineral deposits identified. More and more, the power to say yes or no to applications has been devolved to the local mayor's office. In principal a good idea but open to abuse through influence brokering and bribery.

The government was caught between a rock and a hard place as it had been telling voters and the EU how environmentally aware it was. This statement was partially true, as at the time the country was generating a third of its energy from renewable sources, hydro and wind power being the main components. However, it would not take any action to allow for the exploration of lithium. It did this by indefinitely delaying the tender process it had said it would conduct to award the contracts and licences to explore.

To ensure that we were able to talk sensibly about the ground we had applied for, my Portuguese geologist John and I undertook a field trip to the area around the small village of Almendra. As expected, the rock was granite of the correct age, and there was even an abandoned granite quarry in the area. Its presence would help in the application process as the local community would know that mining could bring employment and economic development to the otherwise remote upland moorland area.

However, there was a problem. We decided to complete a couple of traverses across the moor which had been ravaged by wildfire a few years before and exposed the rocky outcrops. Because the fire had cleared the undergrowth and heather, it allowed us to determine the type of granite and if there was the possibility of finding lithium minerals nearby. As we walked across the land following several ancient paths, I noted a couple of embedded boulders with what may have been runes engraved into the surface of the boulder.

Much as I am a fan of history and in particular Celtic history, my heart sank at the sight of these runes carved into the rock. They were probably associated with the rough pattern of large boulders we saw earlier which could have been associated with a place of worship. As such, mining development would not have been permitted in the area. We took photos, and John emailed them to a friend of his who was an archaeologist.

We decided to carry on and drove along a tiny track to a spot overlooking the Côa River. Again, disappointment: the river valley was quite narrow, and 300ft below us on a small level area, a team of archaeologists were working in three areas where the turf had been removed, and we could see people on their hands and knees; downstream was the famous Foz de Côa archaeological site. The Côa Valley has paintings and engravings from the Neolithic and Chalcolithic eras, and from the Iron Age. The archaeologist friend confirmed that the runes in the rock were probably of Celtic origin. This would not bode well for an application to explore in the area even though there was a small disused quarry on the concession area.

Normally, I would have withdrawn the application fearing that there would have been too many environmental, heritage, municipal, EU and government objections. However, the government beat us to it by suspending all applications for licences for lithium exploration. I believe the application is still in place but the company is no longer active.

Hopefully, exploration activity for lithium in Cornwall will again put Kernow in the forefront of the mining world.

21

ARMENIA AND THE ROAD TO AGARAK FROM YEREVAN

2004-5: Armenia

Casinos, loo without a seat, mines that explode,
Soviet-style managers, and a strange hotel

During the early part of 2004 and through 2005, I was the technical consultant to a group that firstly asked me to assess the worth of a copper molybdenum mine in southern Armenia and subsequently to help them manage it.

The mine is situated close to the border between Iran and Armenia, south of the Armenian capital Yerevan.

It is an extraordinary road that runs south, and at the end of the road lies the open cast copper and molybdenum mine next to the small village of Agarak. The border between Iran and Armenia is defined by rusty barbed wire fence and the River Aras, and Russian troops march along the fence patrolling on the Armenian side. No one seems to know why they are there. Perhaps a remnant of the Iron Curtain or a peace keeping force, a result of the war between Armenia and Azerbaijan?

At the beginning of the road is Yerevan, and in between the two, there are 375 kilometres of road in varying stages of degradation that run along the Turkish border, passing to the east of Mount Ararat with its snow covered flanks. The journey normally takes six hours but that can be extended to twelve or more depending on the road conditions. The road traverses high plateaus which reach all the way to Russia. It runs between steep sided wooded valleys, winds its way down into and out of a canyon as spectacular as the Grand one in Arizona and along a disputed international border strewn with landmines.

But this canyon has far more vegetation than the one in Arizona. I could imagine wolves, bears and boar roaming through the heavily wooded slopes, disturbed only by the occasional shelling from the Azerbaijan militia. At one point, the road skirts the border with Azerbaijan for a number of miles, and there are UN signs in several languages warning of the danger of mines and unexploded munitions. Nearing the end of the road before arriving in the town of Meghri, the road climbs out of a steep sided valley, past the copper and gold mines of Kapan and crosses a mountain pass that would have stopped Hannibal.

Unlike most modern highways, the road to Agarak does not start at a specific point but evolves firstly out of the broad boulevards in the centre of the city, passing a grand roundabout with statues, probably heroes of the Revolution or genocide, their identity known only in Armenia. The road then enters a chaos of partially paved streets which lead to the edge of the city. The road proper begins after you have passed beneath a bridge that supports a rusting railway line. If it rains to any extent, the passage beneath the bridge floods and a high clearance vehicle is required to pass onto the next stage.

The boulevards are lined with crumbling buildings and apartment blocks. All are faced with blocks of light pink volcanic tuff. This stone has been used to build and face almost all of the buildings in Armenia between Yerevan and Agarak. It is an ugly and depressing looking stone; it has no character and looks like badly baked biscuit.

However, unlike the outskirts of many European cities, the buildings in Yerevan have not been subjected to the awful scrawling of demented graffiti artists. The youth are too poor to buy spray paint and if caught would probably be flogged or sent to Russia for re-education.

Since the collapse of the Soviet Empire, few buildings seem to have been constructed here. There are some post-Soviet buildings but they are of the usual concrete slab style, most are whitewashed and are usually low rise. Multi-storey buildings requiring a crane of any height are very few and far between. Adding to the bleak character of the city, almost all of the trees were felled for firewood after the collapse of the Soviet Empire.

On the way to the city from the airport and outside the city limits proper, there are a rash of small town Nevada-style casinos, single-storey and with their name outlined in flashing neon lights. They have the common casino names like 'Caesar's Palace', 'the Nugget', 'the Oasis' and so on. I see no Armenian names, no 'Lucky Karen's' or 'The Ararat Palace', 'Ashot's Hide Away', or 'Maxim's Special Rooms'.

On my first visit to Armenia after passing through immigration, I was met at the airport by a man who spoke little English. I must have looked lost and very British as he picked me out of the assembled passengers standing by the luggage carousel.

"Mr Alan, come, come."

He beckoned me to follow, took my case and left with it, so I had no choice but to follow. We went out to a very cold night where a large black limousine-style vehicle with tinted windows waited. My client had told me he would be at the Hotel Yerevan so I assumed that was where I was going.

After a few miles, the strangest thing then happened. We pulled into the parking lot of the Golden Nugget Casino where a deputation of a dozen or so men, some in black insulated puffy coats, and some wearing formal great coats stood in a group. Most had astrakhan hats and very nice shoes. Odd, because the snow was frozen and it was difficult to walk around in anything but solid working boots.

This group included the mine management, the government representative, and a person who claimed to work with my client. My client was seeking to buy the copper and molybdenum mine at Agarak, and these gents would be greatly affected by the purchase. All were introduced and we shook hands, made suitable greeting noises and pleasantries in what I thought was Russian but it may have been Armenian.

I stuck to English, French and Portuguese which seemed to work for, "hello, pleased to meet you."

After the greetings and salutations, I got back into the car and was driven to the Hotel Yerevan where I was expected. The hotel was built in 1926 and is a good example of Soviet architecture with rooms having high ceilings, elongated single-glazed windows that rattle and let in the cold, a grand staircase and an extremely small lift. There are some other good examples of Soviet architecture in Yerevan but these buildings do not extend to the outer reaches of the city.

Leaving the hotel next morning after a briefing from my client, the driver from yesterday (now known as Arman), myself, and a Russian electrician left for the mine. Vasyli the electrician spoke some Spanish as he had been to Cuba to help with the construction of a hospital. After travelling beneath the railway bridge at the edge of the city, we went south for some 50km where the dual carriageway stops and becomes a poorly maintained two-lane highway. Mount Ararat was on our right, where Noah landed after the flood receded. Rumour has it that he had many more animals in the Ark than reported in the Bible, but on landing, the Armenians stole most of them.

Now I started to worry. We had 275km to go and yet we'd slowed to a more moderate pace after the speedy exit from the city. It was now early afternoon and my math determined we would arrive at Agarak or Meghri or even Kapan after dark. I later learned that those first 50km along the road was the good bit and the road deteriorated from there on.

In the flat lands below Mount Ararat there are small lakes where fish are farmed and harvested. Travelling for about another 60km, we suddenly encountered a roundabout, one of three on the journey. It is imperative to take the first exit and travel east up a big hill. If you go straight on the road will take you to one of the enclaves of Azerbaijan that is stuck on the west of Armenia called Nakhitchivan, a product of the 1991 war between Armenia and Azerbaijan.

The road passes through a few towns and villages, up and down some hills, nothing too bad. The road then enters a wide valley with a river that narrows and narrows, and the road climbs and climbs. It's very nice with willow trees lining the river. There are several Byzantine-style churches perched on rocky outcrops along the valley. Hidden in the foothills beyond Zangakatun is a USAID agricultural station (a development and humanitarian agency). Big trucks frequently appear on the wrong side of the road and there are potholes here that are huge. The road climbs out of the valley onto a high plain classified as 'cold steppe'. It is desolate, almost treeless, and flat. Cresting the hill from the valley, we passed through a monument known as the Gates of Goris.

The road is pockmarked with smaller potholes, and there never seemed to be any attempt to repair them; it took all of Arman's skill to avoid the deepest of these.

This high plateau appeared to last for ever and is the steppe that goes on into Russia. On the high plains between Ararat and Goris, the land in winter is bleak and snow covered; spring comes late to the high plains.

There were a couple of farms along the way that straddled the roadway; communes, at one time. They have a rundown, forsaken look with no physical signs of life other than a few scrawny cattle. During April and May, the local peasants move their cattle out of the barns in which they have been held all winter to feed on the newly sprouting grasses.

There was an internal customs station halfway between the start of the plain and the city of Goris. The post is no longer manned, but in the past, documents would have been required to be produced showing permission to travel, identity papers, and if travelling for commercial purpose, Bills of Lading and so on. There is a clean loo, however without a seat, and I couldn't help wondering why sit-down toilets stop east of Athens. But there was hot water and a person can make tea or coffee without having unwanted strange herbs added to the brew. And a steam-operated television. This was actually a small colour TV mounted on an iron pipe which looked like it could carry steam to the TV set, or so I told one of the other employees of my client on a later occasion. He was a very naïve chap and believed me, for a while.

At this point, you are halfway to Agarak. The road keeps going until you reach the regional centre of Goris in another 45 minutes. On the hills above Goris, the road passes another roadside café. The perimeter fence of the car park surrounding the café is made of mortar shells (expended, one hopes). Set apart from the café on a small mound and sited a little way away is another 'rest stop', again with no seat and slightly raised foot-shaped platforms on which to position your feet.

Passing through Goris, which seems to have only one long main street, the road continues on a downhill run to the bottom of a deeply incised valley. Despite my protest, translated from Spanglish to Armenian, the driver took the car out of gear to coast down the steep hill in an attempt to save petrol.

A German architect once lived in Goris in the early 1900s and is supposed to have influenced the style of building here. There are no signs of any buildings that may have been designed at all. Maybe it was she who introduced the light pink biscuit-lava rock cladding. As you leave Goris, on your left and right are strange geologic natural columns that resemble erect penii (ie. more than one penis). They are columns formed as the result of weathering patterns of the volcanic rocks. They are seen in other parts of the world and worshiped in some primitive societies.

At the bottom of the downhill stretch, the road levelled out and the driver put the car back into gear. For 15km or so, the road follows a river valley sloping down to the west and as it reaches a hydroelectric power station, it crosses the Vorotan and goes up hill, sharply.

This is where you realise how steep the trip was down from Goris. If you are unlucky, you will be stuck behind an Iranian 30-tonne lorry carrying a 40-tonne load grinding its way ever upward. Behind it, we were enveloped in diesel fumes and smoke belching from poorly tuned engines using low quality diesel. Even without the trucks, it takes a good half hour to climb out of the valley. The bends in the road are too tight and the wheels of the Iranian trucks tear the tarmac from the surface of the road as they negotiate the bends. On the map, the road appears as a series of snakes writhing in their death throes, curling back and forth. The slow trip allows one the opportunity to be amazed at the density of the woods flanking the hills.

On reaching the top of this near mile high canyon, respite falsely came in the form of a ridge that sits perched between lesser valleys and woodlands. One side of the road is devoid of trees, and there are UN notices in several languages graphically representing exploding mines maiming cattle and people. The other side is a pleasant wooded valley along which the road passes to the east.

Rocks often fall onto the road from small open-backed 15-tonne trucks carrying lumps of limestone for a cement factory. One night travelling back to Yerevan, we hit one of the rocks and were held up for hours as Narek (a different, more qualified driver) armed only with a large spanner and wheel brace managed to straighten out the steering connecting bar and changed the tyre. We made it back to Yerevan with a troubling *thump, thump,* coming from the front of the Volga.

Armenia prides itself on being the first nation to formally adopt Christianity in the early 4th century. Despite periods of autonomy, over the centuries Armenia came under the sway of various empires including Roman, Byzantine, Arab, Persian, and Ottoman. It was incorporated into Russia in 1828 and into the USSR in 1920. Armenian leaders remain preoccupied by the long conflict with Muslim Azerbaijan over Nagorno-Karabakh, a primarily Armenian-populated region, assigned to Soviet Azerbaijan in the 1920s by Moscow.

Armenia and Azerbaijan began fighting over the area in 1988; the struggle escalated after both countries attained independence from the Soviet Union in 1991. By May 1994, when a ceasefire took hold, Armenian forces held not only Nagorno-Karabakh but also a significant portion of Azerbaijan proper.

Armenia, Georgia and Azerbaijan lie on the south slopes of the Caucasus Mountains. Historically, this region has been (and continues to be) a battleground of different cultures and religions.

As the road winds its way south, it becomes the grand trunk road between Iran and all points north of Armenia. The traffic on the road consists of a few modern, large, transcontinental lorries equipped with sleeper cabs and brakes which are needed on the treacherous mountain passes. I mention 'brakes' as several of the Armenian vehicles seem to have lost the concept of stopping at will rather than crashing into the nearest obstacle capable of arresting their progress.

Most of the Armenian trucks going south carry supplies to the large open pit mines at Zangebour and Agarak, also to the underground copper–gold mine at Kapan. The trucks going north carry copper and molybdenum concentrates from the mines to the smelters and to the railhead in Yerevan. Those going south return with such exotic items as steel grinding balls, floatation chemicals and supplies for the mines.

This seems at odds with a modern air-conditioned passenger bus that daily plies between Tehran and Yerevan. I am sure they contain young Dutch and German gap year students. I have actually only noticed these buses going north from Iran.

Eventually, the road reached Kapan and the Kangesour Mining

Complex and the Shahumyan Gold deposit on the south side of the mountains.

On the first trip after the meeting with the interim management of the Agarak mine in the offices of the Zangezur Mining Combine and leaving the Russian electrician behind, Arman and I set off in the tiny Niva Jeep-type vehicle heading south through the pass over the Caucasus mountains to the mine at Agarak.

The pass over the mountain was blocked with drifts of snow 4m deep and so we had to return to Kajaran.

I waited in the car while Arman went back to the offices at the Zangezur Mining Company, came back and said, "We go hotel."

So we headed back down the valley to Kapan. Halfway down the hill we turned off to the right down a steeply inclined lane which was covered in snow. The road crossed a bridge over the river Voghji and we headed back up the other side of the valley on a switchback road.

In the gathering gloom, I could just make out a couple of lights and a long institutional looking two-storey building. There was a long paved area in front of the building that would have accommodated a hundred cars. As there were no other cars in sight, we parked close to a set of wide steps leading to a tall but quite narrow door. As we mounted the steps with Arman carrying my roll-on and I clutching my briefcase containing my laptop, the doors opened a crack and a small, gnome-like man waved us into a dimly lit hall that had a wide staircase leading to the next level.

"*Dobro!*" said the small man whose name was Vortan. "Welcome, come, come."

He had taken my roll-on, and the driver left with a curt, "*zaftra,*" a Russian word that I learned quickly meant 'tomorrow'.

So I followed Vortan into the depths of the hotel or what I was informed later is called the guest house and was in fact a health resort. Vortan had a little English.

"*Inglesi?*" he asked.

"*Da!*" I said.

"Ah you know Davidov? Davidov stay here, you know him, yes?"

I knew no Davidov other than the cigar and aftershave. But I was wrong: Davidov turned out to be a contemporary of mine from the Camborne School of Mines and was manager of the gold mine at Kapan.

I am still not sure if in Soviet times one was sent to the hotel as a reward for services to the state, or if you were ill and needed to recover in the clean mountain air, or if it was punishment. More likely to be one of the first two options as there were amenities in the rooms that probably would not have been in a correctional institution.

I was given a room on the second storey in what I designated the west wing. I had no idea what direction it was, but it seemed like a good name. A narrow strip of threadbare carpet ran down the centre of the corridor, and every twenty feet, doors led off to what I presumed to be other rooms.

About three-quarters of the way down the seemingly endless corridor, Vortan opened a door and ushered me in to one of the rooms. I had the feeling I was the only guest in the hotel. With mime, a little German and some English, Vortan and I got on quite well and we determined that I would have *kŭken* (chicken) and *kartoffel* (potatoes) for dinner, he would provide me with *Piba* (beer), and the ubiquitous small bottle of vodka.

The door of the room opened onto a small hall with a door leading to a room that held a single bed heaped with blankets; next to the bedroom was a 'lounge' with two sixties-style armchairs, a sofa of the same era, a coffee table, and a carpet that was so thin the wooden planks of the floor could be seen through the weft and weave. The walls were painted halfway up in an institutional shade of green and a whitish cream on the next level. The room was cold. There were no curtains and I could see the snow glistening on the mountains across the valley. In the morning, it proved to be a beautiful view. Vortan opened the valves on the large iron radiators which started clunking and thankfully began to emanate heat.

In addition to the bedroom and lounge was the bathroom. Here was a marvellous piece of plumbing: there was no bath or shower *per se*, however there was a shower system integral to the taps on the hand basin. A flexible rubber pipe connected the taps to a normal handheld shower head. All okay, except there was no shower cubicle; there was, however, a drain in the tiled floor. When showering, I made sure the lid was closed on the toilet and the loo paper was placed on a high shelf.

Dinner was brought by Mrs Vortan, with Vortan smiling and asking if all was okay. There was a TV with one channel not worth watching and no internet or mobile phone service, so I took myself off to bed with a book.

Next morning as per earlier instructions, Vortan brought hot water for tea and I used one of my limited supply of Tetley teabags to make a brew. One lump of sugar and a small jug of possibly long life milk were supplied. I skipped the milk after applying the smell test and determined that its long life had probably ended. A few moments later, Vortan brought two fried eggs, limp bacon and some toast. I was very happy with this repast and just as I had finished, my driver arrived. I said farewell to Vortan and we again climbed the steep hill to the mountain pass.

We didn't get far when we came across a queue of trucks laden with goods for Tehran. This prompted Arman to turn around and we drove off back down the mountain. This was a setback as I only had a few days to spend at the mine and wanted to get the job done and return to the sunny climes of Portugal.

Arman made another plan: we would travel back toward Goris but after passing Kapan we would take a small road south along a river valley that led toward the Iranian border. That seemed okay to me. In fact, I was interested to see that the river came from the huge tailings (mine waste) impoundment from the mines of Kapan and supplied the drinking water for the town. An interesting combination but an issue that can be solved with pumps, filters and cyclones to clean the water. The water flowing in the river did not look so clean to me.

As we went on our way, I did notice there were a lot of large potholes in and along the side of the road. Also a lot of the houses and farms along the way looked like they had been razed or at least subject to devastation caused by war. We saw no animals, no sheep, no goats or even donkeys and almost no humans. We were travelling along the heavily disputed border between Azerbaijan and Armenia. Later enquires revealed that this road and the village of Meghri to which we were headed was a huge area of conflict in the 1994 war.

In any event, unburdened by such knowledge at the time, I carried on and we reached the town of Shvanidzor on the Aras River which formed the Iranian border with Armenia. The road from here to Meghri was good in parts. In other places, it had been destroyed either by detonation of landmines or ordnance, and rough passing places had been constructed around these areas. Some of these were 'point of no return' – if you went past this point, there was no way you could go back to where you had come from.

After five miles, we reached the junction of the road that led to Kapan and the snow blocked mountain pass. This was designated the M2, and after four miles travelling east along it (not at all like the M2 in the UK), we reached the turn off to Agarak. The M2 and the road that we came along from Shvanidzor had a railway line running parallel to it, we crossed the line and several sidings to head uphill to the mine administrative buildings. As noted, the Russian Army guarded the border with Iran.

We arrived at the mine around 10am and I was ushered into what appeared to be an anteroom with a door covered in a brass-studded quilted plastic, presumably to muffle any conversation from the other side of the door; a little like a doctor's waiting room but with no magazines. After a few moments, the door opened and in front of me was a table about 5m in length, at the far end of which was another table at right angles, and about 3m in length with only one chair and one person sitting on it. This layout became familiar to me during my time working in former Soviet countries.

The man at the end of the table was Maslov, the Director of the Agarak mining complex. A man of about sixty, Russian, large of stature and with a ruddy face. He spoke, as it seemed to me that all Russians did, in short angry staccato bursts.

I chose a seat nearest the top table and again was at a loss to say anything as there was no translator, my Armenian was still at zero, my Russian had now expanded to *piba*, *nyet* (no), *da* (yes) and vodka, no translation needed. There was another word I had not realised I knew *chai* (tea). Maslov offered *chai* to me, and I replied, "*Da*."

We sat there for a while waiting for tea, no milk, and a little sugar. Maslov talked and I am sure posed questions to me and mentioned my client's name on several occasions. As I had no idea what he was saying, I just shrugged and sipped my tea. Meanwhile, someone had sent for the translator, a local schoolmaster from Meghri who was incredibly nervous when he arrived.

The large open pit mine had been running on a shoestring for several years after the collapse of the Soviet Union and the state had been trying to fund operations along with other different oligarch sources. I have seen operations run on a tight budget before, but this was ridiculous. The baling wire and string approach was taken to the extreme. The mine truck workshop where the small 30-tonne and larger 45-tonne haul trucks were serviced had no doors and the cold wind whistled around the mechanics. The floor of compacted dirt had become infused with engine oil and was slick in the extreme. In the pit, the haul roads were in such a bad state that the trucks when brought in for repairs were coated with thick mud. The mechanics had to scrape the mud from the part they wanted to repair before getting close to it. Of the forty or so trucks on the mine equipment inventory, roughly fifteen were useable at any one time.

The tailings dam was full, and looked ready to breach its banks and spill its contents into the River Aras which would create yet another international incident.

In the mill, the bearings on the huge rotating ball mills that ground the ore were worn out, and the shaft that was supported by the bearings was giving off smoke as the friction between the shaft and bearing built up. The bearing was poorly seated and at each revolution of the mill the shaft lifted the bearing away from the concrete plinth with a loud thump. The floatation machines that separated the ore from the waste had holes in the side of the tank and concentrate was leaking out onto the floor.

Later that afternoon, returning from the first visit to the mine workings, I went back to the board room and Director Maslov asked me, through the translator, "What did you think of the mine and operations?"

Being in a foreign country, by myself, not speaking the language and with limited telecommunications, I gave very careful consideration to my reply. Did I want to deride the boss of this struggling operation in front of his entire management and risk being left at the end of a very long road back to Yerevan?

"Director Maslov," I began, "thank you for the opportunity to tour the mine, the mill and associated facilities. I know that funds have been short over the past few years, however somehow you and your team have managed to keep the operation running and producing concentrate."

Maslov nodded as the translator passed on my words.

The translator looked even more nervous than ever as Maslov asked, "Will you recommend to your client to invest in the mine?"

I side-stepped the question by saying that there would be another consultant coming to examine the finances and any decision to invest would be made on his recommendation. This may not have been true, but honour was satisfied and *chai* and vodka was produced and we drank a few toasts.

About half an hour later, a call came through on the radio telephone from Yerevan where my client was still stationed in the Hotel Yerevan and he very directly asked, "Well, Alan should I buy the mine?"

I was fairly sure no one spoke English but still gave my guarded reply in the negative, finishing with, "Run away and run away fast."

A slight pause ensued on the line and the client said, "Well, I just bought it so we will need to rectify the situation."

Actually, enjoying the challenge and following four years or so of many visits, a lot of shouting, a new translator, a new but second-hand vehicle to drive from Yerevan to the mine and a lot of money spent by the client, we managed to get the mine back into shape and running on a profitable basis.

Eventually, the client sold the mine and a new project was undertaken in Tajikistan.

22

LETTER FROM PORTUGAL

March 2002: Lisbon, Portugal

Introduction to Portuguese cuisine,
first visit to Jales and the Trás-os-Montes

Lisbon, City of Light during World War Two, once known as Casablanca Two, then a city of spies, desperate refugees, secret police, double-dealing wolfram traders, and one-time store of Nazi gold said to have kept Portugal solvent during the post war period.

Lisbon is an intriguing city and I was also here for the gold – not in the vaults of the Banco Espíritu Santo, but located deep in the earth in the north of the country.

For a couple of years, I had been trying to acquire a licence from the Portuguese State to explore for gold. This involved frequent trips across the Atlantic from Arizona. Then from Lisbon, I would drive to the north to the Trás-os-Montes to look at the projects I was trying to acquire for my company. One of the closed mines was at the village of Jales.

When in Lisbon, I usually stayed at the Hotel Diplomatico, a small, well run, three-star hostelry which was close to the places where I needed to do business, such places being the DGEG (the government department that had responsibility for the mineral and energy resources of Portugal), Empresa de Desenvolvimento Mineiro (EDM a semi-autonomous government-run company that invested in and developed the country's mines), the Registry of Companies, and the lawyer's office. They were all centred around the Marques de Pombal *praca* (roundabout) and close to the hotel.

After checking in, I walked down the Avenida Liberdad to have a pre-dinner beer and, as it was Palm Sunday, to check to see if my favourite restaurant the Riberado Douro was open. It was a hot and humid afternoon and I fancied sitting outside sipping on a *Sagres* beer and watching the Germans and Dutch consult their maps in the pre-Easter tourist traffic before partaking of some fresh fish and football. To my horror, the restaurant was closed, not just closed for Palm Sunday, but closed, finished, gone out of business.

I wonder what happened to João the happy waiter who was a member of the Benfica supporters' club. During my visit the previous December, João and I watched Newcastle play Manchester United in a Wednesday night game on satellite TV. His English was good enough for us to chat about the goals, the fouls and the building of Benfica's new stadium. Time passed quickly and pleasantly, the kitchen served delicious fresh seafood, good wholesome food and great service, an unusual combination to find on the road in a foreign country where you can barely manage to say hello.

So, accepting the fact that the Riberado was closed for good, I crossed one of the three roads that form the Avenida Liberdad to a café resting on an island of trees in the flow of the traffic, had a Sagres and read the *FT* and the Lisbon Sunday *Expresso*. The *Expresso* is now supplied in a plastic shopping bag because it's so big. *New York Times* look out, the Sunday *Expresso* of Lisbon is catching you up in sheer mass; it must weigh 2kg. I only needed the real estate pages and could only understand the headlines anyway. I scanned the ads for a place to rent in Oporto, but most apartments and property for sale or rent seemed to be in the Algarve or Lisbon.

The listings are as strange in Portugal as they are in the United States: 'T3+1, 60m2, bom vista' as opposed to '3bdrms, 2ba, dng+gge', whatever that means. 'T3'? Is that third floor or three rooms? And what is '+1'?

I reverted to the glossy magazine, *Casas de Portugal* and the 'ads in English'. It has nice glossy pictures and concise descriptions of the houses for sale. However, the magazine does delight in defining the material that the house is built of, and in most instances the description will read as: 'house of granite', or 'house of schist' that's fine for me as I'm a mining engineer but what would it matter to the ordinary man in the street? Invariably, the descriptions end with some form of the phrase: 'Good ex posure (*sic*) to the sun' and 'nice views. Peaceful area'. I've noticed the French do that a lot as well, ending with the expression, '*Très calm, près d'un petite village*', but also adding '2 mins from hypermart'.

So, whilst the Portuguese couple next to me whack their small child for sucking the mayonnaise squeegee dry and spilling his coke on the floor, and as the Germans signal frantically to the waiter for the *rechnung*, I decide to go back to the hotel, change, and try the Fabrica Real, an old silk factory converted a while ago to a restaurant. It is just up the road from the hotel, near the old tram terminus in Largo da Rato.

Of course it's Palm Sunday. I don't find the Portuguese a particularly religious nation as much as, say, the Greeks or Spanish, but I guess Palm Sunday means that a lot of places close, including the Silk Factory. Now I am hungry, having had miniscule portions of grilled (charred) lamb the night before and a sandwich of suckling pig for lunch in a motorway café. Yes suckling pig sounds good but it should be served hot with the skin crisp and crackling. The motorway version was soggy and full of fat. I left most of it.

Hah, not what you think. I am not a wimp who won't try the local fare. The day before, I had lunch in a small remote village in the Trás-os-Montes region, consisting of a stew composed of partially identifiable pig parts combined with lots of beans, cabbage and a few carrots for colouring. The bits of pig I could identify were knuckles, sausage and liver. However, it was the thin bi-coloured (two parts beige to one part reddish) of really chewy bits that had me fooled. On inquiry, I found these portions to be the ears. Deep fried with lots of potatoes and a sauce that could disguise most things, the ears may have made it, but not boiled in a stew. They had the consistency of ears: chewy with bits of gristle. I don't know what Tyson was thinking of when he took a piece out of Evander's ear – probably he'd never tasted the 'specialty' of Trás-os-Montes.

The café/restaurant is owned by the mayor of Jales, Celestiano, a man of some thirty years of age. He asks several times if I have had enough. I use my limited Portuguese to assure him that the meal was very tasty, however, I was full. True, I had eaten a lot of beans and recognisable parts of the pig. But the pot that the meal was served in was huge and only a third depleted. João the geologist had eaten quite a bit, and Aderito the workman who looked after the store at the project, had eaten heaps. We ordered coffee to signify the end of the meal. Celestiano kept asking if all was well, I assured him that it was *sabor*, which I hoped was close enough in Portuguese for tasty, adding "tasty" in English just in case.

Well, back to Lisbon: the Silk Factory was closed and the only other place within walking and eating distance was the Rodas, snack bar, *restaurante* third class in the Largo do Rato (my translation being place of the wide mouse, which is apparently wrong).

The Rodas snack bar was a family run restaurant owned by Dereira and Olivera (that's what it said on the bill). It must be *Senhor* Olivera who took the money, as none of the waiters were allowed to present the bill. Instead, they go to *Senhor* Olivera, tell him what you've had, he writes it down and presents it to the waiter who presents it to you. You pay the waiter who takes the money to Olivera who makes the change and the waiter brings it back.

There are seven rows of tables which can seat six either side, a couple of tables in the window, and a marble bar where the regulars sit. Desserts and sweets are displayed behind a glass-fronted counter along with a small, tired offering of less than fresh fruit. It's the sort of place where someone living on their own may go to eat in isolation but with the company of others around them. The café is brightly lit and the walls are tiled. Typically, for Portugal, the tiles form murals. Here they are of wheels: wheels with cogs, wheels with spokes of steel, wheels from trams, an art deco effect, heightened or spoiled by the colours. The wheels are acid green, pink, and a nasty brown. The other tiles are white and they give the room an almost sterile feel, like an operating room for the trams that used to stop at the Largo do Rato. Unlike its French or Greek equivalent, there is no pervading smell of Gauloise or frying fish, just a waft of coffee when *Senhor* Olivera fired up the espresso machine.

I ordered *dorada* – not *dorado* – but a white fish with big bones that tasted a little like mackerel: it was delicious, and served quite elegantly on a stainless steel platter accompanied by chips (or if you prefer, French fries), but in Portuguese *batata fritas*, and a salad of thinly sliced carrots and lettuce. Relatively healthy. Being a travelling man, it's important to know how to order the staples of life: *papas fritas*, in Spanish; *batata fritas* in Portuguese; *heuvos fritas*, *vinho branco*, *cervesa* and so on. The waiter was relatively interested in what he was doing; he wore a white shirt and black trousers, the uniform. When he turned and walked to place my order with the kitchen, I noticed a large brown mark in the middle of his back, the result of overzealous or inattentive ironing.

Just after I arrived, an older looking lady entered, quite prim with grey hair, well dressed in a sleeveless dress and a chiffon scarf. She ordered salmon and proceeded to open a paperback book. I glanced more than once to see the title and author. It's Pascal Quignard *La Frontière*. I will have to look that one up. She sat on the opposite side of my row of tables and was immediately engrossed in the book, whether or not this is just a shield from the common populace was hard to tell.

In the window-seats, a black couple canoodled, and the order comes for a Martini. I am amazed to hear a bar call for Martini here. How wrong one can be? It's Martini: 'the right one, the bright one', Martini Bianco, served over lots of ice with lots of soda. I was imagining the gin Martini of James Bond, stirred not shaken. The couple seemed to be having fun. We individuals turned back to the TV, the soccer goes on, or back to the book.

A family of five arrived, granddad, two sisters, one husband and the grandchild. The genes are strong, and the little girl looks like granddad, and the sisters also share the same DNA. It looked like a regular Sunday outing.

Of the regulars at the bar, one was a man of about thirty-five, with lank, greasy, black hair and thick pebble glasses; there was a small, neat man whose feet dangled above the bar rail; and an older man who I thought was the other half of Olivera and Dereira. Later, they are joined by a policeman in blue uniform wearing a gun. He had a beer and a chat with the lads. The football commentators ranted on about a foul, penalty! Goal! The television shouted the score, and I left, paying *Senhor* Olivera personally, and a tip for the waiter with the ironing mark on his back. Perhaps he will pay his laundress a little more to get it right or buy a new iron.

The next night, I opened the sliding doors of the hotel window and looked down on the late rush hour traffic travelling north on Rua Castillo. A crippled beggar hobbled between the cars and buses, his hand extended in supplication to the uninterested motorists. He is mostly ignored. Traffic delays and frustration for the motorist presents an opportunity to work for him. The lights change. The beggar has an innate sense of timing, shuffling back across the road just before the traffic roars off up the Rua Castillho. I decided to wait a while and go back to the Largo Rato and find another restaurant/café, third class and see what I can see.

We acquired the closed gold mine in Jales and planned to relocate from Arizona to Lisbon or Porto, in August.

I wondered what delights were in store for us.

23

JALES AND GRALHEIRA, PORTUGAL

1996: Portugal

There's gold in them thar hills
We acquire the Jales mine, meeting Aderito,
other golden opportunities, festivals,
provisional permission to mine, the Club, cricket, Geothermal energy
defined

The hills of northeast Portugal are known as the Trás-os-Montes, translated from the Portuguese as 'behind' or 'over the mountains'. A remote and somewhat barren land but home to several Roman gold and tin mines. One of these was located in the small village of Jales.

I was first introduced to the Jales Gold Mine during the summer of 1994 when trying to acquire an exploration licence over the mine and surrounding area from the Portuguese government. This was on behalf of a group called Target Europe of which I was a shareholder. The government owned the concession through a company called Empresa de Desenvolvimento Mineiro (EDM) which developed mining projects on behalf of the state. However, they had been told to divest of the project for reasons unknown to us.

Mining activities in Portugal date back to Phoenician times but it was the Romans who realised the great mineral wealth that led to their conquest of the Iberian Peninsula in about 150 BC. Indeed, it was the Romans who recognised the potential of the Jales underground mine in northern Portugal.

While the Romans are believed to have mined at Jales on several underground levels down to about 140m below surface, more recent operators mined the gold-bearing quartz veins down to 620m below surface.

The concession we were trying to acquire was around 11,000 acres in area and contained the Jales Mine, the Gralheira deposit and the huge old Roman open pit working of the Três Minas mine. All were gold mines, and all still having potential to host significant amounts of gold and silver.

After much paperwork, signing of notarised documents, apostillation of translations, paying an accountant and lawyer in Spain and forming a new company, eventually a portion of the original concession was granted to Target and then transferred to Kernow Mining Portugal Lda. The newly formed Portuguese branch of our Vancouver Stock Exchange listed Canadian company – Kernow Resources and Developments Ltd.

The rights we were granted allowed us to explore the area for gold, silver and associated minerals for a period of five years. During that time, we would have to submit progress reports to the government every six months and annually. The reports would outline what we had achieved, how much money was spent on the project and how much we would spend in the next reporting year.

If we were successful and could prove that the project would be economically viable and we could provide an acceptable environmental survey and management plan, we would be granted the right to mine.

The government decided not to grant rights to explore over the portion of the claim that covered the Três Minas mine. This was a prudent move as any attempt to mine Três Minas would have met with huge resistance from archaeologists, heritage societies and preservationists. I was also pleased as the Três Minas workings were incredible, and highlighted how clever and ingenious the Roman miners were, bringing water from rivers in canals to wash the ore, applying rock breaking techniques still in use today, and stabilising the sides of the pits by using tapered slopes and steps cut back into the slopes known as benches. The combined length of the workings is over 2km and in places over 100m deep. All dug by hand between 27BC and 14AD, and later between 193AD and 211AD. The big mystery of Três Minas is, "where did all the waste rock go?"

There are no signs of typical waste dumps nearby or within any sensible distance.

Between 1932 and 1992, the Jales Mine produced 830,000 ounces of gold, averaging 12.9g gold per tonne and nearly three million ounces of silver. This made it one of the largest gold deposits in Europe. The circumstances surrounding the closure were somewhat obscure as no one seemed to know the real cause. Some said it was because the company failed to pay the electricity bill, some that the miners were demanding higher wages, and some that as the mine went deeper the mining conditions became more difficult with too much waste diluting the ore.

The closure was a severe blow to the economy of the village and the district, as the mine employed over 800 men at the time. Most of the mine buildings were still in place along with the headframe of the Santa Barbara shaft, its winding ropes hanging slack and drooping into the winding house.

The tailings from the mill and treatment plant were stored on an unconfined dump. When it rained, which is quite often in northern Portugal, the run off from the dam flowed in gullies on down into the Tinhela river which eventually ran into the Douro River. The tailings dealt a double blow to the environment as during the summer when it was dry the wind whipped the fine dust from the surface and spread its load over the village and country side.

The Tinhela was no stranger to the workings of the gold miners as the Romans used its waters to wash and treat the ore they had taken from the narrow surface veins at Gralheira and the shallow underground works at Jales. Their presence was marked by numerous millstones which were used to grind the ore for further treatment. They were of granite and were now mostly cracked in half across the diameter of the stone. These were partially buried in the ground and also used in the walls of the hedges. There was also a small beehive shaped furnace of great antiquity. It stood 2m in height and about 3m in diameter, and was made of a cement composed of slag and a coke like material. Once, a consulting geologist took a swing at it with his geological pick. Luckily, I stopped him just in time.

The tailings had a minor amount of gold contained in them but on receiving a grant from the EU, the government decided to rehabilitate the dam and cover it with top soil. This was a blessing for the villagers and for us as holders of the exploration concession; it was now in no doubt that we were not responsible for the tailings.

The work on the tailings was funded by the EU and completed by a consortium led by a French company, and for a while the village came to life with the contractor's workmen taking their lunch at the local cafés and staying in lodgings, either in the few available rooms in the village or in the nearby towns of Vila Real and Vila Pouca de Aguiar.

Our plan was not to put the Jales mine back in to production, but to develop and mine the Gralheira deposit which lay just beyond the Jales Mine. The veins from Jales were striking to the west in the same direction as Gralheira.

Many of the old mine buildings were purchased by *Senhor Vegas*, a local opportunist entrepreneur who sold shoes at the local markets. Being a tough old character he was known locally as *Senhor Torgo* the Portuguese word for 'root'. We rented a warehouse or *armazém* from him for many years.

. . .

The Gralheira Deposit

I decided that although the Jales mine was a worthwhile target, we would concentrate on the Gralheira – a new prospect that had been explored and drilled by Rio Tinto Zinc (RTZ) in the 1970s, and had the potential to host as much gold and silver as the old Jales mine. Actually, it was a continuation of the Jales deposit.

Rio did a huge amount of exploration all over the Iberian Peninsula during that time. At Gralheira, RTZ drilled some fifty drill holes and completed a tunnel 350m long of good working dimensions. They were meticulous in their recording of the sampling and geological mapping of the tunnel giving us a great deal of data to work with. After RTZ decided not to pursue any of its projects in Iberia, they passed this to Bureau de Recherches Géologiques et Minières (BRGM) a state-run French geological service who developed the project in conjunction with COGEMA, a French industrial conglomerate involved in mining. They also completed many diamond drill holes, mapped and sampled the tunnel.

The cost of all of this work amounted to many millions of Euros and generated a huge amount of data. The entire drill core from these operations was stored in the warehouses of *Senhor* Vegas.

Originally, some of the more recent drill core was stored in a small *armazém* which had formerly been a garage for *Senhor* Vegas's lorry in which he took his shoes to the local markets. The store was in the village square which had the usual central pillar carved from granite. Next to the *armazém* was *Senhor* Pinto and Aunty Marie's coffee shop, and at the rear, a tiny convenience store. In summer, we would take a break and have a cool Sagres outside the café on rickety tables. The café was very small and in winter provided warmth and hot coffee from the Sambal Espresso machine.

Senhor Pinto had a club foot and spent much of his day carving clogs from chestnut wood. His main product line was miniature clogs that people used as Christmas decorations, key rings, or hung from the rear view mirror of their car. The larger clogs for people to wear were made to order.

Our geologist, Dr João Damiao, was very small man, balding,

with a large hooked nose. His job was to examine and record the mineralisation seen in the core. To ensure he had the best light possible, we placed the core boxes on tables just outside the *armazém*, and João used a very small hand lens to examine the core. People seldom think of Portugal as being cold in winter but Jales in January was freezing with temperatures dropping below zero. Doctor João would pore over the core with his hand lens in the bright sunshine, so cold his hands would shake while holding the rock core in one hand and the lens with the other, trying to control one or other of them. To enhance the visual contrasts of the minerals contained in the core, we would brush it with water. In winter, this would often freeze before we had a chance to examine the core. In winter, João seemed to have a permanent nasal drip hanging from the end of his nose that would eventually gather enough mass and fall onto the core.

Aderito

Aderito was, "a man who can play many instruments," the Portuguese equivalent of a Jack-of-all-trades.

Aderito had been working on the project for several years. A carpenter by trade, he was the guardian of the core and holder of all unwritten knowledge of the Gralheira deposit, as well as holder of the keys (to this very day) of the *armazém* where the entire drill core from the project was held in boxes. He knew them well as he had cut the core in half lengthways for examination by one of the other geologists, and he had also made the core boxes.

The other half of the core was sent away for assay either in Spain or Ireland.

Many people in Portugal speak English or a little French, but in the far north, it was quite common for people not to speak English. Aderito was the first Portuguese I had met by myself in a work situation, and he spoke no English. So with no translator or helpful friend, I had to communicate with him, even though I'd only been in the country for a few weeks. I did have a small, trusty English–

Portuguese dictionary and had learnt a couple of phrases. After a while, Aderito and I developed our own lingua franca, a mixture of Portuguese, Spanish and a few words of English. We got on extremely well and understood each other, but people would ask, "What language are they speaking?"

Getting to know the mine and deposit took up a lot of my time, and for the first couple of weeks I would travel back and forth to the mine from Porto almost daily on one of the most dangerous roads in Portugal. After a while, to avoid this perilous journey, I took up residence in the Hotel Miracorgo in Vila Real which was a fifteen minute drive to site. At this time, Linda was still in the States while I looked for an apartment helped by José Lino, a real estate agent who worked for Remax Portugal.

Travels with Bear

To familiarise myself with the topography and geology of the Gralheira deposit which extended along a length of over 2km, our faithful workman Aderito, myself, and Bear our jet black Labrador-Pit Bull-cross would hike over the surface of the deposit.

The first time Bear came to the mine and village, Linda took him for a walk. Unfortunately, he took a shine to a local chicken and chased it. Linda managed to save the chook from the crushing jaws of, what our vet in the US called, 'not' a Pit Bull-cross. We related this incident to Paulo, one of our geologists, who said that the manager of the former developers of the project for whom he worked had a dog that once killed a village chicken. Apparently, the chief paid a few Escudos to the owner of the chicken, and for several years after that, the chicken-man would come to the village office at regular intervals with a dead chicken and demand recompense. This carried on until the chief kept the dog at home.

We brought Bear with us from the States, having some trepidation when he went through the veterinary check in Lisbon airport as Portugal did not allow American Pit Bulls into the country. Our vet in the US had described him as a Labrador-cross on his travelling papers.

"Hmm," said the vet. "Labrador-cross? Seems like there is a hint of Pit Bull in him."

Bear wagged his tail and licked the vet's hand.

"Sit!" I said, and Bear did so. "Paw!" I said, and Bear offered his right paw and then his left.

"Okay," said the vet. "I can see he is a good dog."

We put Bear and his travelling cage into the back of the rental vehicle and set off for Porto. Twenty kilometres along the road, we stopped in a rest area to let Bear have a pee after the 18-hour plane ride. Bear leapt from the cage, headed to the grass and peed and peed and peed and peed. Two minutes at least. Talk about relief.

Bear was very pleased to see us, and demonstrated this at bedtime by curling up in the lid of Linda's open suitcase, using her clothes as a cushion.

Toward the conclusion

Over the years, we advanced our knowledge of the Gralheira, undertaking geophysics, drilling more holes, taking large samples that were sent to Porto for metallurgical testing, and developing a model to show that the project was economic.

Some of the results were extraordinary: the geophysical survey showed the veins extended to 2,000m below surface; two of the holes we drilled were over 1,000m below surface and there were good gold values at that level!

There were also several exciting moments working on the project; seeing free gold in the drill core from the deep hole intersecting the vein further along the length of the system, allowing us to expand the estimate of gold that might be contained in the veins.

One of these memorable moments was when we took the large 800kg sample of the mineralised rock from the project to the government-testing facility in Porto. Aderito and I had hewn the sample from the roof of the tunnel every fifty metres. We used scaffolding to reach the roof, and chipped away at the hard quartz vein with a compressed air pick, and often a mallet and chisel. Dusty, noisy, hard work. It took a few weeks, and we put the samples in 50-litre plastic drums and had them delivered to the National Laboratory of Energy and Geology (LNEG) in Porto. The man in charge of the facility, Dr Machado Leite, was excited to be working on the project because the entire mining community of Portugal wanted to see mining recommence, and he had laid out a plan to see if we could recover the gold from the rock samples we had collected.

This was to be done in his pilot plant that he had at his laboratory. It was small unit but would achieve what we needed. The work programme included crushing the rock to -10mm then milling it to yet a smaller size, using floatation machines, and then passing the mineralised material over a full size shaking table.

The culmination of several years of effort was realised when after milling and the staged floatation, the shaking table did its work. Several small particles of gold could be seen on the surface of the table with the pyrite and other heavy minerals (zinc and lead). These made their way across the table to the collection point where I gathered the concentrate into a small glass jar. Dr Machado Leite was very excited, as was I. Along with the concentrate we recovered from the floatation machines, this proved that there was gold at Gralheira that could be recovered by conventional means. The tests would now allow us to submit a Mining and Treatment Plan to the government to apply for a Provisional Mining Licence.

We formulated financial models, devised a mining plan, designed a processing plant with the data from LNEG, and calculated the amount of money we would need to raise to put the mine into production. We had approval from all of the multitudinous government departments to commence with the Provisional Mining.

And then...

Circumstances in the financial world severely curtailed our progress.

I had gone to London to meet a financier who had expressed an interest in the project on the very day that Morgan Stanley and the other financial institutions started to collapse.

We were very pragmatic about it and decided we would have lunch and I would fly back to Porto that afternoon ... with no pockets full of dough.

Boticas

Prior to the financial collapse and as we had progressed well at the Jales/Gralheira and to ensure a flow of projects that would keep investor interest high and enable us to raise money, we applied for a new exploration licence to the north of the current Jales site. The area covered another Roman mining operation. Perhaps not as extensive as the one at Três Minas but one that had the same characteristics.

The deposits near the small town of Boticas were known as Pozo Romano and Limarhino, two open pits excavated by the Romans. Pozo Romano was filled with water and had become a fairly large lake and bird sanctuary, so we excluded that from our exploration work.

We applied to the Instituto de Geologico e Minerio and the Mines Department for a Licence to Explore. In respect of 'European transparency', they had to solicit opinions on the advisability of granting such a licence from the many local and regional authorities. The man in charge of our application in the municipality of Boticas was the local architect and planning officer. He asked us to mark the boundaries of the exploration permit on their Plano Developmento Municipal (PDM).

Unfortunately, they did not have any copies available to mark up because their photocopier was broken. So, they had to send the plans to Chaves, 30km away. This happened in early September and they received the copies mid-November. I was invited to Boticas to mark the boundaries on the new copies (for which we paid €96.84). I rushed to Boticas to pay the money and mark the boundaries.

The assistant to the architect in charge of planning applications, already had a file 25cm thick relative to our application, and his secretary had more waiting in the wings.

The boundaries were marked and the plans returned. Foolishly, I thought that I would be able to mark the boundaries there in Boticas but realised that this was a major task as I had to mark up eight copies for submittal. I thought that we might hear from them relatively quickly, perhaps four weeks or so, but feared for the application's welfare when it reached the Department of the North, the Inter-Provincial Roads and Transport Department, the Nature Conservancy Council, and the Archaeological subcommittee on post-Roman development in the Chaves region. Perhaps an exaggeration, but the number of bureaucratic institutions that needed to review our plans for exploration was staggering.

However, the benefit of driving to Boticas to collect and return the plans was that I was able to drive from Boticas to Salto on National Route 311. It is one of the most spectacular roads I have driven on in Europe (and that includes the northern parts of Corsica, the Peloponnese peninsula in Greece and mountainous bits of Austria).

There is grandeur on a large scale when the road climbs out of Boticas onto the spine of the Barroso range of mountains. The country is wild and remote but the road is well surfaced, empty and fun to drive on (in sunshine). I saw only a few villages and all of them had been bypassed by the 'new' road. After thirty minutes of whizzing around tight curves in the Fiat Palio Weekend, I had the impression that Bear – with all four paws clamped to the floor in the back of the car – may need to throw up, or at least pee. So I stopped at one of the bypassed villages and went for a walk. The brown *tourismo* sign on the main road pointed to '*castro*' which usually refers to an ancient village, one that in the past provided accommodation for the workers in a Roman mining operation.

Bear and I began walking up toward the hills, following an ancient track that was paved with granite slabs, some of which had been roughly chiselled with ridges, allowing bullocks' hooves to grip the road. Granite hedges bordered the road with monoliths spaced at metre intervals, and the paving stones clearly bore the ruts from the passing of a million cartwheels.

The weather was mild, the sun shining, and the only sounds were the tinkling of cowbells and the stream channelled into a millrace – a sign that there was a mine here somewhere. Eventually, the track we were following became a full-blown stream where a breach in the millrace had allowed water to flood the pathway.

Not having the Wellington boots to hand, we turned around and headed back to the car where we met an old lady, a veritable crone swathed in black and holding a hazel walking stick, her face complete with hairy wart and very few teeth. She took great pride in telling me that she was 94 years old. In my limited Portuguese, I wished her a good afternoon and asked her a little about the village. It seemed she owned most of it, and it looked as though all but two houses had been built around the time of Christ. The two new houses were owned by her son and grandson, both living in Lisbon. The old houses were of granite blocks, small and stout, tucked into a cleft in the hill. I told her it was beautiful and peaceful here and asked her if there were any Roman mine workings nearby. She launched into a history of the village which I did not fully understand but she told me of several '*cortas*' (open cuts) where there had been mining, and that the old ones had washed the ore here, right next to the mill race. She really knew her stuff.

She bemoaned the fact that her children only came in the summer and that the winters were cold. I eventually bid her goodbye but she carried on talking and pointing things out with her hazel stick. As Bear and I got in the car, she realised we had gone and burst into a high pitched, wailing song and went back toward the village still singing at the top of her voice.

On we went across the high tops, with views for miles and miles. This was where the remnants of Napoleon's army met their demise after their retreat from Porto in 1809. It was easy to see how a commander would be daunted by the mountain ranges of

Portugal and Spain ... not to mention filling out all the forms to cross the border.

It was hard duty, even for Bear, as we drove along the contours of the huge granite mountains back down toward Braga and on to Porto.

The second summer we were in Portugal it was hot, 36°C hot; it was even hotter in the hinterland where the temperatures rose to over 40°C several times during August.

No one works in Portugal in August.

Other golden opportunities

We also looked at several more gold prospects, acquiring two in the Alentejo at Barrancos and Alandroal, and one just outside Porto which also had a past producing antimony mine within the boundaries of the Exploration Licence. They were all fascinating.

Barrancos is on the border with Spain where farmers raised the famous *Pata Negra* pigs for Iberian ham, also the only place in Portugal where the bull is killed in the bullfight, and the bullring is manufactured with barriers and gates in the main square. It is close to the medieval Castle of Noudar with a lone guardian who would magically appear during a visit like a wraith from the dungeons that were next to the castle bakery. For a very small fee, he would guide you around the three remaining walls and castle keep, pointing out where there was a shaft that led down to the river, supplying water for the castle. The castle and surrounding houses were abandoned in the 19th century and all moved to Barrancos.

The Barrancos concession had it all: an abandoned copper mine from the 1930s, workings for gold and copper on the edge of the town from the 1950s, and Roman workings that had tunnels from the time of Emperor Augustus (circa 14 AD). The pits from the Romans provided excellent assays for gold but had no extent.

Another project, Alandroal, included the Miguel Vacas open pit mine that had produced in the past and had plenty of potential but did not provide any encouragement after drilling several holes.

Closer to Porto was Alto Sobrido, again covering an area mined by the Romans for gold, and at the turn of the 19th century, it was mined for antimony. Some of the remaining engineering work from the 1800s was beautiful to behold – an inclined shaft plunging down at an angle of 30°, some 300m in depth, 4m in diameter and brick-lined. Parts of it had collapsed, but there was access to the old workings from other tunnels.

One day, my geologist Paulo and I were exploring the old Roman tunnels and workings at the Banjas deposit, part of the Alto Sobrido complex. The tunnels and shafts were very small but there were reports of people finding small gold nuggets and flakes in the black graphite seams in the stopes.

We went along the flat tunnel which was running with water. Paulo climbed a very, very old ladder up a raise then along a horizontal sub-level, up another small raise, and then to a branch tunnel that led to an inclined stope, with me following behind. The stope had probably not seen any human life for millennia. Lying on our sides with the stope that was only 90cm high, we started to hack at the black reef. I stopped and thought for a moment. No one knew where we were: if Paulo passed out or was injured, I would never be able to find my way back to the main tunnel. There was no support for the roof of this opening made hundreds of years ago.

For probably the only time in my entire career, I felt vulnerable, in fact, scared.

I called a halt to the digging and we went back to surface with a few two-kilo sacks of the black reef. Later, after panning, we recovered about 20g of gold.

Festivals and Saints Days

The Jales mine village, Campo de Jales, had a market on the 18th and 19th of every month. Travelling vendors would set up open-fronted stalls with tarpaulin covers and rickety tables along the side of the road leading from the village square to the mine site. They sold shoes, clothes, linens, pots and pans, wicker baskets, umbrellas, and an assortment of goods from Hong Kong and China – just about everything you need for everyday life in the country. Oddly, there was little produce for sale. Perhaps the country folk had no need for it, as they probably grew their own. I realised that this event was directly analogous to a travelling department store. Perhaps not as salubrious as John Lewis or as well-equipped as Selfridges, but probably as effective in supplying the local needs.

The event also represented a grand social occasion, with the cafés full of husbands taking a coffee with Croft brandy while waiting for wives to finish the shopping.

Our *Senhor* Torgo was always in attendance with his shoe wagon even though his warehouse was only a couple of hundred metres away.

The vendors travelled from town to town throughout the week, setting up their stalls early in the morning and packing up in the early afternoon. I suspect the *festa* has been taking place on the 18th and 19th of the month since the Middle Ages. It did rain on occasion, and the vendors shut up shop at 12.00 noon. One February it snowed, and the village was cut off from the main roads – one of the few times that the market didn't take place.

During the second weekend in September, we saw the celebration of the mother of all *festas*. It took place in Ponte de Lima, some 80km north of Porto. The celebration is known locally as *Ferias Novas*, 'new fair', with its origin in the 12th century. I wondered what the old fair was.

It lasts for three or four days and has a medieval flavour to it. People come from miles around to sell cattle, horses, dogs and sheep, Chinese junk (which had come a long way), basket work, locally produced honey, wine, herbs, lace and handmade leatherwork, including extremely uncomfortable looking saddles, bridles and kit for horses. The *ponte* or bridge at Ponte de Lima spans the Lima River and is of Roman origin; you can still see the masons' marks or signatures on the key stones supporting the arches.

The river is quite wide and has large shingle banks on its south side. To the west of the bridge, the banks were covered with stalls selling the hardware; the banks to the east of the bridge are given over mostly to the sale of the livestock and rural produce. Carnival rides of all description line the banks of the river further west, and are complete with amplifiers and speakers that pump out rap, hip hop, country and western, and of course *fado* (a traditional musical genre, not unlike a torch song) to attract their customers.

It hadn't rained for more than a fortnight and the day started out in brilliant sunshine, but at 1pm the heavens opened and it poured.

A blessing to the inscrutable sellers of Chinese merchandise which can no longer be classified as 'junk' because barkers with handheld megaphones contested the noise of the carnival rides shouting,

"*Guarda chuvas, dois por cinco euros!*" (Umbrellas, two for €5).

I'd given up trying to convert Euros to US$ due to the extreme currency fluctuations. In any event, *dois pora cinco euros*, is very, very cheap, and the sellers couldn't keep up with demand. The pavements were littered with the tubular plastic covers in which the umbrellas were sold. The rain came in intermittent bursts of ferocious intensity. One moment, all were walking with their brollies furled, the next, after a few spatters of rain on the awnings of the vendors' stalls, it started to pour and there was a collective raising of newly purchased *guarda chuvas*, much poking of people's eyes and much good natured hilarity as those without *guarda chuvas* rushed to the nearest vendor and handed over their €5.

No serious *festa* would be complete without its parade, and the parade at Ponte da Lima was remarkable, out-doing those of São João, São Bartholomeu and Saint George. It started, as usual, an hour late with the ubiquitous fireworks and loud explosions. Bear was already a shivering jelly, not liking the attention he received from children, sheep, gypsies, old men with cloth caps and long sticks (farmers), and not understanding that the umbrella sellers were not shouting at him. Eventually, we found an elevated (and quieter) spot from which to watch the parade. Bear dived into a small hedge of pyracantha and made himself a nest from which he refused to budge until hauled out to return to the car when the parade was ending.

Probably just as well, because the noise was astounding. The parade started somewhere to the south and filed into the main street, went up one side of the road, down the other, and passed on to the town centre. This routing allowed competing bands consisting solely of very large drums to out pound each other in a cacophony of noise as they passed on the street. These are no ordinary drum bands as they consisted of a group of six to eight drums. Some were 1.5m diameter drums, some were 'war' drums, all being beaten at maximum intensity by youths with energy to spare. The noise was deafening. Bear dug deeper into his nest and continued to look worried.

Preceding the drums, there were carnival floats pulled by tractors decorated with representations of seahorses, people washing clothes in half barrels, forging horse shoes with a real fire, a tableau of a natural spring complete with nymphs and a real granite fountain, hunters perched in trees that were mounted on trailers, people wielding sticks to 'flail' corn, and people trampling grapes in a real wine tub. All in all a complete representation of the country life of northern Portugal, mobilised and passing before your very eyes.

Other memorable *festas* included Día de Santa Bárbara at the tiny church close to Aderito's village of Alfarela and the celebration of *Dos Milagres* (two miracles), when cattle, donkeys, goats and sheep with dogs are herded along the narrow lanes to the small chapel of Saint George just outside the village to be blessed. Nearby, at Vila Pouca de Aguiar was the Fair of Onions and Goats, and the celebration of São Martinho was held in early November with chestnuts and *sardinhas assadas* (grilled sardines) at Aderito's village. In Porto, we had the celebration of the feast of São Bartholomeu where the local faithful manufacture a huge variety of paper clothes and parade beside the River Douro to reach the sea at

Foz, then run and jump into the water, washing away the paper clothes along with their sins.

São João: this was a huge celebration with a fair that had candy floss, merry-go-rounds and food stalls on the edge of the River Douro. People would promenade around their neighbourhoods with plastic hammers that squeaked when hit on the head of a passer-by. Some more traditional folk carried 50cm stalks of garlic with the flower intact. These would also be used as a club to strike passers-by. The São João festival is held on 24th June, although it really gets started the evening before and lasts until dawn of the 25th. It's also the custom to launch paper lanterns that are naphtha flame-propelled and float up in the night sky, almost a conglomeration of small moons rising over the Douro with the boats jostling on the river to get in position for the midnight fireworks.

One could almost feel the trepidation of those owners of the centuries old Port wine warehouses on the Gaia side of the river.

The Club (Oporto Cricket and Lawn Tennis Club)

When I was first in Porto by myself, it was a pretty lonely existence. I was looking for rented accommodation and worked with my Portuguese estate agent José Lino. He told me about what he and most Portuguese called 'The British Club' or *Club Inglese*. In fact, it was the Oporto Cricket and Lawn Tennis Club which was to become a central feature of our stay in Portugal.

The Club was populated mostly by English expats some on temporary assignment and those whose families had been in Portugal for generations. A few well known Portuguese lawyers and professionals were members, too. Most of the established families were involved in the wine trade, or as we know it, Port. Others were school teachers, and several were in the shoe business or textile trade. They were an exceptional group of people, interesting and interested, and heavily involved with committees, captaining the cricket team, and so on. They were amazed to hear there was: a) gold in Portugal, and b) that an Englishman should forsake the

Americas and Cornwall to seek the yellow metal in the Trás-os-Montes.

There were a few special people who took us in to celebrate Christmas with their family. I also had a great business partner, Tim Chambers, who had worked on the periphery of the mining industry supplying specialist clays to a company based in the UK. He was also President of the Club for a while.

The Club had several clay tennis courts, a marvellous cricket pitch, a splendid clubhouse with bar and restaurant. The building was reminiscent of some of the colonial clubs we had frequented in the past. We quickly got involved, attending all of the social events, playing for the cricket team, competing in the tennis tournaments, and after a couple of years, Linda became the Honorary Secretary, a position of great power and influence ... and very hard work.

We had a lot of fun at the Club, practising Scottish country dancing for the annual Saint Andrew's Ball, were we danced until dawn; playing Father Christmas at the Ladies Guild Christmas Bazaar; celebrating the Queen's Birthday; the ball to mark the 150th anniversary of the Club; Trafalgar Day; and singing to the families as an impromptu choir gathered for the Christmas lunch.

A hot property – Geothermal Energy

In 2008, the financial crisis was a severe setback in our financing for the Jales—Gralheira project (the collapse of Northern Rock Building Society, Bradford & Bingley, and the Bank of Scotland where investors and savers were in grave danger of losing their life savings). It also hit Europe, and Portugal and Greece were probably the worst hit.

We had launched a programme to identify and develop a resource of geothermal energy close to the town of Chaves. We were told that financing could be obtained in the current market to finance geothermal projects. This was a result of the interest generated in geothermal energy for a brief moment on the Junior Mining Exchanges.

Kernow, in conjunction with the company that acquired us, developed a resource that would generate 20MW (megawatts) of energy over a period of twenty years: enough to power a small town like Chaves. Geophysics enabled us to measure the resistivity of the ground at great depth which further allowed us to calculate the amount of hot water at depth. We knew there was hot water at surface as there was a spa in the centre of the town, dating from the Roman period.

But once again, local politics got in the way. The consultant to the Mayor thought that the spa would run dry if we tampered with the aquifer. So after ten years of struggling with bureaucracy, we decided to move back to Scottsdale. Fortunately, I was offered a job there by a company of which I had earlier been a director for several years.

But this was not the end of the story. As they say, *it ain't over 'til the lady of generous proportions sings.*

The resource is still there and someone will develop it.

24

DUSHANBE TO MOSCOW VIA NOVGOROD

2004: Tajikistan

Homemade vodka over the Pamir Mountains with a wrestler, an unscheduled stop with Tajik Air, the mine sorted

In order to ensure we had sufficient funds to keep Kernow going and to enjoy life in Portugal, I consulted to various companies in the specialist minerals industry, antimony and wolfram being two minerals in that category. The Anzob antimony mine is close to the border between Tajikistan and Uzbekistan, nestled in a steep-sided valley of the Pamir Mountains, and the northern side is a subset of the Himalayas. At one time, Tajikistan was part of the Soviet Union, and after the collapse of the USSR, ownership of the mine passed to the state.

I was assessing the mine and treatment facilities, and had spent three days completing due diligence and analysing the mine's potential for our client. My colleague, Bryce, a shrewd Scot with a background in accounting for several very large mines, was checking the financial status of the complex.

The mine was reached by a road that started in Dushanbe as a paved highway, then headed up over a 3,200m high pass on a dirt road in the middle of the Pamir Mountains, and finally degenerated into a series of potholes connected by tarmac leading to the mine site. In 2011, the Chinese drove a tunnel under the pass which made the journey a little less perilous, but for years there was no lighting and the road surface was unmade. Skilled lorry drivers negotiated the trail using the technique of going from pothole ridge to pothole ridge and seeking out the less spine-jerking path.

It was a successful trip, and our minder, Ali Khan, an ex-commando from the Tajik army, had ushered us through immigration and customs with no fuss at all. This was good, as I was carrying 500g lump of antimony ore in my carry-on that I wanted to have assayed in Europe. From past experience, I knew that customs' officers do not like lumps of dense rock showing up on their X-ray machines, so I was glad to have Ali Khan with us.

We boarded our Tajik Air 737 flight to Moscow. We had been booked in business class, hoping to avoid the proletariat, but Tajik Air Business Class was a bit like the BA Euro Traveller section where the middle seat is folded down and you are served with drinks first and a slightly better meal, but not much else. Bryce sat across the aisle, and there was an empty seat next to me. Seated by the window was a really rough-looking character with a shaven skull and of muscular proportions. I suspect he just took the seat and the crew were not going to ask him to move.

In any event, he was friendly enough, grinning and nodding at me every time I glanced in his direction. The stewardess spoke a little English and not much Russian as she and the plane were on hire from a Czechoslovakian-based charter airline. Between us, we established that my seat companion was a wrestler of some renown on his way to compete in Moscow.

About an hour into the flight, he reached under the seat between us and pulled forth a large canvas bag. After a great deal of unwrapping and grinning at me, he produced what was possibly cake and probably a lump of meat. He laid this repast out on the seat top between us and began to pull pieces of meat from the lump and stuff portions of the cake-like substance into his mouth.

During this process, he would offer me a piece of cake/bread or a lump of meat. I managed to decline the first few offers but he became more instant and a little aggressive. He had a couple of words of English, "Eat, good, yes."

I used all of the ways I could think to decline his offer, mostly by miming actions, shaking my head, rubbing my tummy indicating I was not hungry or that I was sick. I tried to deflect his attention by indicating that he should offer the repast to Bryce who studiously ignored us. The wrestler then reached into the bag and brought out a bottle of vodka. He took a swig from the bottle and then thrust it at me. Straight vodka from a dubious looking container was not my idea of fun. I sought to appease him by asking the stewardess for a glass of Coke into which I poured a small amount of the clear liquid. Ivan the wrestler was now happy, and we toasted each other with cheers and whatever the Tajik for 'cheers' is. After a while and a fifth of the vodka, he fell asleep, and I had my very nice airline lunch brought by the stewardess on a plastic tray.

The tray contained a starter, main course, and dessert. Each course wrapped individually, served with cutlery and wine of your choice. The starter was fresh figs with yoghurt; the main course cold cuts with salad (not to be eaten – who knows what it had been washed in); and dessert was chocolate biscuits and a small bar of chocolate. The tea and coffee were served from the trolley.

The flight remained uneventful until the stewardess came on the PA and said that there was bad weather in Moscow and we were being diverted to Nizhny Novgorod where we would wait until the weather cleared. My first reaction was panic because I was supposed to board the next leg of my flight to Frankfurt within two hours of the scheduled landing. Bryce, who was overnighting in Moscow, was unconcerned and told me that the city was on the Volga and that the Vikings had sailed there in longboats. Apparently, it was not uncommon for the flight to land there to refuel, or for the crew, including the pilot to come through the cabin asking for funds to pay for the refuelling.

In any event, we landed, were refuelled and took off again within the hour. It turns out that the unscheduled stop was very close to the Domodedovo Airport in Moscow where the weather was fine. After disembarking, and with no minder to guide me, I had to push my way through the crowds. I hurried through customs and passed into a totally empty transit lounge. My carry-on was subject to a scan, and of course the lump of antimony was detected and confiscated with much finger-wagging and scolding from the stern-featured lady security guard. I escaped, found my gate, rushed to the plane and boarded just before the cabin door closed.

The Lufthansa crew were a very welcome sight, offering G&Ts and comfortable seats with no wrestlers in sight. The flight to Frankfurt was surprisingly short – it's only 1,200km to Moscow from the Polish border and 2½ hours from Domodedovo to Frankfurt – and as far as I could see, quite flat. I could understand why an aggressor in the past may have thought they could quickly capture the centre of the Soviet empire.

As my client decided to buy the mine, I travelled back to Anzob and Dushanbe several times, and I helped it reach economic sustainability, despite initial resistance from the local staff which was the result of an internal war going on between new Armenian management, the old Russian technical staff, and the existing Tajik management.

It took a Cornishman to sort them out.

PART V
RAMBLINGS

Back in Cornwall with Max and Minnie

25

DON'T GET SICK

All over the world…

*Greek dentist, Tajik surgeon, Armenian ambulance,
a really good doctor in Papua New Guinea*

The Ok Tedi Mine, Western Province, Papua New Guinea 1985

One of the joys of living in the mining town of Tabubil that served the giant Ok Tedi gold mine on the edge of the remote Star Mountains in Papua New Guinea (aka PNG) was bush walking.

I had been appointed by the PNG government as the resident Inspector of Mines to monitor the Government's 20% interest in the huge mining project, and ensure Health & Safety procedures were followed correctly.

Bush walking was mostly done on Sundays as everyone, except for myself and the few other government employees, worked a six-day week. The small band of explorers included Linda and me, the mining company doctor Paul and his wife Jane, and occasionally a one-legged veteran from Rhodesia and his wife. We had several favourite walks which almost always entailed picking one's way up small boulder strewn watercourses that became streams and often ended in waterfalls with a pool suitable for swimming. Alternatively, we would walk along tracks that led to native villages. These were mostly abandoned as the locals, being largely nomadic, would farm an area and then move on.

Off-piste could be a challenge; faint footpaths were festooned with lawyer vines – also known as 'barbwire vines' or 'wait a bit vines' – that would snag and rip flesh from a hand, as well as razor-sharp pampas-like grasses that could inflict deep cuts. It was, of course, very hot and extremely humid, and any cut was a worry as they could easily become infected by strange jungle diseases.

Dr Paul was an Englishman from Essex transformed into an Australian. At one time, he'd been a flying doctor in the Northern Territories based in Darwin. He was very fit and could easily beat me at squash, but I held my own on the tennis court. This sounds quite civilised to have tennis and squash courts in such a remote location, but we were a long way from civilisation with very few other leisure facilities. Tabubil could only be reached by air from Port Moresby on a Dash-8 dual prop which held twenty-four passengers, sometimes happy and sometimes sad, depending on whether they were coming to or leaving the mine site. There were also small single prop planes that carried vegetables as well as people in from the Highland villages such as Mount Hagen and Wapenamanda, and there was the road to Kiunga, the river port on the Fly River.

On one occasion, I was flying from the bush airstrip at Mount Kare to Tabubil on a potato run in a very small Cessna prop plane. Fifteen minutes into the flight, and after having passed through some very thick cloud, the pilot turned to me and asked, "Any idea where we are, mate?"

He handed me the aeronautical chart of the area with comforting notations such as 'maximum elevation believed not to exceed 12,000ft', or areas in white with the notice 'no data available for this area'.

I managed to locate us and told the pilot to head south to the Hindenburg Wall which was just about visible. The wall, a cliff with a sheer drop of 3,000ft, was very close to Tabubil and so we headed south.

I said to the pilot, "That was close! We could have flown into one of those white areas, got lost and ended up as long pig and chips."

I was referring to the sometime cannibal native tradition of eating humans, also known as 'long pig'.

Most of the pilots were ex-Australian Airforce, and most were pretty competent. The Australian Vietnam vets were often helicopter pilots and some were quite strange, with a penchant for performing 'dog fight' aeronautics over the jungle airstrips.

Many of the mine's supplies came by river on barges from Port Moresby to Kiunga which was 110 miles downstream from Tabubil. To reach Kiunga, you travelled along an unpaved and dangerous road that connected it to Tabubil. Supply lorries coming from Kiunga took up most of the road's breadth as it was essentially single-track. The edges of the road would crumble if the fully loaded lorry got to near the edges, and several lorries had tumbled down into the Ok Tedi river. The empty lorries coming back from the mine hurtled down the road, taking little notice of trucks or cars in their way.

From Kiunga, the highest navigable point of the Fly River and 400 winding, oxbow-laked river miles from the mouth, the river reached the Gulf of Papua and the Coral Sea. A little south of the wide mouth was Daru Island, with a small missionary station, and the local bakery staffed by a lady from Aberfeldy, Scotland, the village we had just left to come to PNG.

Daru is 247 nautical miles from Port Moresby where all of the supplies for the Ok Tedi gold mine were transhipped. The mine was perched at 6,600ft above sea level on Mount Fubilan, high in the tropical rain forest.

Tabubil was constructed solely to house mine-workers, with 4,000 inhabitants or thereabouts, so there was a constant need for a resourceful doc who knew how to operate in remote locations.

Dr Paul was a great fellow and could drink most normal people under the table. However, we were anything but normal. Saturday night Tabubil social occasions involved quite a lot of drinking and tended to be lengthy. Hangovers were frequent and anyone who thought that they would get any sympathy from Dr Paul was sadly mistaken. Minor ailments were also treated with contempt. Dr Paul's mantra to all and sundry was:

"Don't get sick. I'm all you have to keep you alive."

As I said, bush walking could be quite hazardous: the jungle was thick and steamy, the paths were generally muddy and slippery, and the stream beds were ankle breaking territory. But the water was cool, and in a couple of places we could slide over large boulders into clear, deep pools. There were some nasty microbes in the water which Paul would tell us about after the fact, along with mosquitos and an extraordinary number of leeches which seemed to have a knack of attaching themselves to the most sensitive areas of one's anatomy, having crawled up the leg to reach the nether regions. To get rid of them, the good old lighted cigarette-end touched on the back of the little buggers seemed to do the trick. For the non-smokers, salt worked just as well.

On one walk, Paul fell and gashed his knee with his *panga* (machete), stitching up the resultant wound with his first aid kit. One had to have a *panga* to chop away at the vines and vegetation *a là* the hero in a Tarzan movie.

On another walk, I fell and twisted my ankle which began to swell immediately. Jane ripped her blouse in half to provide me with a bandage.

To me, the most memorable event was being bitten by a spider on my finger. It hurt like hell and I received zero sympathy. A couple of days later, the skin around the bite started to die and Paul had to treat it with some strange potion which caused almost as much pain as the bite itself.

A few of the paths were used by Nationals coming into Tabubil to purchase western food or to sell bush produce such as *choko, taro* and other unfamiliar veggies. Occasionally, these paths would lead the Nationals into the open pit mine where 90-tonne trucks were rumbling down the mine roads. In the early days of the mine, it was not unusual to see a native Papuan with his arrows and spears, proudly sporting a penis gourd and leaves covering his rear parts, walking down the mine road to the town. Often, his wife would be walking behind him carrying a baby (or piglet) in a *bilum*, a bag similar to a string vest woven from vines or string, and variously enhanced with small pieces of fur from small bush animals.

Dr Paul and the buxom nurse Shelia would also treat and provide health care to the Nationals in the surrounding villages, and through their sterling efforts, the infant mortality rate dropped by over 60% in the first three years of the surgery being established. Even though *don't get sick* was his mantra, he could and would treat you with utmost skill if you were ill.

On a small island in the Cyclades, Greece 1981

Dr Yiorgi and his partner Nico were a gay couple who lived on the island at the same time as our two year stint in the local barite mine. Yiorgi treated me for a severely strained back and, after a later kitchen accident, stitched up a knife wound in my finger without anaesthetic. The wound got infected, and as antibiotics didn't seem to be available to cure it, Yiorgi would squeeze out the infection on a daily basis, which called for a healthy dose of *ouzo* before and after treatment.

Yiorgi was a good doctor, and I'm sure the other medical fellow on the island, the dentist, was good in his own way, but his equipment was antiquated, and the *don't get sick* rule definitely applied to him.

The dentist's office was on the second floor of a building, the ground floor being a café. The atmosphere from the café rose on the air and up the stairs to the dentist's chamber. In the treatment room, the aroma was a mixture of Greek coffee, cigarette smoke and anaesthetic. It was also right on the harbour front which was thronged with tourists in the summer.

My dentist was young, recently qualified, and had inherited the antiquated dental equipment from the prior practitioner. All the people at the mine assured me that the new dentist was competent and inexpensive. The alternative was to fly into Athens or take the ferry to Siros and be treated by a total stranger instead of someone who was at least known to the mine personnel.

I should have guessed that this was not going to be a lot of fun when mounting the wooden stairs to the torture chamber, I could hear muffled moans.

"Probably the people in the café," I said to myself.

Nevertheless, I kept going and entered a large room with a wooden floor that faced the harbour. There was no receptionist or waiting room and the dentist's chair was bolted to the floor in the middle of the room. The young-looking dentist told me to sit in a chair in the corner and wait while he finished with the patient in the chair. At least that's what I thought he said, because my Greek was not too special.

While waiting, I looked around, and on a glass-topped side table I could see grubby-looking plaster casts of teeth and partially completed dentures. Almost a Frankenstein dental lab.

The dentist finished with the patient and called me forward to a chair that could have served as a prop in a cowboy Western movie. Next to the chair was a pedal-powered dental drill with many cantilevered arms and pulleys, all connected with wires from the pedal to the drill bit. At least he had a sterilising cabinet which looked somewhat like a small toasting oven. There was no nurse or assistant. The dentist spoke some English, and I explained that I had lost a filling and needed to have it replaced.

Completing all the normal dentist pre-ops, he then selected a drill bit, put it in the jaws of the drill, located the tip over the offending tooth, and then began to pedal. Immediately, I began to feel pain and made appropriate noises hoping he would stop but he just pedalled faster which at least focused the pain.

Soon, the dentist recognised that this was not going well and decided that the cavity was sufficiently enlarged, so began to make up a splodge of amalgam on a glass plate which was then pushed into the hole. He stood back smiled and motioned me to leave the chair and go to the desk. I was going to pay and asked in Greek how much I owed him. He smiled and said, *"Plirónei i mitéra,"* which translated as 'mother pays', a common expression on the island because a lot of things were paid for by the mine, and it seems as though we had dental cover, too.

The filling lasted until I went to the dentist when on leave in Camborne six months later.

In sight of Mount Ararat, Armenia, October 2005

Thank the Lord that the Russian-made Volga is a very sturdy car, probably the equivalent to a Mercedes but made with steel plate in the appropriate places. The robust nature of the car proved to be my saviour during a routine journey when travelling to the mine site.

The journey became far less than routine when our driver decided to swerve into the path of an oncoming cement truck. He performed this foolish manoeuvre on the road to the Agarak copper mine which lies close to the Iranian border. The road runs along the shores of Lake Ararat in the shadow of Mount Ararat, the peak of which was covered with snow and is where Noah's Ark is supposed to have struck ground after the flood.

Noah probably never contemplated that his ark would be brought to a crashing halt and pushed backwards for a hundred metres into a shallow ditch on the side of the road by a very large cement truck: the fate of our Volga. I was in the front seat and turned around to speak to Karen, my minder and translator. He was a strapping lad, always dressed in a black leather jacket and formal black trousers, with the required shaven head. His most noticeable feature was his large, brown, bovine eyes with long black eyelashes that any girl would have been proud to own.

As I turned to speak to him, a dog ran across the road. Our canine-loving driver swerved to avoid the dog and into the path of thirty tonnes of cement in motion in a large truck.

As I turned back from talking to Karen, I saw the running dog and the advancing cement truck moving across my vision ... then nothing.

The Volga crumpled, the driver broke both his legs, and it took a great deal of effort to extract him from the car. That all happened while I was unconscious. We were about ninety minutes from Yerevan, the capital, where the nearest ambulance was located. Fortunately, there was mobile phone service and Karen called one of his friends in Yerevan to send aid.

I was unconscious for perhaps ten minutes, dazed and very, very lucky. The Volga had no air bags nor any seatbelts, and my action of turning around to speak to Karen probably stopped me from going through the windscreen. A group of villagers had gathered around the accident site and I saw a man walking off with my luggage. I was very concerned because in my suitcase were my emergency rations consisting of several Ginster pasties that I'd bought at Heathrow. I shouted for him to stop but Karen assured me that it was okay and the man was taking the bag to his house where my briefcase was also located. We followed slowly and awaited the ambulance or aid. The driver was taken to hospital by a Good Samaritan.

After several cups of black, sugary tea I began to feel more human.

Astonishingly, one of the many on-lookers, an old weatherworn man, said in English, "Sometimes a dog decides it's the end of his life and will kill himself one way or another."

Karen's friend arrived in a brand new Mercedes, and we were comfortably and swiftly driven back to Yerevan. On the way, I called my insurance company to ensure I could get private treatment, not wanting to experience the Soviet medical system. However, there appeared to be only one private clinic in Yerevan with the hopefully appropriate name of *The European Clinic*. We were deposited here and examined by a Dr Gulbilkian, or some such name. The doctor, after a brief examination, again muttering in Russian, sent us to the state hospital for X-rays. The doctor told Karen that there were no broken bones but there was a tremendous amount of soft tissue damage to the Englishman.

The journey to the hospital was undertaken in a wheelchair, travelling in the one-man clinic ambulance. Karen and the assistant had to keep a tight hold on the wheelchair as the driver raced to the hospital. I suppose he was used to going as fast as possible.

Apparently, the doctor from the European Clinic had called ahead, and I was wheeled into a waiting area for X-rays. All hospitals have an antiseptic smell, but the stench here was awful, combining an antiseptic, sickly, chemical odour with the smell of cheap aftershave.

My turn came, and I was wheeled into the X-ray room. There were several people and a doctor who motioned me to stand in front of him, and a pedestal which held a vertical X-ray machine. This device rotated around my torso and provided an instant image of my internal workings. Again, there was no sign of any broken bones and we were rushed back to the clinic in the ambulance, this time declining the wheelchair and opting for the stretcher-bed with rails to grip onto.

After another night's stay in the clinic, a representative of my client arrived and took me off to the Marriott where I luxuriated in a hot bath to try and ease the bruising and internal pains. After a couple of days, I felt well enough to fly home via Heathrow and then back to Porto.

Quite the trip!

I went back to the mine again but introduced a policy that:

a) any contractors working at the mine (including myself) were to be driven to site in a suitable vehicle equipped with seatbelts,

b) there was to be communication established with the vehicle every hour, and

c) that the drivers were to undergo a defensive driving course (or the Armenian equivalent).

Oh – the dog died.

. . .

Anzob Mine, Tajikistan 2011

I had flown from Porto to Frankfurt and on to Moscow for an overnight stay before taking the Tajik Air flight down to Dushanbe and on to visit the Anzob Mine in Tajikistan.

Just before leaving Porto, I had noticed a slight swelling in my elbow and thought it was either tennis elbow or something to do with my bowling, a very slow spin, right overarm delivery playing cricket for the club. By the time I reached the mine, the swelling had increased to a size that made me look like Popeye the sailor

Fortunately, it was not painful, but all who saw it tut-tutted and shook their heads. Eventually, the mine doctor was called to the hotel and he made an examination with my minder Karen (yes, the same Armenian that I'd worked with before), translating from medical Tajik, which I don't think he understood, to English.

The doctor wisely decided to send me to the regional hospital in Ayni, a two-hour drive away through some spectacular scenery.

The road passed through gorges where the river had carved its way through the limestone bedrock and the road clung to the side. The gorge provided the pathway for the Zeravshan River which flowed past Ayni and on past Samarkand, eventually sinking into the vast sands of the Karakum desert. Along the road in a wider spot at the side of the gorge, I could see the ubiquitous presence of the Chinese; they were investing heavily in the infrastructure of the country and currently improving the road. Not really a hard task to make an improvement on the potholed narrow track that ran along a ledge cut into the mountain, the other side of which was a rushing white water torrent.

On reaching Ayni, Karen and I were dropped off at the crowded entrance of the regional hospital. It was quite extensive and built in the typical Russian style of the early 1960s. We entered the reception hall, and Karen went ahead distributing local currency to what seemed to be everyone including the cleaner with a mop and bucket. The few Somoni notes he distributed put us in front of several queues and into the office of a doctor. In typical Soviet style, the doctor sat behind a large desk and adjacent table forming a T-shape where we were to sit.

He was dressed in Soviet medical fashion, which I find a little scary, with a surgeon's cap which looked like a smaller version of a chef's toque without the pleats, and a white tunic that buttoned to the side with a high collar. Dr Cutitoff did a quick examination and decided to operate. Karen was a little worried, as was I, but apparently the swelling needed to be drained and the amount of cash Karen had distributed put us at the head of the queue.

We entered a wood-lined room next to the consulting room, with many high windows, a couple of spotlights mounted on pedestals, and an operating table. I was motioned to take off my shirt and lie face down on the table with my arm hanging over the side. As I lay there, looking at the table top, I realised it was oil cloth – the sort of stuff you would have had in your kitchen in the 1960s. I hoped it was clean and not just the lunchroom for the staff.

Karen was not allowed to come in, so what happened next was unexpected. I could see there was another person in the room which I surmised was a nurse, then a sharp scratch, which turned out to be a local anaesthetic, and a few moments later, the feeling of a cut in the elbow, followed by some relief from the swelling and the sound of fluid draining into a metal bowl.

Dr Cutitoff and the assistant then pulled me upright for the dressing and closure of the wound. As preparations were made, he took a surgical glove and cut a small piece of it off and apparently inserted it into the wound to act as a drain and then stitched it up. I dressed, and my arm was put into a sling.

Karen was called into the room, given several instructions and what seemed to be a prescription. My extremely limited Russian allowed me to hear 'da' ('yes') and 'zaftra' ('tomorrow'). I knew *zaftra* because every time I asked for information at the mine they would respond, "*zaftra, zaftra.*"

We were ushered out of the consulting room, with prescription in hand, to the pharmacy. Here, we actually had to wait, but it was not too long a wait. Karen paid out more money and emerged with a small brown bottle of pills which turned out to be antibiotics, and some other medicine – pills in a white paper bag, the name of which he could not translate from the Tajik. We also had to pay to leave the hospital. I have no idea how much the episode cost.

On returning to the mine, the doctor there told us the pills in the white bag were painkillers. The antibiotic pills were very small (2 mg?), probably as small as you can make a pill. I dutifully took the recommended dose and supplemented that with my own supply of antibiotics which I always carried with me when travelling.

So, not being able to go underground and not feeling like instructing the mine staff in how to sample and check assays, we took a day off and went up into the Pamir Mountains to the lake of Iskandar, that's Alexander the Great, who came this way *en route* to India. We also visited the President's other official residence on the shores of the stunningly beautiful lake.

For once, the flight back to Porto was uneventful, but I did see my local doctor to ensure all was okay.

Kapan, Southern Armenia 2012

Close to the open-pit copper mine of Agarat where I had been consulting was the mining complex of Kapan. The blocks of flats were lined with red lava brick, and each flat had a small balcony where washing was hung in the vain hope of drying in the winter air. Wires festooned the apartments to an impossibly overloaded power pole. It's probably a vision of the Soviet apartment block that everyone has.

The mining complex had slightly better accommodation, and there was a recreation area overlooked by an impressive statue of Lenin in the oft seen pose of him striding forward with a book in hand, wearing a long coat and pork pie hat.

A small team of technicians had come to Kapan from our mine in order to meet with their managers who were overseeing the production and management of the mine at Agarat. Every month, a meeting was held to discuss forthcoming production quotas and discuss the terms under which the operation was managed. With the production quotas set and the team from Agarat having failed to negotiate better terms for the management contract, to conclude the negotiations we went to the best (and only) restaurant, which was in a park with yet another statue of Lenin. Generally, I was very careful what I ate on these trips, and tried to stick to fried or baked foods and eggs, steering away from sheep parts that I could not recognise and avoiding raw vegetables.

On this occasion, I dutifully ate the grilled chicken and fried potatoes, and thought I would eat a little of the salad that accompanied it. As vodka seemed to be served with every meal in 250ml 'personal' bottles, part of the strategy was to drink a small sip of vodka after every four mouthfuls. It had worked – up until now.

As I was eating the tomato and lettuce, a voice from the past – could it have been Dr Paul? – shouted in my brain, *don't eat the salad!*

Too late: the salad was consumed.

It did not take long to feel the effects of something awful happening in my stomach. Fortunately, by now we were back at the B&B, and so dealt with the consequences in private.

Luckily, or not, depending on your point of view, the B&B was owned by a medical doctor. On learning of my affliction, and after consulting with Karen, he went downstairs to his portion of the house and came back with three extremely small white pills.

He had only a little English but said, "You take. Very good. Stop everything."

I looked to Karen for confirmation, and asked him to find out from the doctor how many I should take. After a burst of Armenian between them which seemed to go on for a while, the answer was one now and one tomorrow.

The pill was taken, and to my relief, the grumbling and other effects ceased within a couple of hours, and I was able to complete my assignment without having to be in close proximity to a toilet. Two days later, I flew back to Porto.

The pills were effective, so effective that I had to go to the doctor in Porto to get pills to undo the Armenian magic medicine.

Which just goes to prove: *don't get sick in foreign parts.*

26

RETURN TO CORNWALL

May 2017: Home

*Resurrecting old exploration properties in Portugal, forming new companies, closing old ones,
searching for a new house,
the hunt for lithium in Portugal, Spain and Ireland,
Max and Minnie get used to rain*

Incident in Church View Road

The house we had for several years was being let and after spending a few weeks in my mother's caravan and our friends' holiday cottage, we moved into 69a.

69a is in a quiet road with what are known as miners' cottages. There are a few, newer, detached houses and many retirees' bungalows. The road connects Kerrier Way which is a sort of bypass around Tuckingmill to the old A30 at Roskear Church. Very peaceful, with church bells on Sundays and wedding days. Occasionally, we would hear the sound of police cars speeding down Pendarves Street to Tuckingmill Hill to connect with the 'new' A30. Sometimes, a large lorry would get stuck on the bend by the house, having ignored the signs that say 'Unsuitable for HGVs'. Google maps and satnav do not know everything, but drivers of delivery vans seem think they are exempt from reading warnings related to road hazards.

One evening, around 9pm, we heard the sound of multiple police sirens which seemed to be coming closer. At first we thought they were on their way down into Tuckingmill, but after a very short time, the sirens were right on us and flashing blue lights lit up the living room.

Suddenly, there was a crash and a loud bang. I went to the front door, opened it, and was greeted by an amazing scene. A car had crashed into the neighbour's parked car and two police cars were slewed across the narrow road. A young man jumped out of the crashed car, leapt on the bonnet and then launched himself at the advancing policeman.

As they say, the police deployed their tasers. It didn't seem to make much of a difference. They were struggling with the man who seemed crazed. Then a woman emerged from the crashed car and started kicking at the policeman, who with the help of his partner, had the man pinned to the ground. Perhaps it was superfluous, but I called 999 as it seemed to me that it was going to take more than two or three police to handle this.

Shortly, more police appeared with drug dogs and what I supposed were crime scene officers. The guy across the road was really upset as his car had sustained quite a bit of damage. During the winter when the 'Beast from the East' arrived, the corner where the incident took place was a collection point for cars slithering downhill either from Dolcoath or Roskear Road, with the two hills meeting at the corner where our neighbour parked. The road was mostly ice and snow for a week, and he had managed to keep his car clear of damage, but now this.

More police cars appeared on the scene and the man and the woman were brought under control. The police told me that they had chased the man in the car for thirty minutes, but did not say what he was wanted for. The police took my statement, and I was impressed because the officer took everything down on a very small tablet and read it back to me. It was accurate. He said I could be contacted to give evidence.

I suppose what Linda and I both found strange was that we had lived in the US for years and some of the most primitive countries in the world but had never experienced this sort of incident. Ever. Here we were, in dear old Camborne, and, "True stories of the men in blue," happened outside our front door.

In another incident, I was walking the dogs around 8pm one night when a bedraggled lady of middle years lit by the sodium streetlamp shouted at me over the gate from a deserted farmhouse and field where she kept a couple of horses without permission.

"Call the police!" she shouted. "Someone is shooting at me horses!"

I had actually heard two loud reports that sounded like gunfire but had dismissed them; this was after all Camborne, 'Centre for Industry and Tourism' as it was in the day, not LA Central, USA.

At this point, a security van appeared. The driver's company was supposed to check on the land and building every so many hours and chose this moment to appear. The lady and I flagged him down and told him of the incident. He called his supervisor on the radio who told him to call 999. The phone was handed to me and I explained what had happened to the 999 operator who asked how I knew I had heard gunshots. I told her I had just returned from ten years in the USA, which seemed to satisfy her.

We were told to wait and that the police would arrive shortly, which they did. Sensibly, they waited for the Armed Response Unit which they said was on the way. After an hour or so, two police vehicles arrived with police in flak jackets and protective gear and a boot full of guns and ammo! If there had been a frenzied gunman roaming the environs of Kerrier Way, he would have gone home for a cup of tea by now.

The Armed Response Unit had come from Bodmin.

Yet again we asked ourselves, was this really Camborne and not some suburb of Los Angeles?

∼

Max and Minnie, the two rescue dogs from Arizona, came home with us. This was a relatively smooth transition as we had the experience of moving dogs around the world before: Misty from the UK to PNG, then from the PNG to Canada, and then from Canada to the US; then Bear from the US to Portugal. Their paperwork was almost as much as for us when travelling to the US.

Both of them comfortably survived the trip and enjoyed seeing new surroundings and new animals. Both dogs were used to horses but as far as we knew had never seen a cat before nor squirrels. Also they had never seen this much grass or so much rain. Neither of them had seen a set of stairs before and Max loved coming upstairs at night to sleep on the landing. Minnie had no interest in climbing them.

∼

The search for lithium continues, and a company of which I am a director asked me to look at a project in Ireland as well as opportunities in Spain and Portugal. The trip to Ireland was easy as one can fly from Newquay to Dublin. From Dublin we drove to Kells, home of the famous *Book of Kells* which is an illuminated manuscript in Latin, containing the four Gospels of the New Testament together with various prefatory texts and tables. Linda accompanied me, and while I went to look at the prospect, she did a little touring.

One particular place she wanted to visit was, "open seven days a week (closed on Fridays and Sundays)."

Very Irish.

Another opportunity for lithium projects was in Spain but the Aussies had got there before us. By now it was apparent that Portugal was closed for the exploration of minerals, so no more work was done there.

Back in the UK, we had to readjust to distances and perceived distances. It took a while to rationalise that Penzance is only fourteen miles from Camborne, and in the winter it can be travelled in fifteen minutes by road or twenty minutes by train. Before we'd started our travelling, Penzance had seemed a long way away, and Truro was a day trip either from Camborne or Praa Sands. I suppose one's brain is hardwired to the distances and the time it took going from place to place during childhood.

Portugal still figures largely in our lives. Firstly, we resurrected the geothermal project in a new company, Capture Results Lda. One can now acquire a shelf, pre-registered company in one day, and begin operations the next. A strange name, but Portugal has streamlined its company formation procedures and this one was the nearest name we could find in the available list that reflected the objective of the company. Unlike the first time we started up in Portugal, when it took over six months to register and start a company.

As in many things Portuguese, all is not as straightforward as it seems. After the refusal by the municipality to accept our investment plan for the geothermal field in Chaves, we started to close the company. The closure was relatively simple although with a lot of form filling, but closing the bank account took 18 months. This was due mainly to Covid, in as much as the bank would only allow the company account to be closed in person by the signatory on the account; a trip to Portugal post-Covid was required.

We still have many friends in Portugal and all over the world, so visitors to the UK are frequent and in a post-Covid world, we travel to visit those in the USA, France, Portugal and those we met in PNG. Of course, we are privileged to have a great number of friends who we knew before leaving that are still here, and special friends from days at the School of Mines.

. . .

Mac's Boy

One of the great pleasures of being back in Camborne was being able to walk from our house in Roskear to the Camborne Cricket Club, buy a pint of cider and sit on the benches in front of the whitewashed wall.

When my cousin Terry was over from the United States we would go together and just watch, commentate to each other and discuss the team members.

One day, I was alone, watching and listening to a couple of elderly gentlemen discuss the match and goings-on in Troon, a nearby village which had a very famous team. Troon had made the National Village Cup knockout cup for cricket on several occasions, the final being played at Lord's, the home of cricket.

On hearing their discussion, I asked them if they were from Troon.

"Yes!" one of them said.

"My uncle was President of Troon CC for a while," I said. "Leslie Nile."

"Oh, yes," they said, and in typical direct style asked, "Who are you then?"

"Alan Matthews."

"Oh, you're Mac's boy," he said, referring to my father.

The other one then said, "Mac, played for Cornwall," (rugby), "used to go round with that girl Treloar for a while then married that girl Tellam."

They carried on talking.

"Leslie and Lillian lived up Mount Pleasant Road. They had a boy, Terry, wasn't it?" they asked each other. "Yes," they said. "Terry, Leslie's boy."

That was so Camborne, so Cornish. Terry had left Camborne in the early 1970s and went to the States in 1974. Linda and I had been away since 1974, but like Terry, had been back on several occasions.

But here I was in 2017 hearing about my father and mother, uncle and aunty from a couple of gentlemen I had never met.

Now we really knew we were home.

Here, in Cornwall, our view from the house stretches out over the golf course to the sea, includes a mining chimney, dracaena palms and fir trees. The wanderlust is still there and we sometimes wonder, where will the next adventure be?

In the words of John the Fish, and as Brenda Wooton once sang of pasties and cream:

Though we may roam, Cornwall's our home
  The dear old county of Cornwall.

GLOSSARY

Adit – a horizontal or slightly inclined tunnel that is used for drainage purposes

Alluvial – deposits of minerals that have been worn away from their host rock and transported and redeposited in gravels, stream and river beds.

Bantu – Black African speakers of Bantu languages (several hundred indigenous ethnic groups)

Brattice – a partition or shaft lining in a mine, typically made of wood or heavy cloth

BLM – Bureau of Land Management (USA) manages the federal government's nearly 700 million acres (2,800,000 km^2) of subsurface mineral estate (mineral rights) located beneath federal, state and a few areas of private lands severed from their surface rights

Cargo cult – a system where rituals were performed by adherents in the belief that it would cause a more technologically advanced society to deliver goods).

Copper oxide minerals – the main minerals being malachite, azurite, chrysocolla and cuprite; soluble in acid from where the copper can be recovered by precipitation

Copper Sulphide minerals – the main minerals being chalcopyrite, bornite and chalcocite, and are recovered by smelting

Decline/Incline/ramp – an inclined tunnel that descends at usually no more than 33° in inclination or declination

Drift – a tunnel for prospecting purposes and usually follows a vein

Eluvial – deposits that are derived by in situ weathering, or weathering plus gravitational movement or accumulation (as opposed to alluvial where the mineral constituent eg. gold/tin/diamond is carried away from the source by water

Jack-up rig – a mobile platform that consists of a buoyant hull fitted with a number of movable legs, capable of raising its hull over the surface of the sea

Junior mining – a term applied to companies listed on the Australian, Canadian, South African, US and UK venture exchanges. Generally, their market capitalisation is low, not exceeding US$5 million in most cases, and their shares trading below $0.50, usually with projects in development and exploration.

Kiap – a remnant from the time when PNG was administered by Australia and refers to district officers and patrol officers who were travelling representatives of the British and Australian governments with wide-ranging authority in pre-independence PNG

Level – a section of the mine that is accessed from the shaft or decline at a certain point below surface eg. Level 6 relates to the sixth level down from Level 0, which would be surface

Mineralisation – Mineralisation includes chemical alteration, replacement, and enrichment of minerals within igneous, metamorphic, and sedimentary rocks. In the context of the book it refers to economically important metals in the formation of ore bodies

Outcrop – a vein or rock that shows above the soil or grass at surface

Porphyry – a type of igneous rock consisting of large-grained crystals such as quartz and feldspar scattered in a fine-grained groundmass

Raise – a small vertical tunnel used for access

Shaft – a vertical tunnel, usually the main entryway to an underground deposit

Stope – a working area where ore is extracted. These areas are generally narrow and can be near vertical. Others can be flat lying depending on the deposit

Strike – A term used to define the direction of a vein or bed of rock

Tailings (Dam) – fine grained rock that has been processed by grinding and the majority of the valuable minerals removed.

Tramming – moving broken rock from a production area, stope or tunnel to a shaft or ramp for removal to surface

A NOTE FROM THE AUTHOR

August 2022: Praa Sands

The journey of our lives described in this book is from a compilation of notes that I have made over the years while sitting in hotel rooms, in the guest house of mining towns and exploration camps. A large section of the notes are from my 'Letter from Portugal', an account of life in Portugal sent to friends and family after moving there from the US. Initially, I was encouraged by several people including my mother to publish these, and I have included several portions from these letters in the text of this work. Thanks to them.

I would like to thank Jane Harvey-Berrick for the opportunity provided by her to publish this account, and for her excellent editing and guidance. Having a successful published author with her own publishing company living close by was certainly a great help.

Going back in time, my interest in geothermal energy and my branching out into the oil business was fostered by Dr Tony Batchelor, lecturer in Rock Mechanics in my time at the Camborne School of Mines. Doc Batch has always encouraged me throughout my career and in particular in my efforts to bring sustainable energy to northern Portugal. Doc Batch sadly died in October of 2022 and will be sorely missed. Dr Peter Hackett deserves special thanks for allowing me to join the CSM using my Ordinary National Certificate in Engineering qualification from Cornwall Technical College.

Huge thanks also need to be given to my wife Linda for her review of every single story, and her fantastic editing and in particular recognition of repeated passages. Her memory banks are often far more accurate than mine. Her recollections will often trigger a chain of memories that form an important part of the story. Her sister Tracey has read many of the stories and has always provided praise.

I cannot thank enough all the friends mentioned and those not mentioned, who helped along the way to enrich our times in strange lands and life back in Cornwall.

Finally the Upper Gastro Intestinal oncology team at Treliske Hospital in Truro have our heartfelt thanks for their dedication and providing me the opportunity to finish this work. I wish my father was still around to be able to see what a wonderful life we have had.

www.ingramcontent.com/pod-product-compliance
Lightning Source LLC
Chambersburg PA
CBHW060148050426
42446CB00013B/2725